Mexicans in California

Mexicans in California

Transformations and Challenges

EDITED BY
RAMÓN A. GUTIÉRREZ AND
PATRICIA ZAVELLA

with the assistance of
Denise Segura, Dolores Trevizo,
and Juan Vicente Palerm

University of Illinois Press
URBANA AND CHICAGO

Manufactured in the United States of America
1 2 3 4 5 C P 5 4 3 2 1
∞ This book is printed on acid-free paper.

Library of Congress Cataloging-in-Publication Data
Mexicans in California : transformations and challenges /
edited by Ramón A. Gutiérrez and Patricia Zavella.
p.   cm.
Includes bibliographical references and index.
ISBN 978-0-252-03411-4 (cloth : alk. paper) —
ISBN 978-0-252-07607-7 (pbk. : alk. paper)
1. Mexican Americans—California—Social conditions—
Congresses. 2. Mexicans—California—Social conditions—
Congresses. 3. Immigrants—California—Social
conditions—Congresses. 4. Mexico—Emigration and
immigration—Congresses. 5. California—Emigration and
immigration—Congresses. 6. California—Ethnic relations—
Congresses. 7. California—Social conditions—Congresses.
8. Social change—California—Congresses.
I. Gutiérrez, Ramón A., 1951– II. Zavella, Patricia.
F870.M5M495   2009
305.868'720794—dc22   2008034993

Contents

Acknowledgments   vii

Introduction   1

PART I. WORK AND POVERTY

1. Poverty, Work, and Public Policy:
   Latino Futures in California's New Economy   15
   Manuel Pastor Jr.

2. Working Day Labor:
   Informal and Contingent Employment   36
   Abel Valenzuela Jr.

PART II. EDUCATION AND ACHIEVEMENT

3. Understanding and Addressing the California Latino
   Achievement Gap in Early Elementary School   61
   Russell W. Rumberger and Brenda D. Arellano

4. Reaffirming Affirmative Action:
   An Equal Opportunity Analysis of Advanced
   Placement Courses and University Admissions   77
   Armida Ornelas and Daniel G. Solórzano

5. Chicano Struggles for Racial Justice:
   The Movement's Contribution to Social Theory   94
   Ramón A. Gutiérrez

6. "Lifting As We Climb":
   Educated Chicanas' Social Identities
   and Commitment to Social Action   111
   Aída Hurtado

   PART III. CULTURE AND SELF-REPRESENTATION

7. The Quebec Metaphor, Invasion, and Reconquest in
   Public Discourse on Mexican Immigration   133
   Leo R. Chavez

8. Prime-Time Protest:
   Latinos and Network Television   155
   Chon A. Noriega

9. The Politics of Passion:
   Poetics and Performance of *La Canción Ranchera*   168
   Olga Nájera-Ramírez

   PART IV. CULTURE AND VIOLENCE

10. Conflict Resolution and Intimate Partner Violence
    among Mexicans on Both Sides of the Border   183
    Yvette G. Flores and Enriqueta Valdez Curiel

   Bibliography   217

   Contributors   243

   Index   247

Acknowledgments

The editors would like to thank the University of California Institute for Mexico and the United States (UC MEXUS), which, along with the UC Committee on Latino Research, sponsored the conference "Latinos in California II" on September 11–12, 2003. Many of the chapters included here are based on research presentations made at this conference, and we thank the authors who contributed their research articles to this volume. With support from the Chicano/Latino Research Center at UC Santa Cruz, research apprentices Sonja Diaz, Christa Erasmus, and Adrian Flores did very helpful work on the bibliography.

Introduction

This book is about the present, past, and future of California's ethnic Mexican population, and by implication, the fate of our republic. Of the 36.5 million people living in California today, approximately eleven million are of Mexican ancestry, representing by far the largest single national group in the state and largest component of the state's thirteen million Latinos. With ethnic Mexicans representing close to one-third of the state's population, and Latinos accounting for 35.2 percent of its total, California naturally has become the epicenter for one of the most factious debates of the moment, the regulation of immigration and its long-term social, economic, and political consequences for America's future. What language will be spoken? What social services will be provided to ethnic Mexicans? Should those in the country illegally or without authorization be granted legalization, or what some decry as amnesty? And if ultimately granted permanent residency status and citizenship, how will their votes affect the political processes of the state and the republic? How will this largely young population be educated to sustain California's long-term viability and the inevitability of having to rely on them for the transfer payments necessary for an aging white population? In short, what sorts of cultural citizenship will ethnic Mexicans enjoy in California's present and future?

Since the end of the U.S.–Mexican War in 1848, when California incorporated some ten thousand Mexican nationals into the polity as citizens, as dictated by the terms of the Treaty of Guadalupe Hidalgo, the many paths leading to California from Mexico constantly have been traversed. At no moment since 1848 has the flow of immigrants ever really stopped. At the end of the nineteenth century, Mexicans headed for the United States seeking work and greater economic opportunities, having been displaced from their ancestral farms through the rapid modernization and mechanization of mining and agriculture. They found work in California, as in other states of the Southwest, in the construction of railroads, in the tilling of land, and as menial laborers in a host of industries. From 1900 to 1930, Mexicans found refuge in California as they fled the violence that preceded and followed their country's revolution between 1910 and 1917. As in previous generations, they arrived to sow and to harvest, to clean and to cook, to service and to tarry, the majority of them as poor peasant farmers but a number of them as skilled craftsmen, as businessmen, as intellectuals, and as entrepreneurs. Many of these Mexican immigrants entered the United States legally before 1924, when few restrictions or physical barriers tempered the movement of Mexicans into the Golden State. Numerous others came as exceptions created in American immigration law to provide cheap labor to those industries deemed vital to the republic's war efforts and to sustain economic growth. From 1942 to 1964, for example, the United States created a guest worker program, which became known as the Bracero Program (*brazo* in Spanish means arm), which contracted some 4.6 million Mexican workers for temporary labor in agriculture, mining, and transportation. Under the Bracero Program, the United States Department of Agriculture acted as the official contracting agent, negotiated salaries, set the levels of work, monitored its conditions, and oversaw the workers' return. But to many owners of American firms, such regulation seemed onerous to the free flow of capital. They preferred instead the hiring of illegal Mexican immigrant labor, which was more pliable, less rebellious, more easily deported, and exploitable without much recourse. Since the end of the World War II, some twenty-five million Mexicans have entered the United States illegally, to perform the same types of work that their legal compatriots have done and continue to do, but under the shadow of lawlessness and without legal succor of any sort. And yet they come—many by overstaying their visas. They come attracted by the prospect of a land celebrated for its opportunities and vaunted as a place where dreams of prosperity can become realized. They come escaping misery, exploitation, and hopelessness. And they come knowing that death has taken many of their compatriots along the way.

Mexicans in California: Transformations and Challenges is a volume designed to offer readers a comprehensive survey of the principal issues affecting this population, exploring the social, economic, political, and cultural transformations engendered by the growth of *mexicano*, ethnic Mexican, and Chicana/Chicano populations of California. Herein scholars, policy makers, elected officials, and citizens concerned about the health of the body politic will find extensive discussion of important issues of concern: the concentration of ethnic Mexicans in the lower rung of society, mostly among the working poor; their contingent and informal labor and its modest rewards; the tensions family members face when they join the migrant stream; the effects of education on upward mobility; the educational achievement gap between ethnic Mexican, white, and black students in public schools; the segregation of Mexicans and Mexican Americans in low-performing schools that have no access to honors or Advanced Placement (AP) courses; the social movement for appropriate curricula for ethnic Mexican students; and the underrepresentation of ethnic Mexicans in various fields of creativity. These are some of the themes this volume addresses, looking at the complexity of the Mexican population in California, challenging the assumption that the story of these immigrants is comparable to that of white European immigrants, and that with time they too will eventually assimilate and participate fully and equally in the body politic.

The rapid growth of California's ethnic Mexican population has been greeted enthusiastically in many places, with ambivalence in others, and with open hostility in many sites. Undoubtedly because the growth of the Mexican immigrant population in California has been so profound over the last three decades, the state has spawned some of the most virulent and xenophobic responses to immigrants, at the extreme attempting to deny them access to state-sponsored social services. In 1986, for example, the California electorate voted to declare English the state's official language through passage of Proposition 63. Since then, California's electorate has passed a number of draconian voter-initiated propositions, all aimed at regulating the ethnic Mexican population. In 1994, Proposition 187 was passed by voters, putatively designed and marketed as a measure to "Save Our State." It banned access to education and health services by undocumented immigrants except in emergency cases. The proposition would have required teachers and health-care providers to check the legal status of students and clients. The proposition ultimately was nullified and deemed unconstitutional by the courts, but it nevertheless became a major political flash point, mobilizing thousands of nativist and pro-immigration groups in radical opposition to each other. These politics raise questions about who belongs in the nation and how large states like California should support those who enter the United States illegally or who overstay their work visas.

California Proposition 209 was voted into law in 1996. Officially known as the "Prohibition against Discrimination or Preferential Treatment by State and Other Public Entities" law, it prohibits discrimination or preferential treatment in access to public education, employment, or contracting on the basis of race, gender, ethnicity, or national origin. Bilingual education was similarly targeted by nativist groups in 1998 with the passage of Proposition 227, popularly referred to as the "English Only" initiative, which required the placement of all public school students in "English-language classrooms" and severely restricted funds available for foreign language instruction. Similar anti-immigrant measures have been proposed in a number of other states, including Texas, Arizona, New Mexico, and Michigan, with varying levels of success. In Arizona, for example, voters passed Proposition 200 (popularly dubbed California's "Proposition 187 on Steroids") in 2004. This measure requires proof of citizenship to register to vote, demands proof of citizenship through a birth certificate or passport to access public services, and enjoins all of Arizona's public employees to report to the United States Department of Homeland Security anyone seeking public assistance suspected of being an undocumented immigrant.

The fears that propel voters to severely constrain the opportunities of the very immigrants who clean their houses, nurse their babies, cook their meals, and construct their homes for a fraction of what citizen-workers would demand, are not well understood. Nor do we know much about the citizen children and grandchildren of Mexican immigrants. What we do know is that as the citizen children of Mexicans come of age in the United States, they are becoming increasingly politically active in resisting nativist practices against their relatives and fellow ethnics, as the massive demonstrations in Los Angeles and other cities on May Day 2006, in favor of new comprehensive immigration legislation, so amply testified (Bada, Fox, and Selee, 2006). The majority of babies born in the state of California (50.6 percent) now have mothers of Mexican ancestry (Hayes-Bautista, 2003). If one simply does the math (something that strategists for both the Republican and Democratic Parties have done), these children are quickly transforming the impact of the ethnic Mexican vote in state and national politics. Presidential candidate George W. Bush clearly understood this in 1999 while stumping for Mexican American votes in California, New Mexico, Arizona, and Texas. He repeatedly emphasized his deep cultural connections to Mexico, reminding voters that he spoke Spanish, that his brother Jeb Bush, then Florida's governor, was married to a Mexican American woman, and that while he was governor of Texas he had visited with Mexican officials all along the border to improve political relations and spur economic development. Bush's slick Spanish-language advertising and his Mexican American voter-outreach campaign wooed and mobilized a significant numbers of voters. For as he and his chief political strategist, Karl Rove, so clearly understood, this was a rapidly growing population that was predicted to represent 35 percent of the country's total by the year 2020. If the Republican Party was to remain a viable national party capable of winning elections, it needed the Mexican American vote, a fact that has not changed.

By most statistical standards, California's ethnic Mexican population is largely concentrated at the bottom of the socioeconomic ladder, with very few of them in the ranks of the wealthy. Indeed, when the magazine *Hispanic Business* identified "Hispanic millionaires" in the United States back in 1995, it found only seventy-five. The largest number of these, twenty-seven, were Cuban Americans; twenty-five were Mexican Americans, eight were Spaniards, seven were Puerto Ricans (five lived in the United States and three on the island), and one each were from Chile, Colombia, Costa Rica, the Dominican Republic, Ecuador, Uruguay, and Venezuela. Their collective biographies showed that the majority had arrived in the United States already wealthy or with significant economic resources, which allowed them to launch businesses. The exceptions to this trend were the ethnic Mexican and Mexican American movie stars, singers, and athletes who had occasionally been able to amass significant fortunes on the basis of their own talents.

The number of ethnic Mexicans who have entered the corporate elite in the United States is just as small. Again, *Hispanic Business* reported that between 1990 and 1995, the number of Hispanics (broadly defined) on the boards of directors of Fortune 1000 companies did not exceed 1 percent of all corporate directors. In 1990 they numbered forty, and in 1995 fifty-one, with roughly one out of every five of these a female. Analyzing the personal histories of these individuals, sociologists Richard L. Zweigenhaft and G. William Domhoff found that the majority had been born into middle-class families and had access to elite education. "Only a few people on the list of directors could be considered genuine bootstrappers, making their way to the top of corporations without the benefit of family backing or an elite education." The majority of these rags-to-riches stories were of individuals of Mexican American origin (Zweigenhaft and Domhoff, 1998:124, 126).

Mexican American movement up the corporate ladder has been extremely slow. In 1990 there were no Mexican American CEOs of large corporations. In 1995 there were five, a number that has not grown significantly since. Between the years 1990 and 2000, the number of Latinos (again, broadly defined) at the level of vice president or higher in Fortune 1000 companies went from 167 to 217, representing about 1.4 percent of the top management in telecommunications, commercial banking, and ethnic food production. Ethnic Mexican corporate managers fared quite poorly in companies that did not have to meet Affirmative Action targets to win federal contacts. A study of the number of Latinos listed in Poor's *Register of Executives and Directors,* listing the top managers and directors of fifty thousand public companies, found that between 1965 and 1995, the number had gone from seventy-eight to 374. Latinos had thus progressed from representing 0.1 percent of all managers and directors in 1965 to 0.5 percent in 1995. This statistic reflects the growth of Latino-owned business rather than higher levels of employment by Latinos and Mexican Americans in non-Latino companies (Zweigenhaft and Domhoff, 1998).

Ethnic Mexican–owned businesses are extremely important for a community's economic development because they tend to hire ethnic workers, address unmet consumer needs (for example, food products), and frequently serve as anchors for community development and political empowerment. From 1987 to 1992, U.S. Latino-owned businesses grew by 83 percent, with their gross receipts rising by 195 percent. Despite this rate of growth, they still only represented 4.5 percent of all firms in the United States and only 2.2 percent of all receipts. Almost half of all Latino-owned firms had receipts of less than $10,000; average receipts for Latino businesses were $94,000, compared to $193,000 for all firms. Mexican Americans in California owned the majority of Latino businesses, with 249,717 firms, and receipts totaling $19.6 billion. The Los Angeles–Long Beach corridor was home to the largest number of these firms (109,104), followed by Miami (77,300), where the ownership was largely Cuban American.

Studying the relationship between sectors in which Latino-owned businesses were concentrated and the wage dynamism of those areas, economist Manuel Pastor Jr. (2000:13–19) found that while Anglos and Asians were concentrated in high-wage, fast-growth sectors, the majority of Latinos were in the low-wage, fast-growth sectors, portending dire consequences for the long-term economic future of Latinos. Elías López, an economist at the California Research Bureau, similarly found in 1998 that Latinos, the vast majority of whom were of ethnic Mexican origin, had the state's lowest median wages. The median wage for California's 15.6 million workers was $21,000; for whites it was $27,000, for Asians $24,000, for blacks $23,000, and for Latinos $14,560. The low level of educational achievement among ethnic Mexicans explained most of this wage disparity. Seven percent of white workers lacked a high school diploma, as did 7 percent of black workers, 12 percent of Asian workers, and 45 percent of Latino workers. When it came to the earning of a bachelor's degree or higher, the story was much the same. Only 8 percent of Latinos had a bachelor's degree or above. Twenty-four percent of black workers had achieved this level of education, as did 33 percent of whites, and 43 percent of Asians. Projecting the size and composition of California's population forward to the year 2025, López predicted dire fiscal consequences for the state if investments in Latino educational achievement were not radically increased. In 2025, Latinos would constitute 43 percent of the population, whites 34 percent, Asians 17 percent, and blacks 5 percent. If roughly 50 percent of Latinos continued to drop out of high school, this would account for about one-fourth of the state's population (López, 1999).

Mexicans in California: Transformations and Challenges, which consists of ten essays by a number of this country's leading scholars of the Mexican American and Latino experience in the United States, explores issues of poverty and work, education and achievement, culture and self-representation. In this anthology's first section, "Work and Poverty," economist Manuel Pastor Jr. explores the worrisome relationship among wage, employment, and educational attainment. What he finds is that ethnic Mexicans over the last decade have had the highest rates of labor force participation of any ethnic group in California. Mexican woman and men alike are working hard everyday but are nevertheless always falling behind. They are the group most impacted by downturns in California's business cycles and increasingly are living in conditions of poverty. Pastor shows that between 1999 and 2004, California's poverty rate for Latinos was 38.2 percent, 30.1 percent for African Americans, 18.2 percent for Asians, and 15 percent for whites. For nearly half of all Latinos in the state, the conditions of economic existence are grim. These patterns of poverty could not be explained away as the difference between immigrants and longtime residents; both groups suffered equally and lived rather bleak lives. Pastor proposes that job training and educational advancement are the only activities that will profoundly change the cycle of working poverty that ethnic Mexicans in California specifically, and Latinos more generally, currently find themselves in.

Abel Valenzuela Jr.'s essay, "Working Day Labor: Informal and Contingent Employment," examines that form of unauthorized Mexican immigrant work that increasingly is being used in California's cities and towns as a way for employers to lower wages, to avoid the payment of any taxes or benefits, to skirt occupational safety regulations, and to escape government detection and sanctions for employing illegal immigrants. Using twenty-five in-depth interviews with Mexican day laborers in Los Angeles, as well as the 1999 Los Angeles Day Labor Survey of 481 workers, and his own participant observation, Valenzuela concludes that the workers are largely young and male, have low educational attainment, are in the United States illegally or without authorization, and lack English-language proficiency. They turn to day labor as a way of gaining work experiences and skills, as a way of gaining networks of friendship and camaraderie, because such work allows them to personally negotiate the terms of their labor, albeit in adverse ways, which more formal work in secondary labor markets would not allow, and ultimately because work of this sort often leads to better and consistent employment.

A great deal of scholarship on the ethnic Mexican and Chicano/Chicana population of California is theoretically driven by models of assimilation, and accordingly focuses on the children and grandchildren of immigrants, seeking the determinants of intergenerational mobility. Although this has been important work, much more attention must be given to the first generation in the United States, and particularly on ways to improve their wages. We know that English-language proficiency is one of the major determinants of wage level for Mexican immigrants in the United States. Thus the continuing challenge is how to teach adult immigrants English. Immigrant second-generation pathologies—juvenile crime, poor health, and low school performance—are largely based on the low and unstable incomes of first-generation parents (Cornelius, 1999).

In the second section of this book, on "Education and Achievement," authors take up these larger questions. In their essay, "Understanding and Addressing the California Latino Achievement Gap in Early Elementary School," Russell W. Rumberger and Brenda D. Arellano examine what difference poverty status, race, ethnicity, disability, and limited English-language proficiency have on the learning of young children in California. Arguing that student achievement is both the product of individual attributes and the combined effects of families, schools, and communities, they show that the achievement gap between Latino and white children during the first two years of elementary school is considerable in reading and mathematics and only grows more pronounced over time, based largely on differences among students, and much less so on the quality of the schools they attend. Most of the initial achievement gap is best explained by socioeconomic status and language background. The personal attributes that best predict measurable improvement in reading and math among Latino children are the pro-learning behaviors that parents can cultivate in children (for example, attentiveness, eagerness, independence), or that are taught in preschool classes. Rumberger and Arellano conclude that two educational reforms would have a tremendous impact on the long-term education and upward mobility of Latinos in California: the creation of state-subsidized child care and of English-language instruction for monolingual Spanish-speaking parents.

Why the citizens of California and of the larger United States must worry about the educational achievement gap between ethnic Mexicans and other ethnic/racial groups is splendidly illustrated in "Reaffirming Affirmative Action: An Equal Opportunity Analysis of Advanced Placement Courses and University Admissions." Armida Ornelas and Daniel G. Solórzano show

how the public school system in California is significantly failing Mexican American students. They chronicle the "leakages" in the educational pipeline with some rather sobering statistics. For every one hundred students that currently enter K-12, for example, only forty-seven will graduate from high school. Of these, only twenty-six will enroll in a junior college or university, and among these, only eight will obtain a baccalaureate degree. Of these eight, only three students will continue to a graduate or professional school, and fewer than one will receive a doctoral degree. Why so few students of ethnic Mexican ancestry are actually matriculating in California colleges and universities has to do a great deal with the discriminatory ways in which educational resources are allocated by school districts, or, more clearly stated, not allocated to large urban public high schools in predominantly minority neighborhoods. Students at such schools have far fewer fully credentialed teachers than their peers in schools serving middle-class and upper-class neighborhoods. Most crucial for admission to the California State University and University of California systems, ethnic Mexican students have access to far fewer advanced placement courses, which have become much more significant in gaining admission to postsecondary institutions. Ornelas and Solórzano offer a number of recommendations to more equitably distribute educational resources.

The political mobilization of the ethnic Mexican population of the Southwest, under the leadership of Chicano students and their movement during the late 1960s and 1970s, had a profoundly salubrious effect on the ways in which public schools educated these students, on the level of participation parents and students were given in the regulation and content of education, on the ethnicity of the teaching staff, and, most importantly, on the curricula fashioned to give Mexican Americans a greater sense of their history and exclusion from American public life. Ramón A. Gutiérrez's essay, "Chicano Struggles for Racial Justice: The Movement's Contribution to Social Theory," offers us a historical genealogy of the dominant theory that Chicanos/as embraced to analyze their historical and material conditions in the United States in the 1960s: the theory of internal colonialism. He shows how the theory largely originated among Latin American theorists of dependency and underdevelopment in Latin America during the late 1950s, how black nationalists in the United States acquired it in the early 1960s through contact with Cuban Marxists and deployed it to understand urban ghettoes as colonies, and how Chicanos propagated the theory of internal colonialism to understand their experiences of marginality and racism in the United States, accordingly invoking it to start Chicano/a studies programs and curricula concerned with community empowerment.

How formative programs in Chicano/a and ethnic studies were for several generations is amply demonstrated in Aída Hurtado's qualitative research on Chicanas with advanced educational degrees, entitled " 'Lifting As We Climb': Educated Chicanas' Social Identities and Commitment to Social Action." Hurtado found that women's access to such courses was pivotal for their development of a political consciousness about their racial, gender/sexual, and class identities, about how oppression was experienced, and about an understanding that it was only through social activism that their communities could be bettered. Hurtado concludes her essay with a number of public policy recommendations that focus on curricular innovations, financial aid, and mentoring programs in higher education.

Mexicans and Mexican Americans in the United States largely acquire a sense of place and of belonging in their local and national communities through a range of cultural expressions, such as literature, dance, theater, music, television, and film (Aparicio, 2004). Popular culture provides important sites for the creation and affirmation of cultural identity, providing opportunities for communal debates about biculturalism, representation, and human agency. In the context of globalization, migration, and marginalization, many *mexicanos,* whether migrants or citizens of the United States, find cultural expressions as key sites for expressing their language, rituals, and cultural memories. Particularly when they are excluded from mainstream cultural productions—such as film or television—access to other cultural forms becomes important. The growing presence of Spanish-language radio stations, fueled by deregulation and the growth of the Latino population, is undoubtedly one of the outcomes of exclusion in other venues. The presences of Latinas/os are creating new identities and patterns of socialization, as well as constituencies and markets, media and art forms, and languages and organizations. Indeed, California sits at the crossroads of demographic shifts where complex social problems associated with migration, settlement, poverty, political mobility, and cultural expressions are in dire need of analysis and are slowly but surely developing analysts.

In the next section of the book, called "Culture and Self-Representation," three scholars present analyses that illustrate the responses ethnic Mexicans craft when they are excluded, represented in patently negative ways, or forced to adapt to new cultural environments. Leo R. Chavez studies the depiction of Mexican immigration in the United States through an analysis of visual and textual discourses in American popular magazines such as *Time, Newsweek, The New Republic,* and *The Atlantic Monthly* in "The Quebec Metaphor, Invasion, and Reconquest in Public Discourse on Mexican Immigration."

He shows that between 1965 and 2000, the tone and tenor used by opinion makers to describe these immigrants became increasingly shrill, constantly deploying words such as "invasion," "crisis," and "time bomb" as part of a larger nativist rhetoric intended to provoke xenophobic response. Central to this alarmist project to curtail the continued entry of Mexican immigrants has been a concerted campaign to depict the concentration of Mexicans in the American Southwest as an invasion that is quickly leading to the area's "Mexicanization," which in time, given high female reproduction rates, Spanish-language loyalty, and increasing political clout, will undoubtedly lead to the creation of a "Chicano Quebec," a separatist/nationalist project destined to challenge the primacy of the United States.

Chon A. Noriega's essay, "Prime-Time Protest: Latinos and Network Television," further explores the theme of ethnic representation by looking at the low level of Latino employment in film and television at all levels: management, production, acting. He shows that while in 1955 Latino portrayals represented 3 percent of all primetime television programming, in the 1990s they represented only 1 percent. Mexican American media activists who were eager to see an improvement in these statistics formed the National Hispanic Media Coalition in 1986 in Los Angeles. Over the years, the coalition has enjoyed a number of successes, gaining memoranda of understanding from networks and local television and radio stations for the employment of greater numbers of women and minorities in every phase of the management and production process. The coalition's victories have been largely predicated on a better understanding of how media conglomerates operate in a global and state-deregulated space, on the creation of broader and more inclusive media reform organizations, and with a comprehensive activist agenda that uses a number of different protest strategies and tactics all at once. As Alex Nogales, the president of the National Hispanic Media Coalition, noted: "How do we get in their way? We're doing it through economics *and* politics *and* existing law."

In "The Politics of Passion: Poetics and Performance of *La Canción Ranchera*," Olga Nájera-Ramírez offers readers an analysis of one form of Mexican popular music, *la canción ranchera*, that highly emotional, energetically charged song about rural to urban migration, with all of its nostalgia for parochial life and bygone times; a musical form so closely equated with Mexican national identity and a longing both for the former mother-fatherland and for a lover. She argues that *rancheras* defy easy classification and are best understood as melodrama associated with themes of "[s]eduction, betrayal, abandonment, extortion, murder, suicide, revenge, jealousy, incurable illness, obsession, and compulsion" and that offer both songwriters and performers a genre with which to challenge gender stereotypes, patriarchy, and communal values and norms.

Finally, in the final section, "Culture and Violence," Yvette G. Flores and Enriqueta Valdez Curiel empirically study the consequences of such passion and apparent love used to rationalize patriarchy in "Conflict Resolution and Intimate Partner Violence among Mexicans on Both Sides of the Border." These scholars examine how often such abuse happens, how often it is reported, and what its principal determinants appear to be. Basing their findings on two survey samples that together totaled 390 heterosexual married couples, they study intimate partner violence among Mexicans residing in Tenamaztlán, Jalisco, Mexico, and recent Mexican immigrants that had lived for at least two years in the northern California cities of Sacramento, Woodland, Davis, and Vacaville. They found that the majority of couples in Jalisco and California reported suffering and/or perpetuating psychological or verbal violence, but vastly less of a physical and sexual nature. In general, couples in Jalisco reported more overall violence of every sort. And indeed, those who suffered or perpetuated partner violence in either country, as immigrants or long-standing residents, generally were quite dissatisfied with their marital partners and held highly chauvinistic and sexist attitudes—what sociologists have long called *machista*—toward members of the opposite sex. Their findings suggest a binational point of view helps contextualize troublesome processes experienced by migrants in the United States.

In sum, *Mexicans in California: Transformations and Challenges* provides a systematic, interdisciplinary inquiry into the lives of *mexicanos,* ethnic Mexican, Chicanas/os, and Latinas/os in California, their economic integration, the prospects for their social mobility, and their forms of protest and cultural production, continually influenced by transnational migration between Mexico and the United States. The methodological approaches herein employed are diverse and include anthropology, economics, education, history, psychology, political science, and sociology as well as interdisciplinary fields such as ethnic studies or cultural studies, and the authors utilize historical, qualitative, or quantitative research in support of their arguments.

PART I

Work and Poverty

1. Poverty, Work, and Public Policy

Latino Futures in California's New Economy

MANUEL PASTOR JR.

Introduction

As recession gave way to a strong expansion in the mid-1990s, many felt California had entered an era of a "new economy." Employment gains over the decade were impressive, with roughly 2.2 million jobs added over the 1991–2000 period. Unemployment rates declined sharply, with the state rate in 2000 dipping below 5 percent even as unemployment in the San Francisco and San Jose areas fell to around 3 percent.[1] When an economic downturn began in early 2001, many felt that it was but a temporary blip in a healthy trend of long-term growth and suggested that California's fundamental strengths in industries such as information technology and biotechnology would help it stay ahead of the national economic curve. The recession did last longer than expected—and was remarkably deep in the high-tech environs of northern California—but by 2005, California's unemployment rate was back around its 1999 level.

Yet the optimism about the overall economy was not matched by hope about progress in terms of inequality in the state. Once celebrated as a sort of land of opportunity for all, by the late 1990s California had emerged as the third or fourth most unequal state in the union, depending on whether one measured inequality as the ratio of the top fifth of households to the middle fifth or the top fifth to the bottom fifth (Economic Policy Institute, 2002). And while California improved its distributional position slightly in the early part of the century—an update from the Economic Policy Institute on income distribution for the 2001–2003 period placed California as the tenth most unequal state when comparing the top fifth of households to the middle fifth of households, and the sixth most unequal in the United States when comparing the top fifth to the bottom fifth—this was hardly a record to boast about (Bernstein et al., 2006:18–19, 23).

Against this backdrop of a robust economy and unequal fortunes, California's Latinos have generally shown up at the lower end of the income profile. Employment rates for Latinos are relatively high, suggesting a strong work ethic and attachment to the labor force. At the same time, Latinos are the poorest ethnic group in California, with disproportionate representation at the bottom of the wage and occupational structure. As I note below, this is not simply a function of the recency of immigration, with a longer period of time in this country likely to produce improved outcomes—even second- and third-generation Latino households find their incomes lagging those of Anglos. And because employment and economic growth do not seem to be doing the trick on their own, Latinos will need to devise long-term political and policy strategies to improve economic outcomes for themselves and their children.

This chapter seeks to contribute to this task by offering a longer-run look at the state of Latinos in the California economy. I begin with a brief review of employment and distributional trends of the last decade and a half. I then profile key economic characteristics of California's Latinos, especially the striking contradiction between high rates of labor-force participation and high rates of poverty, and suggest that a significant portion of this gap has to do with lower levels of job quality and educational attainment. I suggest that Latinos are a disproportionate share of the state's working poor and note how strategies geared to the working poor should therefore be of special interest to Latinos. I conclude with a brief discussion of both the policies and the political will that will be necessary to improve Latinos' fortunes.

A few caveats are in order. First, I do not focus in this piece on Latino small business; in Pastor (2003), I offer a more detailed account of that sector and stress the importance of such businesses in hiring other coethnics and thus enhancing employment. I also note the potential contribution of small business to community and economic development, emphasizing how the flowering of a middle class with sufficient assets and political power can help a general Latino agenda, particularly when that middle class is only one generation and modest amounts of income away from its working-class origins. However, though the number of Latino businesses has grown dramatically, in 2002 the receipts for Latino-owned firms in California were only about 2 percent of total business receipts in the state, slightly down from the 2.4 percent share of such receipts in 1997.[2] This suggests that much of the economic action for Latinos is occurring elsewhere, particularly in the more generalized labor market.

Second, while I note what the literature has told us about the relative importance of immigrant status, education, and other factors, I do not offer any independent regression analysis of the determinants of Latino economic performance in the state (for that, see Pastor, 2003). In general, the bottom line from such statistical studies squares with common sense: though discrimination, networks, and other factors are also extant, immigration, education, and job quality are among the most important variables in explaining Latino well-being in California. This suggests that a Latino economic agenda may wish to focus on those measures as well as accept that the very nature of the "new economy"—despite the glitter and glitz of high tech and bioengineering—is such that improvements in basic labor standards may be an essential part of Latino economic advancement.

Third, I do not offer an analysis of the stock of wealth by ethnicity in the state. This is an important issue because generational advantage is often passed on through wealth, and enhanced private wealth, including home equity, can make it easier for communities to borrow, start businesses, and further economic development. This issue is, however, covered in detail in Lopez and Moller (2003), including an analysis suggesting that the average Anglo household in California has around three times the level of wealth as the average Latino household, with the wealth disparity even larger if one does not include home equity but instead focuses on financial assets.[3] Yet from a broader perspective, even the focus on Latino labor in this chapter is about assets: the state has a population that is working hard every day but still falling behind, suggesting that much economic energy is going to waste and thus compelling us to consider new policies that will aid Latinos directly and therefore all Californians hoping for economic vitality and widespread prosperity.

The General Economic Picture and Latinos

The fortunes of the California economy have seen dramatic shifts over the last decade and a half. The 1990s began with a sharp recession, which given its origins in cutbacks in national spending on defense and aerospace had the sharpest impact on southern California, particularly the Los Angeles metro area. Figure 1.1 shows the unemployment experience in the state as a whole and in several key metro areas: San Francisco (which includes Marin and San Mateo Counties), Oakland (which includes Alameda and Contra Costa Counties), and the Los Angeles, San Jose, and San Diego metro areas, all of which include only the county in which the city is located.[4]

As can be seen, Los Angeles helped lead the state into recession and lingered there longer than the rest of the state, a fact that deeply affected Latino

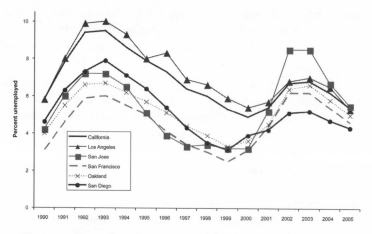

Figure 1.1. Unemployment rates in California and its regions,
1990–2005.

outcomes because nearly 40 percent of the state's Latino population lives in
Los Angeles County (versus fewer than 20 percent of the state's Anglos). As
the recovery proceeded, the San Jose and San Francisco metro areas—that is,
Silicon Valley—led the boom, but as 2000 turned to 2001, that region also led
the bust (particularly the San Jose/Santa Clara heart of the valley). Although
most recessions start with a slip in consumer spending, the recession of this
decade was largely triggered on a national level by a decline in business investment, particularly in high-tech spending. Because so much of the state's
employment was in that sector and had been rising during the 1990s—with
even more of Silicon Valley's employment high-tech dependent—the national
recession was felt early and hard, particularly in the Bay Area.[5] The high-tech
recession also led to problems for every resident because the state had become
highly reliant on income tax revenues from the richest residents, many of
whom were paying higher taxes because of boom-induced high incomes,
but saw them slip sharply downward, along with the value of stock options
and the vibrancy of the economy itself.

What did this pattern mean for distributional outcomes? To get at this,
I use the March Supplement of the Current Population Survey (CPS) to
calculate changes in income at various points in the income distribution.
Income was inflation-adjusted to reflect 2004 dollars—the iteration of the
March CPS available at the time of writing was from 2005, and so the most
recent income data available was from 2004. California's income distribution
started off quite unequal: in 1989, a peak year for the California economy,
the two-year moving average income for those at the 25th percentile of the

income distribution was just below $26,000, the income level for the median household was just over $49,000, and the income level for those at the 90th percentile was about $122,000.[6] Distribution worsened over the next fifteen years: by 2004, those at the 25th percentile had slipped by $1,000, those at the median had gained only about $600, and those at the 90th percentile had gained nearly $15,000 in real inflation-adjusted income.

Of course, these end-to-end comparisons poorly illustrate the impacts of the business cycle along the way. Thus, in Figure 1.2, I normalize the income levels at one hundred for the various income distribution points discussed above and track the yearly changes (using a two-year moving average)— remember that despite the fact that all the series start at one hundred, they represent very different levels of initial income. The chart highlights that the recession of the early 1990s had very little impact on high-income households but caused a sharp decline in incomes for those in the middle, and even more for those at the 25th percentile of the distribution. The recovery in the latter 1990s did yield strong benefits for richer households but the buoyancy of the economy also led to strong gains for those at the 25th percentile. The recession in the early 2000s had a strong impact on those at the top end—the sectors hardest hit, after all, were higher tech—but there were big losses at the bottom of the distributional pyramid as well.[7]

The overall pattern suggests the importance of a strong economy to those in the lower half of the distribution.[8] And this, as it turns out, is especially salient for Latinos: in Figure 1.3, I look at the ethnic composition of households by income deciles in California for the period 2002–2004.[9] As might be expected, the Anglo share of households steadily rises in the higher deciles, peaking at

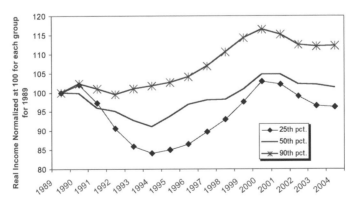

Figure 1.2. Income shifts at various percentile breaks for California households, 1989–2004.

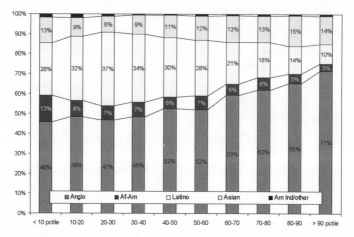

Figure 1.3. Ethnic composition of households by household income deciles in California, 2002–2004.

71 percent of households; African Americans have a very high representation in the lowest decile; the Asian community is bifurcated, with significant representation at the lowest and highest deciles; and Latino households peak in the second, third, and fourth deciles. This is exactly the group whose income appears most sharply affected by the state of the business cycle.

But it is not just economic growth that produces wage gains—policy matters as well. For example, while the federal minimum wage fell nearly 12 percent in real terms between 1997 and 2002, California's real minimum wage rose more than 13 percent over the same period as a result of state-mandated hikes. Alongside this state-level policy came the adoption of numerous living wage ordinances throughout the state—measures that required both local authorities and contractors to pay their own workers above a certain standard—as well as a growing movement to raise local minimum wages (for example, in San Francisco). Even market-oriented critics have concurred that such living wage ordinances did tend to improve income outcomes for the targeted low-wage workers (Neumark, 2002) and early studies suggest no evidence of employment losses owing to local minimums (see Dube and Reich, 2005, on the San Francisco case). Of course, neither the minimum wage nor living wages could protect households against the slack labor demand from a slowing economy, but the measures provided crucial floors and suggest much of what needs to emerge from future policies.

What did this changing economic and distributional picture mean for Latinos? Once again, I turn to the Current Population Survey data and chart the two-year moving average for household income, this time for Anglos,

Latinos, and African Americans.[10] In the results pictured in Figure 1.4, two patterns stand out. First, Latinos and African Americans are both at the bottom, with a substantial gap relative to Anglo households and with one group occasionally switching places to replace the other as the "leader" in low incomes. Second, the experience of both groups, in keeping with the discussion above, seems more susceptible to the state of the business cycle— the ups and downs of African American and Latino incomes track the state level of employment.

In analyzing the experience of Latinos, it may be useful to look not just at household income but also poverty rates. As Rodriguez (1996) notes, the majority of foreign-born Latino households contain three or more workers, twice the number for Asian immigrants and more than three times that for Anglos. Thus it is possible, depending on the number of earners and dependents, to be both below the poverty level (which controls for the number of people in a household) and squarely in the middle of the household income distribution (which does not control for the number of people or earners in a household).[11] In looking at poverty, I use as a benchmark the 150 percent poverty rate—that is, persons are designated as poor if the households in which they live have incomes that, if adjusted for household size, would place them below 150 percent of the federally determined poverty line. This poverty level is becoming more common in economic analysis, partly because the calculation of the federal poverty line has not been adjusted for years and seems absurdly low in the context of California's high housing prices. To afford the

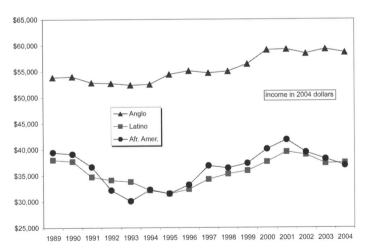

Figure 1.4. Median household income by ethnicity in California (two-year moving average), 1989–2004.

readers a sense of what this means, the 150 percent poverty threshold was around $28,000 in 2004 for a family of four, a level most observers would associate with hardship in high-cost California.

As can be seen in Figure 1.5, Latino poverty rates—pooled over the 1999–2004 period to smooth out any business cycle fluctuations—are the highest in the state, well above those of Anglos but also exceeding the poverty rates for African Americans. The chart also shows that poverty rates for Asian Pacific Americans exceed those for Anglos; the latter may surprise some who also know that Asians have relatively high household incomes, but it is a pattern that reflects the experience of some subgroups—that is, the higher Asian poverty rates are determined by the experience of Southeast Asian immigrants and Filipinos, both of whom fare less well than other Asian Pacific Islander groups. Still, the striking fact is that the Latino poverty rate is nearly 40 percent—almost half of California's Latino population lives in conditions most observers would term quite challenging.

While some may assume that these high poverty outcomes largely owe to the presence of low-earning immigrants, this is not a full explanation. Figure 1.6 displays the household income data for the two largest groups, for which the larger sample size makes the data the most reliable: Anglos and Latinos. The figure shows that immigrant Latino households are low earners, but even households headed by U.S.-born Latinos earn only about 80 percent of their Anglo counterparts. Something besides the generational immigrant experience is factoring in here.

The other key variable, it seems, is education. Over the last few decades, the

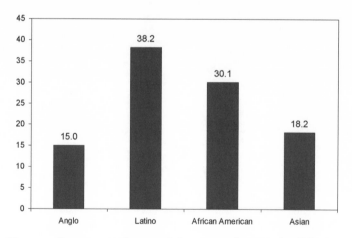

Figure 1.5. Poverty rates (percent below 150% of poverty level) by race for California, 1999–2004.

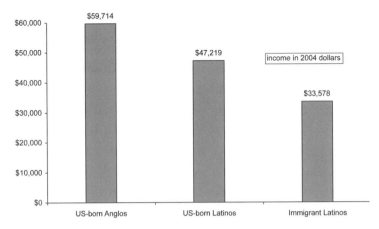

Figure 1.6. Household income of U.S.-born Anglos, U.S.-born Latinos, and immigrant Latinos in California, 1999–2004.

returns to education—that is, the additional income yielded from an additional year of schooling—have been on the rise. Data from the Economic Policy Institute, for example, indicate that real wages for those with less than a high school education declined by nearly 18 percent between 1979 and 2005, while wages for those with a college degree rose by more than 22 percent over the same period—in short, the earnings gap between the more- and less-educated got even wider.[12] Figure 1.7 shows the educational levels for California's civilian labor force by race, ethnicity, and immigration. As can be seen, nearly 60 percent of Latino immigrants in the labor force lack a high school education, clearly a factor in the earnings disparity for immigrants. What is perhaps more striking is the extraordinarily low presence of college graduates in the U.S.-born Latino workforce, even when compared to African Americans, as well as the relatively high percentage of those who have not completed high school.

Steve Trejo (1997) has suggested that this educational disparity accounts for virtually all of the difference in economic outcomes between Anglos and second- and third-generation Mexican Americans, in particular. I have argued that for a variety of reasons, this likely overstates the contributing role of education and diminishes the impact of both social networks and ongoing discrimination (see Pastor, 2003). At the same time, it is clear that raising the educational profile of U.S.-born Latinos is a necessity if one hopes to see any decline in the poverty and income gaps depicted in the various figures above. The other must-do, however, is tackling the basic nature of the jobs being generated in the California economy, and for this I turn to a deeper analysis of the poverty and job-creation pattern.

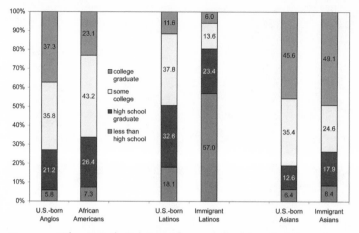

Figure 1.7. Educational attainment for work force by ethnicity and immigration, California, 2000–2005.

Working Poverty and Latinos

Latinos are, as noted, the poorest group in the state. The usual story with regard to poverty is that it stems from low levels of attachment to the labor force—that is, that individuals become poor when they are not able to obtain employment, perhaps because they have inadequate skills, live far from available jobs, or are saddled with significant child-care responsibilities (Wilson, 1996). Yet as many authors have noted, Latinos do not fit this mold, with California males exhibiting the highest rates of labor force attachment of any ethnic group and females on parallel with other groups, with the latter particularly impressive because Latinas are far more likely to have children and therefore have various reasons to stay out of the workforce (see Hayes-Bautista, 1993 and Melendez, 1993). Instead, it seems, the key issue for Latinos is working poverty: having a job but being unable to garner sufficient earnings to support a family.

The nature of poverty matters for several reasons. The remedies for poverty are different depending on its cause. If the problem is nonworking poverty, connecting people with their first job is crucial; if it is working poverty, connecting workers with career advancement is more significant. If the challenge is nonworking poverty, unions could be an impediment, as they often limit entrance to a field; if it is working poverty, unions are crucial because they can lift the wages of organized workers. If the problem is nonworking poverty, daytime classes that build hard and "soft" skills for employment are essential; if it is working poverty, classes should be scheduled at night and focus on hard skills (because, presumably, those already employed have already acquired a working base of "soft" skills such as showing up on time, behaving appropriately in the workplace, and so forth).

The nature of poverty also matters for reasons of politics. Whether one agrees with this sentiment-or not, the general mood of the U.S. public is not generous toward those who do not labor and are receiving public welfare. On the other hand, numerous polls and focus groups suggest a deep sympathy to those who labor but still fall below the poverty line. Many policy measures that have proven popular in California—such as increases in the state minimum wage as well as living wage ordinances in Los Angeles, San Jose, and elsewhere—were predicated on building political momentum by creating the image of hard-working residents who, owing to the vagaries of the economy, did not see their efforts translate into more productive outcomes. Not only does this imagery square with values deeply held by many in society, it also tends to connect with the insecurities of middle-class Californians who feel they are one paycheck away from destitution themselves. For all these reasons, working poverty has surfaced as a major focus for both analysts and advocates.

As can be seen in Figure 1.8, work is certainly a major antidote for poverty. Following census definitions, I define full-time work as having worked at least fifty weeks a year and at least thirty-five hours a week. I also offer a definition for significant work as having worked less than full-time but more than thirty-five weeks a year and more than twenty-five hours a week. Part-time work is defined as having worked less than a significant worker but more than

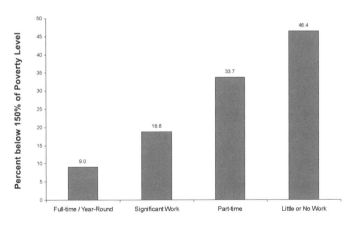

Figure 1.8. Household poverty rate by householder work status, California, 1999–2004.

ten weeks a year and more than ten hours a week; those in the little or no work category have worked less than ten weeks a year or less than ten hours a week.[13] I focus here on the work experience of the householder, although I take the poverty level from the household as a whole; though there are potential problems with this strategy (particularly if others in the household are actually the primary earners), it is a useful way to identify ethnicity, poverty, and work experience all at the same time, and more complicated analyses yield very similar patterns by ethnicity and other variables (see Pastor and Scoggins, 2006).

In any case, the figure illustrates that those who work are far less likely to fall into the poverty trap. But it also shows that nearly 10 percent of full-time year-round workers, and almost 20 percent of those who are engaged in significant work, head households that fall below the 150 percent poverty line. Who are these working poor, that is, those falling below the poverty line but still involved in full-time or significant work?

Figure 1.9 helps us understand the demographics by contrasting the ethnic composition of those householders who are nonpoor, those who are poor but not working poor, and those who are working poor; again, for improved accuracy for the subpopulations, I pool data from 1999 to 2004. The pattern is striking: Latinos rise from 22 percent of the nonpoor households, to 38 percent of the poor but nonworking households, to nearly 60 percent of the working poor households. This trend of overrepresentation in the working poor outpaces that of all other groups and is a striking difference from the

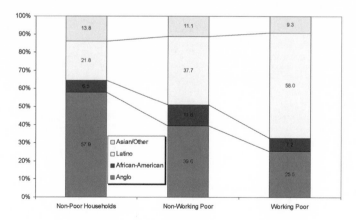

Figure 1.9. Composition of non-poor, non-working poor, and working poor households headed by working age person in California, 1999–2005.

pattern for African Americans: in California, African Americans constitute about 7 percent of the nonpoor and the working poor, but 12 percent of the nonworking poor.

Another way to look at the same phenomenon is to ask how important the experience of working poverty is to each ethnic group. For this view, the focus is on what share of the poor households in each ethnic group falls into the category of working poor. The results are depicted in Figure 1.10. As can be seen, half of the Latino poor fall into the working category; for all other groups it ranges between 28 and 36 percent. In short, strategies to improve the situations of the working poor would have disproportionately positive influence on Latinos: they constitute more than half of the working poor, and about half of the Latino poor are working.

The need to focus on this part of the Latino poverty problem is reinforced when looking at the unemployment patterns by race. The usual story in a recession is "last hired, first fired"—that is, minorities will be laid off more quickly in a downturn, and so the unemployment experience is more volatile for them than for Anglos. But, as Figure 1.11 points out, there is a very different experience unfolding in California. Using official state statistics for each month and adopting the state's practice of taking a twelve-month moving average to smooth out fluctuations owing to small sample sizes by ethnicity in any particular month, the figure illustrates that Latino unemployment is higher than that of Anglos but has actually been quite stable in terms of its relationship to Anglo unemployment. Indeed, the average gap between Anglo and Latino unemployment fell from 2 percentage points in 2001 to 1.5 percentage points in 2005; the gap between African American

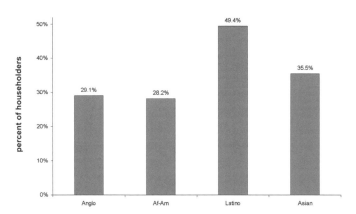

Figure 1.10. Percent of poor by ethnic group with full-time or significant work, age 25–64, pooled 1999–2004.

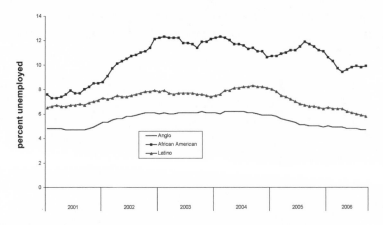

Figure 1.11. Unemployment rate by race, January 2001 to September 2006, not seasonally adjusted, 12-month moving average.

and Anglo unemployment actually rose from 3.4 percentage points in 2001 to 6.2 percentage points in 2005.[14]

The relative stability of the unemployment rate suggests that Latinos, particularly immigrants, have become "embedded" into the structural demand for low-wage labor in the California economy (Cornelius, 1998; Marcelli and Cornelius, 2001). Another way to see this is to examine the composition of the working poor in terms of immigrant status, particularly the recency of arrival. This is done in Figure 1.12, with a contrast offered to the immigrant composition of the nonworking poor. Two trends emerge. One is the structural embeddedness story, with an interesting twist: Immigrant households that came in the 1980s are even more likely to fall into the category of working poor, probably because they have not moved on significantly economically but perhaps also because they have fewer earners per household as time in country goes on, and so household pooling of income declines. The second significant fact is the very large share of U.S.-born residents in the ranks of the working poor; apparently, this is a phenomenon that affects many Californians and it is one on which common ground can be built.

Economic Futures and Latinos

The discussion of structural embeddedness suggests something very important to Latino futures: low-wage work seems to have become a permanent part of the California economy. This may, at first glance, seem surprising:

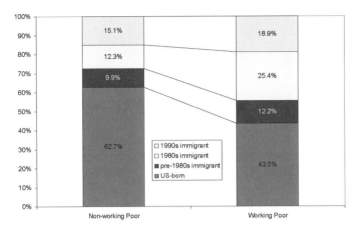

Figure 1.12. Immigrant status of nonworking poor and working poor in California, 1999–2004.

after all, I started this chapter by discussing the state as the center of the new economy, complete with its high-tech industries and highly trained population. But low-wage jobs in the local-serving sector have often been the flip side of high-tech growth: computer programmers and Web designers working sixteen-hour days wind up needing restaurant, laundry, and child-care services, and these are jobs filled by large numbers of Latino, immigrant, and other minority workers.

Temporary and contingent work has also been an important part of the vaunted new economy: nearly 16 percent of the total net increase in private employment between 1991 and 2000 occurred within employment services or temporary help agencies, and contingent or part-time employment (including off-the-books day labor) was skyrocketing outside these agencies as well. While the recession led to a cutback in temporary help—part of the reason for hiring workers who are not permanent is exactly so they can be laid off more easily—temporary work was back on the rise after 2003. Both the aforementioned service-sector jobs and this temporary employment have not been high-quality, and the service sector has been an area of the economy with high numbers of low-skill Latinos.[15]

The future looks to be bringing more of the same unfortunate mix of job quality. Table 1.1 relies on the occupational projections of the state's Employment Development Department to cast light on the twenty occupations projected to have the most growth in job openings between 2004 and 2014. The

Table 1.1. Top twenty occupations with the greatest number of job openings in the California economy, 2004-2014

Occupation	Number of Openings	Educational/Training Requirements
Retail salespersons	288,300	On-the-job training (30 days)
Cashiers	205,700	On-the-job training (30 days)
Waiters and waitresses	158,400	On-the-job training (30 days)
Laborers and freight, stock, and material movers, hand	143,400	On-the-job training (30 days)
Office clerks, general	134,200	On-the-job training (30 days)
Combined food preparation and serving workers, including fast food	130,700	On-the-job training (30 days)
Registered nurses	109,100	A.A. degree
Janitors and cleaners, except maids and housekeeping cleaners	93,300	On-the-job training (30 days)
General and operations managers	85,900	B.A. degree and experience
Elementary school teachers, except special education	83,000	B.A. degree
Customer service representatives	82,300	On-the-job training (1-12 months)
Teacher assistants	76,200	On-the-job training (30 days)
Counter attendants, cafeteria, food concession, and coffee shop	75,700	On-the-job training (30 days)
Carpenters	73,100	On-the-job training (1-12 months)
Landscaping and groundskeeping workers	69,400	On-the-job training (30 days)
Sales representatives, wholesale and manufacturing, except technical and scientific	69,400	On-the-job training (1-12 months)
Executive secretaries and administrative assistants	68,800	On-the-job training (1-12 months)
Farmworkers and laborers, crop, nursery, and greenhouse	68,500	On-the-job training (30 days)
Stock clerks and order filers	66,100	On-the-job training (30 days)

striking fact is that none are in the high-tech industry (with the possible exception of some of those in the category of general managers and executives), and seven of the top ten require no more than short-term on-the-job training.[16]

These state-projected trends square with the findings of Milkman and Dwyer (2002). Using an innovative technique to focus on the quality of jobs being created—an approach that focuses on the demand side of the market rather than on whatever may be happening with the skill set of workers on the supply side—they find that there is increasing polarization in the job structure itself. They also find that this is likely to have especially severe impacts on Latino workers, given their concentrations in certain low-wage occupations and industries. In such an economy, it is critical for any program focused on Latino well-being to include attention to basic labor standards that will attach to any job, as well as to the paths for future advancement.

Of course, labor standards are not enough. In general, there are three paths to better labor market outcomes for Latinos in California: rapid economic growth and its side effects; targeted education, training, and placement; and the aforementioned improvement in labor standards. Growth is a sine qua non, although it is an issue often left aside by progressive thinkers and advocates. Despite the doom-and-gloom pictures offered by those who point out that inequality increased during the 1990s, it is also clear that after a long shakeout by class and race, distributional improvements were finally emerging in the latter part of the decade. Unfortunately, the party stopped just as new guests were arriving—and getting the economy humming again is an essential part of any economic program that will lift Latino incomes and better position them for the future.

This progress involves the need for a Latino voice in the various macroeconomic decisions that set the path for the state, including the need to balance environmental and growth goals and the nature of the state's fiscal system. Latinos should be especially interested in reversing policies that tend to favor the expansion of business over the creation of new jobs; for example, that Proposition 13 has led many localities to depend on retail sales tax revenue rather than property values has led to a push for big-box retail rather than industrial development and retention. The effect of this distorted fiscal structure on job quality is quite negative, with communities struggling for sales tax leftovers in order to pay for the social services and support systems needed by poor residents working in those same retail industries. Though such tax and development policies have not traditionally been "Latino issues" in the state, they should be, particularly given their importance to the working poor, the recent tendency for Latino leaders to occupy important decision-making positions in state government, and the general need to rekindle growth to improve Latino outcomes.

Education, training, and networking are also important parts of economic and individual development. Educational attainment must be improved, particularly in the public schools that train the lion's share of Latino youth. As noted, econometric and other evidence suggests that there is a very high payoff from a college education: outreach programs for the University of California and the California State University systems are therefore especially important for Latino economic advancement. Unfortunately, these sorts of programs and public education in general have been very much threatened by the state's current fiscal problems, as well as a lack of political will—year after year, such programs are forced to survive on soft and insecure funding.

Education must also go beyond a focus on K-12 and the university system. Critically important for the advancement of working people is the community college system: it both prepares individuals for university and provides a plethora of practical training activities for both job-seekers and incumbent employees. This is an especially important entry point for the immigrant population, both those with and without high school degrees who seek advanced job skills, as well as for the large mass of U.S.-born Latinos who lack a college degree and need convenient access to higher-education resources. Yet a 2004 study found that California's community colleges ranked forty-fifth out of forty-nine states in terms of revenues spent per student. It also found that the previous thirty years had seen increases in real per-student revenue of nearly 25 percent for the University of California, while the community colleges saw only a 4 percent increase in real per-student revenue (see Murphy, 2004). The crisis in the community colleges should be of special concern to advocates for Latino interests.

Latinos, particularly immigrants, also need an expansion of adult education and basic job training. English skills for adults are especially important: they can boost wages for full-time workers by more than 15 percent, even controlling for education, immigrant status, and other factors that usually impact wage outcomes (Pastor and Marcelli, 2000). Training also needs to be regeared to those who are already working, that is, to the working poor, if it is to truly help the population profiled here. This should involve new thinking with regard to the design of the workforce development system, particularly community representation in the emerging structure of workforce investment boards, as well as more mundane matters like the timing of classes, the desirability of on-site training, and the need to couple vocational English training with worker education about basic labor rights. It would also be useful to consider incentives for employer provision of on-the-job training, something that would be particularly helpful to incumbent workers; this sort of tax break would seem far superior and more helpful to economic development than, say, reducing vehicle licensing fees.

Networking is also a crucial, if often overlooked, component of workforce improvement strategies. Studies have found that most people obtain employment through connections with others; Latinos are no different, but because so many of their connections are with coethnics who are no better placed in the labor market than they, the placements they get are often to lower-wage employment (Falcón, 1995; Pastor and Marcelli, 2000). Many Latinos, in short, would do better to rely on sympathetic agencies than on sympathetic friends—but this will only improve outcomes if the agencies are also effective and well-rooted in the worlds of both business and community (Benner,

Leete, and Pastor, 2007). Public policy could help by steering workforce development dollars to innovative community-based groups.

Finally, there is the matter of labor standards—measures that range from minimum wage laws to health insurance guarantees to enhancements in the capacity to join a union. These sorts of actions are generally opposed by businesses, who believe that they will bring higher costs and strangle investment. But while this may be true of an individual enterprise, lifting the society's floor in general can actually help protect firms from cutthroat competition and steer regional economies onto "high-road" growth paths.

What is practical in this regard? The state minimum wage is already 30 percent higher than the federal level, and further hikes are planned for 2007 and 2008 as a result of an agreement between the governor and the legislature in 2006. Though this will be helpful, wages are only one part of job quality—and companies can compensate for higher cash outlays by trimming back health insurance, increasing work intensity, and other measures. In this regard, it is critical to expand health insurance, and this would be especially helpful to Latinos: over the 2001–2005 period, the percentage of Latino households lacking health insurance was 40.1, about twice the rate of Anglos.[17]

Of course, the government could help matters and improve labor conditions simply by encouraging worker representation through unions. Latinos, ensconced among the working poor, are increasingly sympathetic to union representation and unions, and are aware that most of the net growth in the future workforce will consist of Latinos. They are receptive to new organizing efforts focused on both U.S.-born and immigrant Latinos; in fact, labor's most dramatic organizing successes in recent years—including janitors and home health-care workers—have come about with largely Latino immigrant workforces. The government could help this through modest changes in labor law that would make it easier for workers to seek union representation—for example, regulations that would call a union election quickly after cards are signed, rather than allowing companies a lengthy period of time to convince workers to either vote for the company or face quiet harassment and/or firing. Unions will also continue to make gains if they stick with an emerging emphasis on how to support the incorporation of immigrants into economic and civic life.

What is fascinating is that very few of the issues mentioned above are "Latino" in the traditional sense of an ethnic agenda. This is not to say that such traditional issues are unimportant: bilingual education has helped many to transition to English, affirmative action has proven quite helpful to the creation of a middle class, and civil rights enforcement is necessary to prevent the sort of bank redlining that prevents Latino businesses from growing to their full potential and impedes Latino families from sharing in the dream of home ownership. Yet the fact of the matter is that Latinos are disproportionately working poor, and strategies targeted to lift this group may prove most crucial in the hard times likely to occupy policy makers' attention in the coming years.

Finally, it may be tempting for some to put aside issues of Latino advancement in favor of a "broader" agenda of simply keeping the state economy vibrant and growing. But while equity is often helped by growth, growth does not always deliver fairness, and equity is not a luxury good to be purchased only at the peak of a business cycle. Indeed, it is precisely because Latinos are so emblematic of our state's economic future—one filled with polarized employment, insecure health insurance, and lagging wages—that a focus on helping Latinos achieve their economic potential may be a way to ensure a better future for all Californians.

Notes

1. Unemployment data is taken from the Labor Market Information Division of the Employment Development Department of California; see http://www.labormarketinfo.edd.ca.gov/.

2. Data on Latino share of state receipts from the 2002 Survey of Business Owners, Statistics for All U.S. Firms by State, Hispanic or Latino Origin, and Gender, as downloaded from American Factfinder, http://factfinder.census.gov. 1997 share from the 1997 Survey as reported at http://www.census.gov/epcd/mwb97/ca/CA.html.

3. For more on home ownership rates among Latinos and the obstacles to raising those rates, see Kotkin, Tseng, and Ozuna (2002).

4. Employment data from the state's Employment Development Department, Labor Market Information Division (see www.edd.ca.gov). I do not include the Central Valley in this picture partly because inclusion of the very high and persistent rates there tends to distort the detailed picture for other metro areas. The experience of Latinos in agriculture and rural areas is important and unique and deserving of a treatment separate from what is offered here.

5. For example, in the years 1999–2001, 27.6 percent of employment in the San Jose metro area was in the tech sector, with the comparable figure for the state being 7.2 percent, and for the nation 4.3 percent.

6. I use a two-year moving average to control for volatility in the series. I also use the income levels at various breaks in the income distribution rather than calculating the share of total household income because the early years of the data used for this exercise include a "topcode" that reduces accuracy at the very top end of the income spectrum.

7. Some might suggest that this shifting income distribution is simply the result of migrants entering the labor force at the bottom and thus dragging down certain deciles simply by their low-earning presence. This is difficult to disentangle over the whole period, mostly because the Current Population Survey did not start collecting immigration status

data until 1993. Looking at the income distribution for just the U.S.-born from 1993–94 and 2003–2004, I find that the shifts in that period for the 25th percentile and the median were roughly the same for just the U.S.-born; however, the gains at the 90th percentile were even larger when I exclude immigrants. In short, the inclusion of immigrants in the data presented does not seem to distort the underlying pattern in the economy itself.

8. In Pastor and Zabin (2002), we use state-provided data from the Occupational Employment Statistics Survey to show the changes in wages at various points on a wage distribution—for the worker at the 25th percentile, one at the 50th percentile, and one at the 75th percentile—and also find that the latter part of the boom brought great gains for those on the bottom.

9. Anglo households for this period were 55 percent of all households, while African Americans were 7 percent, Latinos 25 percent, and Asians 12 percent; note that the Anglo share of households is larger than their share of population, and the Latino share of household is lower than their share of the population, mostly because of differences in household size. The household composition numbers are actually from the 2003–2005 period because the income figures for those households are reported for the year before.

10. I do not picture Asian household income here, partly because the sample size is so small that the series is very volatile. In general, Asian household income exceeds even Anglo household income, albeit slightly.

11. This realization does not prevent Rodriguez (1996) from making what I think is a misleading analytical decision—using median household income as a cut point for determining whether a household is middle class. This results in counting many large households with multiple low-wage earners as part of a growing Latino "middle class" in southern California. In fact, household income may be moderate, but resources per person can be low.

12. Data from the Economic Policy Institute, http://www.epi.org/datazone/06/datazone_2006-full.xls. The shift in earnings was particularly strong for men in the labor market—those with less than a high school education saw a decline of 22 percent in their real hourly wages, and even those with a high school education saw a 10 percent decline in real wages. Propping up the returns for high school graduates overall were women, who saw a 10 percent increase in their real wages over the period as more job opportunities opened.

13. This work breakdown is developed and utilized in Pastor et al. (2000).

14. As the chart shows, there was some improvement in the gap between African American and Anglo unemployment rates in 2006, but at the time of writing, the full year of data was not yet available for a more careful comparison. In comparing years in the discussion in the text, I take the December figures for each, as they are a twelve-month moving average for the whole year.

15. I discuss other measures of job quality later in this chapter when I review data on health insurance and unionization.

16. The data came from the California Employment Development Department; see http://www.labormarketinfo.edd.ca.gov/.

17. Data on health insurance is taken from the Current Population Survey, March Supplement, various years.

2. Working Day Labor

Informal and Contingent Employment

ABEL VALENZUELA JR.

Introduction

A review of all articles related to day labor[1] appearing in the *Los Angeles Times* between 1986 and 2006 overwhelmingly portrays this type of employment as unstable, illegal, underpaid, and fraught with employer abuses (Reyes, 1991; Mozingo, 1997; Rosenblatt, 1997; Aubry, 1993). Light and Roach (1996) present day laborers as part of the informal employment growth of Los Angeles, with street-corner labor markets as a form of marginal self-employment. Parker (1994:63) describes day labor as bottom rung for wage earners in pay, with no benefits and inadequate to provide workers with enough income to afford housing, thereby concluding that the majority of day laborers are homeless. In their study of Chicago's temporary employment industry, Peck and Theodore (1998:658) describe the hiring halls and the day labor contractor as typical of the "bottom end of the temporary industry . . ." Media and academic accounts of day labor in part reflect the dramatic growth of this market, where large concentrations of recent arrivals, predominantly men, partake in this burgeoning labor exchange. Even though the growth of temporary or contingent jobs paid informally or "under the table," or with large concentrations of unauthorized immigrants, is not adequately captured by the census and Department of Labor Statistics, other evidence suggests that in recent years, paid temporary day labor has increased (GAO, 2000; Valenzuela, 1999, Valenzuela et al., 2006).

As a result of the modest academic attention to day labor and the mostly negative media coverage on this job market niche, we have little empirical evidence about this growing market, the workers who participate, and the employers who seek this type of labor. In fact, with the exception of a few studies (see Valenzuela, 2003, for a review of the literature), scholars have neglected to empirically investigate this urban labor market, and as a result, it remains understudied and undertheorized.

Drawing on participant observation, in-depth interviews, and a survey of day laborers in metropolitan Los Angeles, I explore the utility of informal and contingent labor-market theory to explain participation in day labor. These two frameworks drive explanations for understanding participation in day labor work. I pose this question: Why, given the boom in Los Angeles's economy and the abusive and difficult nature of day labor, would so many workers participate in this economic exchange? Using informal and contingent employment as a conceptual framework, I contextualize day labor and argue that even though this occupation is unregulated, unstable, and prone to workplace abuses, the characteristics of the day laborers, their limited job experience and skills, their development of friendships and networks, their ability to negotiate a fair wage with their employers, and the structural and other barriers to the formal market allow a sizable number to earn a modest living. As a result of these and other factors, I conclude that informalization falls short of an adequate explanation, while contingent employment, particularly when analyzed in concert with immigrant labor-market disadvantage, provides a better framework of worker participation in day labor. Empirically analyzing the unique characteristics of the day labor force and the day-to-day experiences of this occupation provides additional information on this topic and contributes to our understanding of day labor, informality, contingent employment, and the motivations for participating in this employment niche.

Day Labor: Bottom of the Barrel?

Gathering every morning in a public open-air venue to secure work is, on the face of it, a desperate attempt at employment. Day labor is unstable, the potential for employer abuse is great, and for most, securing a job is similar to winning a $75 lottery ticket; the adrenaline is high, the payoff relatively low. Serious threats at hiring sites, such as harassment from police, residents, and merchants, and the possibility of ICE (formerly the INS—Immigration and Naturalization Service) sweeps seem to always exist as a result of the market's attraction to recent arrivals, the majority of whom are undocumented. Securing work on a street corner is frantic and can be physically dangerous, as moving cars come to a halt and men eagerly surround them, aggressively drawing attention to themselves in the hopes of being selected for a day of hard work.

For employers, hiring day labor is also not without risks. Unclear are the legal sanctions for hiring an illegal worker from the street. One of the attractions of this market exchange is the savings from not paying taxes—this is accrued to both the employer and the worker. Failure to pay taxes may result in legal sanctions to both. For an employer, hiring day labor is also like playing the lottery, but with fewer risks; unless one hires the same worker regularly, an employer does not know if the hire will produce good or skilled work. Employers have few telltale signs of a day laborer's work ethic or experience—traits that all employers prefer to know prior to hiring someone. Few if any women participate as day laborers.[2] As a result, female employers can only hire male day laborers. Hiring and entrusting a stranger of the opposite sex in your home or worksite is potentially dangerous.

Other factors make this market difficult for both employers and workers. Workers regularly compete with each other for the infrequent jobs secured at open-air hiring sites, aggressively getting the attention of prospective employers. Irregular employment may prompt desperate actions to obtain work. In a public setting with similar men, securing work becomes increasingly frenzied. Unscrupulous employers, knowing the volatile nature of this market, often take advantage of this desperation and abuse workers by refusing to pay the worker altogether, or by paying the worker an amount less than agreed, or having the worker perform dangerous or difficult tasks without proper safety equipment and for inadequate pay.

Despite the difficulty in finding daily work in this market, the potential for abuse, and the unknown legal sanctions of hiring a temporary, likely illegal worker from a public setting, this employment exchange has grown rapidly and is visible throughout the United States (GAO, 2002; Valenzuela et al., 2006). In Los Angeles alone, more than one hundred hiring sites exist, representing approximately eighteen thousand to twenty thousand workers (Valenzuela, 1999). Day labor also exists outside the United States, in places such as Mexico (Vanackere, 1987), South Africa, South America (Townsend, 1997), and Japan (Fowler, 1996; Marr, 1997; Giamo, 1994; Gill, 1994, 2001; Valenzuela et al., 2002).

Given the unstable, low pay and difficult nature of this employment exchange, a simple question emerges: Why do so many workers participate? In this chapter, I demonstrate that day labor, though mostly a desperate and unstable occupation, does provide semiregular employment opportunities, competitive wages to a sizable number of participants, and other important work attributes such as job experience, possibilities for permanent employment, and social networks including camaraderie and friendship. As a result, successful job seekers in this market earn a modest living consistent with if not better than other forms of marginal or secondary-sector jobs, and even for those who are unable to earn a living, other benefits such as information sharing and networking arise from participation in this line of employment.

Day Labor: Informal and Contingent Employment

Two related labor-market theories help explain participation in and the contemporary development of day labor in the United States: the informal economy (Williams and Windebank, 1998; Portes et al., 1989; Portes, 1994) and the advent of nonstandard and contingent work (Kalleberg, 2000; Smith, 1997; Beard and Edwards, 1995; Belous, 1989). To be sure, both informality and contingent employment can be found at the high and low end of the hourglass job strata, both have grown considerably since the 1970s, and both can trace their contemporary emergence to broader and more complex changes in the economy. Within these two frameworks, but especially within the contingent framework, participation in day labor is better understood. Missing, however, is an explicit discussion of the workers in these types of jobs and the characteristics that mediate their participation. Therefore, in order to maximize the utility of contingent work for understanding day labor participation, a discussion of immigrant labor-market disadvantage is critical to make sense of this market.

Informal Employment

Informal work variously referred to as the "underground" sector, "hidden" work, or the "shadow" economy (see Williams and Windebank, 1998) is paid work beyond the realm of formal employment. This work involves the paid production and sale of goods and services that are unregistered by or hidden from the state for tax, social security, and/or labor law purposes, but that are legal in all other respects (Williams and Windebank, 2000; Feige, 1990; Portes, 1994; Thomas, 1992). Therefore, paid informal work includes all legitimate activities where payments received by individuals are not declared to the authorities. Informal employment also includes work in illegal activities such as prostitution, the large-scale manufacture and sale of illicit goods, and drug peddling.

Castells and Portes (1989:12) demonstrate alternative or informal income-generating activities characterized by one central feature: "it is unregulated by the institutions of society, in a legal and social environment." As a result of the absence of institutional regulations, different work processes are ignored, changed, or amended. For example, labor may be clandestine, undeclared, paid below the minimum wage, or employed under circumstances that society's norms would not otherwise allow. The conditions under which we work also fall under the control of institutional regulations and involve land-use zoning, safety standards, hazardous or toxic dumping in the workplace, and other health-related work issues. Informal employment often does not adhere to institutional regulations of these types. Several immigrant-concentrated occupations come to mind: the garment industry, piecework, street peddling, domestic help (Hondagneu-Sotelo, 2001; Hondagneu-Sotelo and Avila, 1997; Hondagneu-Sotelo and Riegos, 1997; Ibarra, 2000), and day labor. Day labor is unregulated by the federal and state government, although momentum is gaining to locally regulate the industry (Valenzuela, 2000; Toma and Esbenshade, 2001; Esbenshade, 2000; Calderon et al., 2002). Employment in day labor is dangerous, safety standards go unchecked, and workers are frequently injured (Quesada, 1999; Walter, 2000; Walter et al., 2002; Brown et al., 2002; Worby, 2002).

Are immigrants more prone to informal employment? According to Williams and Windebank (1998), they are. However, this conclusion is mostly based on U.S. research, the vast majority concerning the extent to which immigrant and minority populations engage in informal employment and the type of paid informal activities. Most work on this topic focuses on low-paid, labor-intensive, nonunionized, and exploitative occupations in poorer areas with high concentrations of immigrants, ethnic minorities, or both (see Fernandez-Kelly and Garcia, 1989; Lin, 1995; Portes, 1994; Sassen, 1989; Stepick, 1989). As a result, informal employment is closely associated with immigrants and minorities. Day labor in Los Angeles is overwhelmingly immigrant (99 percent), unauthorized (84 percent), and of Latin American origin (98 percent) (Valenzuela, 2001). Nevertheless, informality falls short in its explanatory power because day labor is a highly visible market where the search is done publicly, the work undertaken is almost always legal, and because most workers are hired for one or two days, employers are not required to pay typical payroll taxes or to check for legal documents. In essence, day laborers function as self-employed contractors, shielding them from certain legal standards and employer tax requirements.

Contingent Work

The growth and visibility of the informal economy occurred simultaneously with labor flexibility—the process whereby the standard core employment relationship in industrial mass-production enterprises has changed from predominantly secure (full-time employment for an indefinite period, with a single employer) to insecure (self-employed, part-time, temporary, and sub-contract) nonstandard work (see Kalleberg, 2000; Smith, 1997). Early work on this subject by Portes and Benton (1984) and Portes and Sassen-Koob (1987) shows that from the post–World War II period until 1980, Latin America experienced a rapid and sustained process of industrial development that also included informal and self-employed work. Tilly (1996:13) also documents the growth of part-timers in the workforce, stating "since the 1950s, the proportion of part-time workers has grown gradually, climbing from 13 percent in 1957 to 19 percent in 1993." Finally, employers, in their attempts to reduce costs, have increased their use of employment intermediaries such as temporary help services and contract companies, and are relying more on alternative staffing arrangement such as on-call workers and independent contractors (Polivka, 1996; Henson, 1996).

In response to these changes, perceived or real, in full-time, single-employer, long-term jobs and simultaneous increases in "disposable" or "hire on-demand" temporary workers, a new category of workers emerged, known as contingent workers. First coined in 1985 (Polivka and Nardone, 1989) the term describes a management technique of employing workers only when there is an immediate and direct demand for their services, such as during a temporary layoff or spurt in demand for a particular product. Since its initial use, the term has been applied to a wide range of employment practices, including part-time work, temporary-help service employment, employee leasing, self-employment, contracting out, employment in the business-services sector, and home-based work. It is also often used to describe any nontraditional work arrangement, differing from the norm of a full-time wage and salaried job, such as day labor.

To make sense of this new employment category and to provide specificity on its possible size and impact, the Bureau of Labor Statistics (BLS) developed a conceptual definition of contingent work (Polivka and Nardone, 1989; Polivka, 1996). Its focus is on job security and unpredictability in hours worked. According to the BLS, any work arrangement that does not contain an explicit or implicit commitment between the employee and employer for long-term employment should be considered contingent. The BLS also added another category, "workers in alternative work arrangements," under the broad rubric of contingency. Workers in alternative work arrangements are independent contractors, on-call workers, temporary-help agency workers, workers provided by contract firms, and day laborers.

To better assess the status and numbers of the contingent workforce in the United States, the Bureau of Labor Statistics operationalized their definitions and collected data on this population from the 1995, 1997, 1999, and 2001 supplements of the Current Population Survey. As a result, the BLS has the most extensive and detailed data on contingent workers, bringing to light for the first time important differences among nonstandard work arrangements, characteristics of workers, and differences between contingent work and traditional work arrangements. Relying on this survey to analyze day labor is problematic because of definitional variations of the term, making it difficult to distinguish between informal "open-air" curbside, formal temporary staffing agency, and other types of day labor.

Employers use contingent workers for a variety of reasons. Houseman (1996) finds that employers hire contingent workers to accommodate work-load fluctuations, fill temporary absences, meet employees' requests for part-time hours, screen workers for permanent positions, and save on wage and benefit costs, among other reasons. Employers also use contingent workers to avoid paying benefits or employment taxes, to reduce workers' compensation costs, to prevent workers' attempts to unionize, or to lay off workers more easily. Finally, the ease and flexibility in hiring contingent workers make this supply of workers especially attractive. Cumbersome personnel procedures are circumvented through temporary agencies or by simply driving by a temporary hiring site and securing labor.

Workers participate in contingent work for a variety of reasons. Some workers prefer a flexible schedule because of school, family, or other obligations, and they are willing to forego steady work at a higher wage for the flexibility afforded in this type of work. Others partake in this market for additional income, supplementing their full- or part-time employment elsewhere. Still others are unable to find a steady job and hope that work in this market will lead to permanent employment.

Immigrant participation in contingent employment, particularly in day labor, is consistent with these reasons but also shares at least two other important factors. First, immigrants often seek an alternative to the formal, noncontingent labor market where their pay is low. Immigrants participate in the flexible or contingent labor market because they have adapted to the lower incomes generated from their "regular" jobs' low pay and wish to supplement their take-home pay. Contingent work is at the very least a supplement, if not an alternative, to their participation in a low-skill, low-pay job in the formal, albeit secondary, sector of the economy.

Second, immigrants, particularly Latino immigrants, often have no other employment options but to participate in this labor market as a result of their labor-market disadvantages (Light, 1979; Min, 1988). Poor labor-market outcomes among Latinos are attributed to several factors or characteristics that immigrants bring with them, or are prevalent among the native-born Latino. They exhibit, for example, lower educational attainment and youthfulness, a lack of English proficiency, unauthorized or illegal status, a lack of experience in this country, their concentration (segregation) in low-wage firms, industries, and occupations, and their racial (phenotype) and gender background. These factors adversely affect wages, joblessness, and employment opportunities for Latinos. Higher rates of unemployment for Latinos are of special concern because researchers have found that differences in unemployment are not primarily explained by personal characteristics or education. Rather, Latinos have a higher probability of experiencing one or more spells of unemployment and, interestingly, have a lower average duration of unemployment. That is, job turnover is high and rapid with Latinos and immigrants entering in and out of low-skill jobs. This latter fact is the result of Latinos having a lower reservation wage—a greater disposition to accept a lower-paying position after losing a job. They also have a higher proportion of involuntary part-time work, indicating that Latinos tend to stay in less-desirable jobs rather than face unemployment.

Informality and contingent models provide theoretical clarity that helps explain worker participation in day labor. In the following sections, I analyze empirical data about this occupation, the search for employment, the hiring and wage negotiations that take place, and different survival strategies. This approach provides further insight into worker motivation in a highly unstable, volatile, and public labor market. In addition, it helps us reconcile the seemingly desperate nature of day labor work, the men who participate, and other factors that bring together employers and workers in this informal and contingent labor exchange.

Research Description

The primary data used for this chapter come from twenty-five in-depth interviews undertaken by two graduate students and myself. In addition, I draw on participant observation at several official and unofficial hiring sites[3] where my research team and I spent significant time learning about this labor exchange. Finally, I also draw on the Los Angeles Day Labor Survey (LADLS) to explore this market. The Los Angeles Day Labor Survey is a face-to-face random survey of 481 day laborers administered in 1999 at eighty-seven different hiring sites throughout southern California. All but ten surveys were administered in Spanish, and each respondent was provided with a modest incentive ($25) to complete the query. This survey is statistically representative of all day laborers in the Los Angeles metropolitan region.

Worker Characteristics

Based on the random sample survey of day laborers in southern California, a demographic portrait of this workforce reveals three important insights that help explain their participation in this market. First, while variegated on several key demographic characteristics, day laborers are primarily under-educated and have limited English proficiency, which severely disadvantages them socially and economically. Second, a significant proportion are unauthorized and recently arrived, placing them in a vulnerable position in the formal labor market. Finally, almost all participants in this market are male, Latino, and young, traits that characterize this population's participation in low-skill, low-pay, unstable jobs.

On the other hand, more than one-third of day laborers have between nine and twelve years of education—the equivalent of some college in countries such as Mexico, Guatemala, and El Salvador. Day laborers are not all uneducated, and indeed, a significant number show modest to impressive human capital characteristics with regard to education. Further analysis of data reveals that educational attainment measured by number of years may not necessarily mean degrees. Indeed, the majority of day laborers (even those with many years of education) were not degreed. The relatively high proportion of day laborers with more than nine years of education (38.6 percent) belies their concentration in this market. On the other hand, their low degree rates perhaps more adequately explain their participation in day labor work. In addition, almost one-quarter (23.4 percent) of day laborers have been in the United States for more than eleven years, with 10 percent having been here longer than twenty years. Even though this labor market is overwhelmingly immigrant, a dichotomy between recent arrivals (that is, less than one year) and older immigrants (that is, eleven-plus years) clearly exists. Though a small minority of day laborers have the necessary documents to be in this country legally, the overwhelming majority do not have legal documents, which plays a major factor in their participation in the day labor market. The demographic characteristics of day laborers, particularly those traits related to legal status and skill, point to their likely participation in either informal or contingent employment.

Why Day Labor?

Observing a group of men convening daily, often early in the morning and well into the afternoon, in search of unstable employment reveals important insights about day labor not readily apparent in survey data. In-depth

Table 2.1. Day labor characteristics

Characteristics	Percentage
Country of Origin (*n* = 481)	
Mexico	77.5
Central America[a]	20.1
Other[b]	1.1
United States	1.3
Recency of Arrival (*n* = 479)	
Less than 5 years	52.3
6–10 Years	24.4
11+ Years	23.4
Nativity and Legal Status (*n* = 481)	
Foreign-born	98.7
Unauthorized	84.0
Age (*n* = 479)	
18–27	37.9
28–57	58.7
58+	3.5
Mean age	34
Educational Attainment (*n* = 481)	
No education	5.1
1–6 years	51.5
7–8 years	4.9
9–12 years	34.4
13+ years	4.2
Mean	7.0
Highest Degree Obtained (*n* = 481)	
None	79.5
High school diploma	14.3
GED	.14
Tech degree/certificate	1.7
AA	1.4
BA/BS	.78
Advanced graduate degree	.41
Adult school certificate	21.6

Source: Valenzuela, Los Angeles Day Labor Survey, 1999.

[a] Includes day Laborers from El Salvador (7.2%), Honduras (2.9%), and Guatemala (10%).

[b] Includes day Laborers from Zimbabwe (.1%), Morocco (.3%), South Africa (.2%), Peru (.2%), and Colombia (.3%).

interviews similarly reveal the day-to-day interactions, labor exchanges, and other processes that give meaning to this occupation. Through these methods, I find four important characteristics of day labor that help us answer why workers search for employment in this market regularly. Day laborers participate in this market because (1) they lack the work experience and job skills needed in similar occupations in regular or non–day labor work, (2) of other structural and human capital barriers (for example, lack of documents, poor transportation options, low English proficiency), (3) social networks and friendships channel workers to this occupation and provide camaraderie and support, and (4) the opportunity to barter and earn competitive, albeit irregular, pay exists. Each of these four factors likewise provides insight into the mechanisms and characteristics that help delineate day labor into informal or contingent employment.

Obtaining Work Experience and Skills

Lack of work experience and few skills to entice regular employers make the prospect of employment more difficult for immigrant workers. As a result, many recent arrivals and older immigrants who have been in the United States for several years are employed in underskilled jobs that pay poorly and offer few opportunities for mobility. Day labor affords many of these new arrivals work, but perhaps more important, an opportunity to obtain valuable work experience and skills in construction and related (for example, roofing, plumbing, painting, landscaping) industries that might lead to stable and long-term employment in an industry that is both robust and pays well. Alfredo, a day laborer from Mexico, refuses to work at a restaurant or factory as his roommates do because there would not be an opportunity to learn new trade skills that could lead to better employment and wage prospects. "Before, I did not know how to work certain types of machines used in construction. I also did not know of the different types of cement . . . in other words, you learn a lot of things in this industry. You learn how to do that, and this, and how to utilize different tools. And in the types of places [restaurant, factory] where those men [roommates] work, they are never going to do or learn anything beyond what they are already doing there."

The acquisition of skills, rather than the competition for jobs based on skills, seems to drive many of the participants to this occupation. Though most respondents mentioned improving their human capital by obtaining work experience in different trades, the majority of day laborers did not see the lack of a specific skill as a hindrance to their employment as a day laborer. At the same time, clearly marked day laborers (for example, those wearing painter pants or brandishing their own tools) are better able to secure skilled jobs than those who have no markings. Workers have other ways of informing would-be employers of their work experience. For example, many workers verbalize their work skills by shouting the names of the trades they can perform, sometimes exaggerating their "years" of experience. Employers often prefer workers who can communicate in English, and will often diminish work experience for the ability to communicate well with the worker. Potential employers will also discriminate blatantly against small, skinny, or well-dressed workers, preferring to hire large, gruff, and seemingly work-experienced laborers.

The structure of day labor may not be the most advantageous for skilled workers, for several reasons. First, in most instances, employers of day laborers are not necessarily looking for skilled work. Because day laborers are usually hired for menial or labor-intensive jobs, skill in a particular trade may be negligible. Day laborers in the construction industry (broadly defined) were largely employed in light construction, gardening (which included digging holes, cutting shrubs, and landscaping), painting, cleaning and maintenance, and loading and unloading in the moving business. The majority of workers we interviewed served as assistants to skilled foremen or to a primary worker or licensed contractor. When probed about specific duties, we found that day laborers mostly performed tasks that involved assisting a skilled worker rather than actually performing the skilled job itself. Of course, there are many instances when a skilled worker is required, particularly when an individual (that is, home owner or noncontractor), rather than a contractor, is looking for assistance to complete a complicated or skilled home-improvement task. Based on our survey, employers in the day labor market in Los Angeles are either contractors (43 percent) or individuals (42 percent), and while workers preferred contractors for the possibility of securing repeat or permanent employment, they spoke positively of working for individuals.

Second, beside obvious markings, it is very difficult to "advertise" or make known your skill level, much less the degree of experience in that skill. As a result, workers often creatively attempt to get the attention of prospective employers, sometimes aggressively pointing to themselves, or entering their vehicle. Last, workers who are not skilled can easily claim that they are, and employers really have no way of verifying until the worker performs the job task. This is done for an obvious reason, to acquire work, but sometimes deceiving employers comes at a cost of getting paid an amount less than agreed, or being returned to the site once the agitated employer discovers the level of inexperience. Leon, a day laborer of three years, relates a typical response to my inquiry of how much experience he has in different occupations: "If they ask me if I know construction, I say yes. If they ask me if I know about roofing, I say yes—I tell them I can do it all. In this manner I gain work experience in different jobs."

Day labor, though rarely providing stable work, does offer opportunities to gain employment experience and to hone job skills in the construction and related industries, thereby increasing the human capital of the participants and improving their prospects for permanent employment elsewhere or more consistent day labor. So though day laborers seek experience and employers seek flexible, short-term employment, a ready supply of men provides the "low-end" of the contingent market with temp workers. The bottom of the temp market, day labor, was one of the fastest growing sectors in the 1990s, more than doubling in size between 1990 and 1997, and now represents one of the most important sources of work in low-income neighborhoods (Peck and Theodore, 2001:474). The "high-end" of the day labor temp market is well documented by Jamie Peck and Nik Theodore (1998, 2001) and is primarily the formal temporary staffing agencies who charge employers a rate to supply a worker who is paid at or slightly above minimum wage. The primary benefit to the workers of this market is clearly not the wage rates but the higher probability of securing steady (everyday) employment. The majority of workers in this market have documents, have taxes deducted from their pay, and need to search for work daily. Contingent working arrangements are commonplace in the United States, and workers hoping to maximize their skill acquisition can do so easily, more or less regularly, and without question through day labor either at informal hiring sites or through formal temporary staffing agencies.

Barriers to Permanent Work

The majority of day laborers prefer to work in the permanent market for jobs considered to be at the lower end of the occupational strata, with the majority preferring to work in the permanent labor market regardless of the quality of job (Carvajal, 2000). Stability seems to be the driving factor. Luis, a day laborer from Guatemala, comments, "Sometimes you work and sometimes you don't. You sometimes work three days or you can be without work for four days. Well, I think it's different because you don't always get work everyday. You need a permanent job, it's the only thing that's secure."

Determining which factors prevent day laborers from employment in the regular or formal labor market is important because it provides insight into the workers' circumstances and the constraints they face in seeking employment outside this industry. More important, it suggests that underemployment and labor market disadvantage are primary factors that induce day laborers to seek self-employment as temporary workers in the day labor market.

Predictably, lack of documents was the primary factor preventing day laborers from finding other types of employment. Alfredo, a Mexican national who immigrated to the United States in 1997, describes the frustration of lacking documents and the quality of non–day labor jobs, both of which compel him to seek employment in day labor. "The permanent jobs that I'm offered are badly paid, even those that are [better] paid—in the end it doesn't matter because I don't have papers. I have nothing else left to do but to work there at the canyon [a day labor hiring site]. There are no other good jobs, they always ask for papers, and in those where they don't they are badly paid and they are very grueling jobs."

Several other key labor-market disadvantages were important as well. For example, low pay rates and unavailability of jobs were mentioned by almost 20 percent of all day laborers. In addition, labor market and human capital disadvantage factors were likewise reported. Finally, the inability to speak English was ranked highly as a constraint in job acquisition outside day labor, and lack of requisite skills for a particular occupation or not knowing certain customs or U.S. work norms emerged as a barrier. Zeferino, a day laborer from Mexico who has been working as a day laborer for eight years, states that the lack of English proficiency is one of the reasons why he cannot find permanent work: "Because I don't speak English well, I work as a day laborer. . . . I have to find money to pay my food." These factors prevent day laborers from participating in formal labor markets and relegate them to day labor work. The barriers to employment in permanent work also suggest the draw to informal and contingent employment.

Though lack of documents clearly limits a worker's employment options, participating in day labor is not jeopardized. Lack of documents also makes unclear the legal ramifications of hiring men from storefronts or curbside hiring sites and is one of the primary reasons why day labor is considered informal.

Searching for Daily Labor: Networking and Friends

The role of social networks for day laborers is important and should not be understated in understanding worker participation in this market. While social networks are important in other job markets and social settings, they play a particularly important role for understanding job acquisition at open-air hiring sites and why day laborers continue to work in this type of market. To be clear, social networks are not the only mechanism workers use to secure jobs at hiring sites. As described earlier, hustling and aggressively drawing attention to oneself, waiting expectantly, and participating in job queues at official hiring sites are other ways to secure employment in this occupation. As a result of infrequent employer contacts, the day labor market depends on friendships and networks at the sites, and a culture of reciprocity among day workers during periods of unemployment.

For example, based on our field research, most employers of day laborers hire between two and five workers on any given workday. The selection
of workers is often done by one of the day laborers that perhaps worked
with the prospective employer the day before, or who was merely chosen as
the "broker" or lead person because of his aggressiveness, ability to speak
some English, or by luck. The lead person then goes about selecting his loyal
friends to join him for that particular job. This individual usually serves in a
liaison-type role in which the employer communicates work orders, breaks,
wage negotiation, and other work-related communiqués to the lead, who
in turn relays the information to the other day laborers. Another scenario
is a contractor or prospective employer who has already established a prior
relationship with one of the day laborers. That worker is asked for and told
to select, for example, three or four "strong, dependable, and hard-working"
men. As a result, a day laborer's relationship with different workers, especially
those most experienced, is advantageous in securing employment.

Friendships among day laborers are important for other reasons. Day laborers often seek each other for companionship, camaraderie, advice, and favors.
For instance, workers lend each other money for different purposes, including
rent and food during low bouts of employment. One interviewee described
a situation in which a *coperacíon* (loan or money contribution) was collected
for a proper burial for a fellow day laborer from Oaxaca who had passed away.
Day laborers have also supported themselves by housing each other.

There are many different types of reciprocal favors and sources of information that day laborers negotiate among themselves at day labor sites. For
example, money pools are often created to help a day laborer get back home
for a special event or family emergency. Similarly, money pools are used
to purchase a bus ticket for a family member or friend trying to get to the
United States, or to hold someone over until their next job. Communication
and networking at day labor sites also aid in providing and organizing social
and sporting events where workers and their families meet for recreation. No
doubt, establishing friendships at day labor sites is important for economic
reasons, including small loans and other forms of reciprocal favors that make
settlement easier and collective. Social networks also provide a clue to why
day laborers return to this line of work daily, where a sense of community and
mutual respect exists when compared to similar work in the regular market.
Even though the vast majority of day laborers expressed a desire to secure
full-time steady employment, returning to day labor provided the social
contact and networking needed for settlement, subsistence, and opportunity,
however unstable, for employment. Tomas, a day laborer of ten years, sum-

marizes well the role of networks in this occupation: "Coming together every day at this site is good. We help each other; keep an eye out for bad *patrones* [employers or bosses], share our food, laugh, and hang out when we don't get work. My friends at the site also help me get jobs, sometimes—good ones that last several weeks."

The use of networking and friendship is important in all types of job acquisition. It certainly makes life easier on men who primarily participate in contingent work, where instability is the norm and making ends meet is a daily challenge. Day labor has a significant amount of "down-time" as workers wait for jobs or undergo bouts of unemployment. As a result, ties to friends and others facilitate their survival, their job procurement, and insights into how the industry ebbs and flows. Social networks, described in the work of Pastor and Marcelli (2000), channel low-skill, immigrant workers to this low-skill, unstable industry and sustain their day-to-day activities in this contingent and informal market.

Social networks in part also explain the overwhelming preponderance of Latinos in this sector. As this industry has grown, so has the participation of Latinos and, to a lesser extent, non-Latinos, aided in part through social contacts and the norm that day labor or *jornalero* work is "Latino." Although a sprinkling of whites and African Americans search for work in this manner, they are at best 2–3 percent of the entire day labor force. Based on my observations, the overwhelming participation of Latinos in this industry is related to three other factors: employer preference, documents, and stigma. In Los Angeles and other high-immigrant cities, employers have a clear preference for migrant Latino laborers over white or African American workers (Waldinger, 1997), particularly in low-skill jobs, where this is clearly playing itself out in Los Angeles's day labor market. Lack of documents, clearly a phenomenon that overwhelmingly affects Mexican and other Latino immigrants,[4] relegates Latinos without papers to the most marginal of jobs in Los Angeles's occupational structure. Most observers know that day laborers do not have documents, and this in part also contributes to the third reason that Latinos overwhelmingly work in this industry: the negative stigma of day labor and Latino migrants' willingness to work at almost any job for a wage that, relative to where they come from, is good. Day labor is viewed as a desperate, "bottom-of-the-barrel," migrant occupation that is unstable and difficult to secure regularly. The day-to-day activities of this market, its structure, and pay mechanism make this market extremely unattractive for many nonimmigrants and, by extension, non-Latinos. As a result, you see few African Americans or white Americans participating.

Bartering and Earnings

The flexibility in negotiating a wage and the range in earnings make this market both extremely risky and attractive to the participants. What determines the pay scale for day labor work? There are no government regulations, corporate guidelines, pay scales, unions, or even a minimum wage in this industry. In most instances, day laborers informally negotiate their wage with their prospective employer for the day. At least two important conditions play into wage negotiation. First, the wage rate that a day laborer attempts to negotiate depends on several factors, including the job to be performed, their ability to effectively communicate their work capabilities, their size and perceived strength (for difficult manual jobs), and sheer ability to barter. Second, trust matters between an employer and a prospective worker. Most negotiations for a job are done at the hiring site or in a car en route to the job site. Therefore, a large degree of trust is necessary when an employer describes the size, length, and difficulty of a job. Despite a nonexistent pay scale or regulations by the state, social interactions and strategies among the day laborers serve to informally regulate pay at many hiring sites.

The majority of day laborers at each surveyed site knew each other and often mingled in groups of three or five. They talked openly with one another and often discussed past jobs, abuses, and pay. More experienced day laborers often spoke of their ability to negotiate a fair wage for a day's labor, extolling their experience and deft ability to call a successful negotiating bluff or to walk away from a job. Learning how to negotiate pay for a day's labor is not easy, especially with a seasoned employer or contractor who is unwilling to be flexible. Day laborers were quick to draw on their experiences and provide useful tips on negotiating ploys to fellow job seekers. A common procedure at one particular site was the setting of a minimum wage (for example, $7.00) among all day laborers. This would have the effect of not undercutting each other whenever a prospective employer sought a lower rate from a different worker.

Only those men who have semisteady day labor employment, or who are able to obtain higher-paying day labor jobs, are able to aggressively bargain for a better wage rate. Clearly this option is unavailable for the recently arrived immigrant who knows little about this market, or for the desperate day laborer who has not landed work in several days or weeks. Jimenez, who had several years' experience at a particular site and who had his own tools, often turned down jobs that paid poorly, or that he simply felt overqualified to do. He was clearly the exception rather than the norm. "Whenever I negotiate, I tell the boss that I'm experienced, that I'm a good worker, and that I deserve a fair wage. If they don't like it, I walk away; I only work if I'm paid what I'm worth."

Determining a minimum wage for day labor is impossible to accurately calculate because there is no federal- or state-mandated provision for day labor wages or for other types of informal work. One way to determine a minimum wage of sorts for day laborers is to ask them their reservation wage. A reservation wage is the lowest amount (usually per hour) a person is willing to work for in a particular job or task. The mean hourly reservation wage of the respondents interviewed for this study was $6.91. As a result, on average, day laborers in my sample refused to work at a rate lower than $6.91 per hour, about two dollars higher than the federal minimum wage in 1999, when this survey was undertaken. The reservation wage under low-demand conditions (that is, winter/rainy season, and/or consistently bad luck securing jobs) fell to $6.21 per hour.

The average wage a day laborer received for a day job (nonhourly) was $60, though it was not unheard of for workers to earn upward of $80 and $100, depending on the job. Regardless of pay rate and arrangement, the pay earned each week is highly variable, and the weekly job schedule is constantly in flux because of up and down swings in demand, weather, and supply of workers. Adding to this variability are uneven rates of pay from different employers and the ability of day laborers to secure employment consistently. Far from stable, day labor work is difficult to obtain on a consistent basis, can pay relatively well but is usually offset by bouts of infrequent employment, and depends highly on the ability to deftly negotiate a fair wage.

Earnings of day laborers are mixed. On the one hand, the mean yearly income ($8,489) is slightly above the poverty threshold for a single person in 1999. On the other hand, the mean day labor hourly rate of $6.91 seems promising. That wage is about $1.15 higher than the California state minimum wage and slightly below the city of Los Angeles's Living Wage Ordinance when the survey was administered.[5] Calculating the mean reservation wage for day labor, a full-time, year-round worker would earn about $14,400, almost 175 percent above the federal poverty threshold for a single person for that year. Because day labor is insecure and unstable, the mean yearly income of $8,489 more likely reflects actual earnings for this type of work. It captures cyclical and seasonal variations in employment and hourly rates below and above the average. We also know that on average, day laborers find work three (2.95) days out of a typical week. Thus day labor, when secured and when a good wage is negotiated, can provide a worker with the possibility of earning a modest living. It is certainly comparable to other types of low-skill, low-paying jobs in the formal market, including that of farmworkers,

Table 2.2. Earnings among day laborers

	Estimated Yearly Income
Mean	$8,489
Median	$7,200
Standard deviation	$5,064
Monthly Wages	
January '99 (mean)	$568
Typical "good" month	$1,069
Typical "bad" month	$341
Hourly Wage	
Day labor	$6.91
Federal	$5.15
State	$5.75
Los Angeles "living wage"	$7.25

Source: Valenzuela, Los Angeles Day Labor Survey, 1999.

who (77 percent) earn salaries between $7,500 and $10,000 (Villarejo et al., 2000). The primary difference here is that day labor is urban, meaning a greater social safety net infrastructure and better employment prospects, including the possibility of long-term employment. Other factors suggest that employment in day labor is preferred not only to farmwork but also to employment in other dead-end and low-paying jobs.

Other wage-related reasons push workers to day labor. First, day laborers are usually paid daily and in cash. They are also usually provided lunch—a basic cold sandwich or a fast food burger and fries. Providing lunch is clearly a throwback to the old industrial mill-town days when food was provided to workers, clearly a practice that no longer exists, with the notable exception of contemporary day labor. Not all employers, however, provide lunch or, for that matter, breaks or water. For reasons not fully understood by this author, day laborers receive lunch during most of their daily employment ventures. This fact did not differentiate between employers who were contractors or individuals. In interviews with contractors, many provide lunch to their crew, and if a day laborer is hired, they become part of the crew. Individual home owners perhaps feel a sense of obligation to offering a lunch break or guilt at not providing a meal for a worker. Finally, the fact that most day labor work is in the construction trades in neighborhoods, some of which are in isolated locations, perhaps miles from a fast food restaurant or grocery store, also might explain why employers oftentimes provide lunch. A hungry worker is a less productive and grouchier worker than one that has been fed and rested during the lunch hour.

Second, because day labor work is effectively tax-free, a dollar of casual wages is worth more than a dollar of formal wages. In tax-free terms, the $6.91 casual wage is significantly higher than the federal minimum rate of $5.15, about $2.50 higher if you assume a 15 percent tax rate. Similarly, the estimated mean yearly income for day laborers ($8,489) is worth about $1,300 more than a formal income. For a recently arrived immigrant or someone who has worked for minimum wage for many years, this difference is significant. Zeferino, a day laborer of eight years, speaks highly of being paid tax-free and in cash at the end of a workday. "I get paid cash and one sees the money and distributes it according to what one needs. I don't like permanent jobs because they take out taxes and you end up getting paid $5 in the end. Then when you go cash the check, you pay the ride to get there, then the check-cashing place takes about 3 percent of the total. The employer that hires you on the street takes you to their home, gives you lunch and a ride back; if you work at a factory, you don't get that." Finally, the majority of day laborers negotiate their wages. Being able to negotiate a day's labor well is key to successful day laboring and is not lost on Latino immigrants who come from countries where bartering is commonplace.

Clearly, the relatively low-pay, cash-based, and tax-free structure of earnings in day labor is consistent with informalization. In addition, haggling for wages, refusing to work for a particular job assignment, and the inherent abuses of this industry, such as wage theft, also speaks to the informal nature of this market. When compared to the formal temp agencies that dispatch low-skill day labor (Peck and Theodore, 1998; 2001), informal or street-curb day laborers earn better wages, another trait that draws workers to this industry and helps differentiate between day labor in formal or temporary staffing agencies and day labor in informal street-curb markets. Though both markets are similar with regard to exploitation, poor pay, and instability, policies to regulate both would have to differ. Indeed, a day labor bill of rights, introduced by Congressman Gutierrez of Illinois, though not yet passed by Congress, is mostly symbolic for day laborers who search for work on street curbs. It has more than symbolic meaning for day laborers who search for employment in temporary staffing agencies because these agencies are regulated by the state, and therefore have to abide by any legislation that targets them. Informal day laborers, however, fall below the radar of such regulations, maintaining their status as marginal or at the "low end" of the day labor industry.

Conclusion

Two theoretical models help us understand worker participation in day labor: informalization and contingent employment. Both models provide a unique perspective on day labor's growth and its participants. However, informalization on its own fails to capture adequately the unique attributes of this occupational niche, whereas contingent employment, coupled with an understanding of labor market disadvantage, provides an adequate explanation of the workers who participate and the labor processes that give meaning to day labor. A close analysis of this market reveals that worker participation is complex and at the same time highly rational when workers consider other options available to them in a low-skill, poorly paid, and unstable formal or secondary labor market. Day labor exhibits characteristics and processes that are captured by both informal and contingent models of employment.

Because day labor is unregulated, the wages are primarily paid in cash and "under the table" abuses are commonplace, and most participants are undocumented immigrants, the industry is often dismissed or simply discussed as informal. However, day labor also exhibits key characteristics of contingent employment: it is highly unstable and temporary, poorly paid, increasingly regulated through temp hiring halls and official curbside worker centers, and primarily concentrated in the construction industry—a major employer of "low-end" contingent workers.

The participation of workers in this enterprise is not altogether different or less desirable than work in the formal or non–day labor market. In Los Angeles, where immigrant laborers and low-skill exploitative employment is commonplace, day labor may be a rational alternative to other forms of work in the region. Day labor may also serve as a springboard to better or consistent employment, as a buffer from a layoff or firing, or as a supplement to part- and full-time work in the regular market.

Day labor is one example of how immigrants are transforming the spatial and economic geography of large cities as they struggle to incorporate their populace economically, socially, and politically. Though seemingly desperate to most observers of this occupation, day labor, when considered alongside other employment opportunities for immigrant Latinos, may be a viable alternative. It certainly competes if not betters employment in textiles, garment, or other immigrant-concentrated jobs. The participation of so many workers in this occupation, and the processes involved in securing work, obtaining valuable skills and work experience, fostering friendships and establishing networks, and earning a relative living tell us that day labor is much more than meets the eye.

Notes

This project was supported by the UCLA Chicano Studies Research Center, SCR 43, University of California Committee on Latino Research Grant. I also received generous support from the Ford Foundation. I gratefully acknowledge the research assistance of Fabiola Vilchez and Maria Cardona. I also thank Lawrence Bobo and Pierrette Hondagneu-Sotelo for constructive remarks on an earlier version of this paper. Finally, I thank Patricia Zavella and Ramón Gutiérrez for their excellent suggestions on this chapter.

1. I use the term "day labor" in reference to the occupation where men congregate on street corners, empty lots, or parking lots of home improvement stores to solicit temporary daily work. These sites are unregulated and seemingly chaotic, with several hundred men competing with each other for jobs with employers who drive by in search of cheap labor. Some sites are "regulated," in which a designated spot (empty lot, freeway underpass, park trailer) is provided (often by the local municipality) where workers and employers can safely convene to exchange labor for wages. The negotiation of wages is undertaken by the workers and employers, no fixed rate is assumed, and work opportunities fluctuate on any given day. Day labor in this context is distinct from the more formalized "hiring hall" definition used by Peck and Theodore (1998; 2001:473) to describe the temporary staffing industry in Chicago. Their use is in reference to neighborhood-based temporary staffing agencies that supply day laborers (and other workers) usually at or around minimum wage for manual work assignments.

2. Day labor, similar to other jobs in the informal economy, is gendered. For example, it is primarily women who work in the domestic and caretaker occupations, while men participate in gardening and day labor. As a result, the interaction between day laborers and their employers, local residents and merchants, and other intermediaries takes on a distinct male environment that further shapes their lives and day-to-day activities and processes in this market.

3. During the course of my research on day labor, I identified two basic categories of "open-air" hiring sites: official and unofficial. Official or regulated sites are formal hiring places where workers and potential employers come together to exchange labor for wages. These sites are usually sponsored by local municipalities and controlled or organized by a city agency or a community-based organization. Workers who use these sites are usually provided shelter, bathrooms, modest sources of food (for example, coffee, pastries, fruit), tool exchanges and borrowing, and assistance with wage disputes. Unofficial sites include two broad types of gathering places: connected and unconnected. Connected sites are gathering places "connected" to some specific industry, such as painting (Dunn Edwards, Standard Brands), landscaping or gardening (nurseries), moving (U-haul), and home improvement (Home Depot). Unconnected sites do not have any connection to a specific industry but may very well exist for other reasons, such as foot or vehicular traffic, police cooperation, or historical reasons (for example, the site has existed for many years).

4. By far, California receives the largest share of unauthorized immigrants—about one-half. In addition, almost one-half of all unauthorized immigrants come from Mexico—no other country comes close to this figure. After Mexico, El Salvador and then Guatemala follow as the countries that send the most unauthorized immigrants to the United States.

5. The Los Angeles Living Wage Ordinance (No. 171547) requires that nothing less than a prescribed minimum level of compensation (a "living wage") be paid to employees of service contractors of the city and its financial assistance recipients and to employees of such recipients. As a result, not all workers in Los Angeles qualify for the living wage.

PART II

Education and Achievement

3. Understanding and Addressing the California Latino Achievement Gap in Early Elementary School

RUSSELL W. RUMBERGER
AND BRENDA D. ARELLANO

One of the most pressing problems in California is improving student academic performance. This is especially true for the state's Latino students, who now represent the largest ethnic group in the state,[1] but who generally have much lower achievement levels than white or Asian students.[2] If California is going to maintain its economic competitiveness in the global economy in the twenty-first century, it is going to have to effectively educate its increasingly diverse student population, and particularly its rapidly increasing population of Latino students.

Historically, policy makers have attempted to improve academic achievement for all students irrespective of their ethnicity or other characteristics. But in 2001 the federal government enacted the *No Child Left Behind* (NCLB) Act, which requires states to document progress in eliminating the achievement differences among students who differ by poverty status, race, ethnicity, disability, and limited English proficiency (U.S. Department of Education, National Center for Education Statistics, 2006). These differences are sometimes referred to as the *achievement gap*.

Because of NCLB and an increase in state accountability systems (Fuhrman and Elmore, 2004), there is a growing interest among scholars, educators, and policy makers to better understand and address the achievement gap. This paper examines the extent of the achievement gap between California Latino and non-Latino white students in early elementary school; the individual, family, and school characteristics that account for those differences; and some educational policies that could help close the gap.[3]

Explaining Disparities in Achievement

Researchers have long sought to understand and explain the vast racial and ethnic disparities in achievement that have always existed in the United States (Coleman et al., 1966; Jencks et al., 1972; Jencks and Phillips, 1998; Lee, 2002; Ogbu, 1992; Rothstein, 2004; Steinberg, Dornbusch, and Brown, 1992; Thernstrom and Thernstrom, 2003). Although numerous investigations have been undertaken, there is no consensus about the primary cause of these disparities. Rather, researchers have identified a wide range of factors that contribute to educational achievement and have tried to determine the extent to which differences in the amount or effects of these factors explain differences in achievement. These factors vary along two primary dimensions.

First, they vary with respect to whether they focus on the attributes of individual students or the attributes of the three primary settings in which they live: families, schools, and communities. Although student achievement is clearly the result of individual attitudes, behaviors, and experiences, these individual attributes are shaped by the institutional settings where people live (National Research Council and Institute of Medicine, 2000). One challenge, therefore, is to determine the extent to which attributes of individuals explain educational outcomes versus the attributes of institutional settings. Addressing this challenge is important not only to better understand achievement differences, but also to help determine where policy interventions should be targeted. If educational outcomes can largely be explained by individual attributes, such as ability and motivation, then policies should largely focus on altering the attributes of individual students and their families. If, however, educational outcomes can largely be explained by attributes of schools, such as the quality of the teachers and educational programs, then policies should largely focus on altering the attributes of schools.

Addressing this challenge has also generated considerable controversy among scholars and researchers. The controversy began with the publication of the landmark "Coleman Report" in 1966. In the largest study of school effectiveness ever undertaken, Coleman found that schools only accounted for 5 percent to 38 percent of the total variation in student test scores among different grade levels, ethnic groups, and regions of the country (Coleman, 1990, p. 77). Since that time, virtually every study of school effectiveness has confirmed that most of the variation in student achievement is attributable to differences between students (and their families) rather than differences between schools (Lee and Bryk, 1989; Rumberger and Palardy, 2005; Reardon, 2003). Yet despite the common interpretation that the Coleman Report and subsequent studies show—that "schools don't make a difference"—research clearly demonstrates that schools can still have a powerful effect on student achievement. For example, one recent study found that students learn twice as much in some high schools as in other high schools (Rumberger and Palardy, 2005). A more reasonable conclusion from existing research is that student achievement results both from the actions and attributes of individuals and from the actions and attributes of their families, schools, and communities.

Second, the factors that contribute to educational achievement vary with respect to the types of attributes they identify. Although a wide array of specific attributes has been identified, they primarily are of two types. The first type concerns material resources. Many researchers have argued that the major factor that explains differences in student achievement has to do with disparities in material resources and conditions that exist among students, their families, and their schools (Armor, 2003; Rothstein, 2004). In the case of Latino students, for example, one critical resource is language. Students whose first language is not English have substantially lower levels of educational achievement than students from English-only backgrounds (Gandara, Rumberger, Maxwell-Jolly, and Callahan, 2003). Because more than half of elementary-age Latino students in California come from non–English-only households (Rumberger and Gándara, 2000:table 1), this may help explain achievement differences between Latino and white students. But to what extent the relationship between language background and achievement owes to characteristics and practices of families (for example socioeconomic status [SES], literacy practices) and to schools (qualified teachers, language of instruction, proper assessments) is less clear (August and Shanahan, 2006; Rumberger and Larson, 1998).

Material resources within families and schools also matter. Research has consistently found that parental socioeconomic status, most commonly measured by parental education and income, is a powerful predictor of student achievement for students from all racial and ethnic backgrounds (Betts, Rueben, and Danenberg, 2000; Entwisle, Alexander, and Olson, 1997; Guo and Harris, 2000; Lee, 2002). Because parental education and family income, including poverty, vary greatly between whites and blacks and Latinos,[4] these differences contribute to differences in educational achievement at school entry, during the school year, and over the summer (Duncan and Magnuson, 2005; Entwisle and Alexander, 1995; Lee, 2002; Roscigno, 2000). Differences in family income also contribute to differences in access to preschool, which has been shown to impact school readiness and may contribute to differences in early school achievement (Barnett, 1995; Magnuson and Waldfogel, 2005). School resources have also been shown to affect student achievement (Betts et al., 2000; Darling-Hammond, Berry, and Thoreson, 2001), although there is considerable controversy over whether financial resources matter or simply human resources, such as the quality of teachers (Hanushek, 1997; Hedges, Laine, and Greenwald, 1994). Because ethnic and language minority students are more likely to attend schools with fewer resources, including qualified teachers, these differences also contribute to differences in student achievement (Betts et al., 2000; Rouse and Barrow, 2006; Gandara et al., 2003).

The second category of attributes that contribute to student achievement are attitudes and behaviors of students, families, and school personnel. At the student level, research has shown positive attitudes and engagement toward learning, as well as prosocial and attentive behavior, promote learning in early elementary school for all students, regardless of their socioeconomic status and racial backgrounds (Alexander, Entwisle, and Dauber, 1993; Burchinal, Peisner-Feinberg, Pianta, and Howes, 2002; Finn, Pannozzo, and Voelkl, 1995; McClelland, Morrison, and Holmes, 2000). Relatively little research has documented any marked racial differences in school attitudes and behaviors in early childhood. One recent study found that black students had poorer teacher-assessed learning behaviors in kindergarten compared to white and Latino students (Xue and Meisels, 2004). Yet to what extent these differences can explain observed differences in achievement among ethnic and racial groups in early elementary school is unclear.

Differences in parental beliefs and practices may also contribute to differences in student achievement. Among adolescents, research has found that parenting styles, such as communication patterns and supervision between parents and their children, impact academic achievement (Dornbusch, Ritter, Leiderman, Roberts, and Fraleigh, 1987; Sui-Chu and Willms, 1996). Yet while research has also found racial and ethnic differences in parenting practices, these differences do not appear to explain differences in adolescent achievement (Sui-Chu and Willms, 1996). Similarly, among young children research has demonstrated that parental beliefs and parenting practices, particularly literacy practices, contribute to early academic achievement for all children (Bennet, Weigel, and Martin, 2002; Guo and Harris, 2000; Burchinal et al., 2002; Snow, Barnes, Chandler, Goodman, and Hemphill, 1991). Research has also demonstrated that these beliefs and practices are related to both socioeconomic factors, such as income and parental education, and cultural factors (Brooks-Gunn and Markman, 2005; Gallimore and Goldenberg, 2001; Guo and Harris, 2000). For example, one longitudinal study of 121 Latino families found that Latino parents were more likely to practice a cultural model that emphasized moral development rather than literacy development (Reese and Gallimore, 2000). Research has also demonstrated that differences in parental beliefs and practices can explain between 25 and 50 percent of the racial and ethnic achievement gap (Brooks-Gunn and Markman, 2005).

Finally, a number of school practices have been shown to affect student achievement, such as teacher beliefs, instructional practices, and social interactions with students (Ashton and Webb, 1986; Schacter and Thum, 2004; Pianta and Stuhlman, 2004; Xue and Meisels, 2004) and parental involvement (Domina, 2005; Griffith, 1998). There is also evidence that some of these practices, including instructional practices within classrooms and parent involvement practices within schools, vary by the racial and socioeconomic composition of the student body, which could also lead to differences in student achievement among racial and ethnic groups (Stipek, 2004; Griffith, 1998).

Differences in the relative importance of material resources versus attitudes and behaviors also have important implications for policy. If material resources are most important in affecting student achievement, then policies should be aimed at improving the material resources of students and the settings in which they live: their families, schools, and communities. If, however, attitudes and behaviors matter most, then policies should be aimed at improving the attributes and behaviors of students, their parents, and school personnel.

The Present Study

The present study investigates the achievement gap during the first two years of elementary school in California. The study was conducted using data from a large, ongoing federal study known as the Early Childhood Longitudinal Study of the Kindergarten Class of 1998–99 (ECLS-K) (U.S. Department of Education, National Center for Education Statistics, 2000). ECLS-K is a longitudinal study of a sample of about twenty thousand kindergartners who were enrolled in about one thousand public and private schools in the fall of 1998. The present study is based on a subsample of 1,612 California students in 127 schools from the larger study who were followed through first grade and for whom comprehensive student, parent, teacher, and school data are available.[5] Comparisons with available California State Department of Education data show that the subsample is quite representative of the state's population of kindergartners (see Rumberger and Arellano, 2004, table A1).

The study examined two measures of educational achievement: reading and mathematics. The ECLS-K reading assessment measured basic skills (print familiarity, letter recognition, beginning and ending sounds, rhyming sounds, word recognition), vocabulary (receptive vocabulary), and comprehension (listening comprehension, words in context); the math assessment measured skills in conceptual knowledge, procedural knowledge, and problem solving.[6] Each assessment was administered up to four times: in the fall and spring of kindergarten and in the fall and spring of first grade.[7]

Students identified by their schools or teachers as coming from a non-English background were given an English language proficiency test to see if they were able to understand and respond to the assessment items in English. At the time of each assessment, children who passed the language screener received the full ECLS-K direct assessment battery. Children who did not pass the language screener, but who spoke Spanish, were administered a Spanish-translated form of the mathematics assessment. Other language minority children received a reduced version of the ECLS-K assessments.[8] The present study used scale scores for reading and math in order to examine changes over time.[9]

A series of independent or predictor variables was created from the ECLS-K data to measure characteristics of students, their families, and their schools, identified in the literature review as important predictors of student achievement for this study.[10]

Because students in the ECLS-K data are nested within classrooms and schools, hierarchical linear modeling (HLM) was used in this study (Raudenbush and Bryk, 2002, chapter 6). In the current study, we tested a series of statistical models with different sets of predictor variables to estimate initial achievement in reading and math upon entry to kindergarten, and achievement growth in reading and math during three distinct periods: kindergarten, first grade, and the summer in between (see Rumberger and Arellano, 2004).

The Size of the Achievement Gap

We first examined the size of the achievement gap by comparing differences in estimated achievement between Latino and non-Latino white students during the first two years of elementary school.[11] Differences in reading achievement are illustrated in Figure 3.1. They show that Latinos scored 3.2 points lower than whites on the reading assessment upon entry to kindergarten, and by the end of first grade the gap had grown to 4.2 points.

But how big of an achievement gap does this represent?

One way to answer this question is to compare the size of the achievement gap with how much the average student learns during kindergarten, which can tell us how far behind Latino students are when they start kindergarten, compared to white students. We estimated that students increased their reading scores by about 1.7 points per month, which means that Latino students began kindergarten almost 2 months behind their white peers.

Another way to measure the size of the achievement gap is to represent the difference in achievement test scores as a fraction of a standard deviation

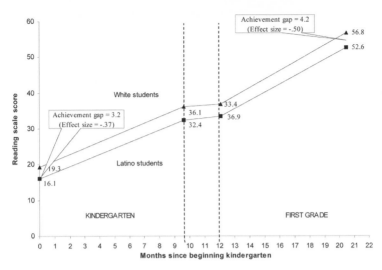

Figure 3.1. Estimated reading achievement for Latinos and whites from kindergarten through first grade, fall 1998 to spring 2000. Source: ECLS-K California sub-sample (*n* = 1612) weighted (Y2COMW0).

(SD), which is known as an effect size (Cohen, 1988).[12] One of the benefits of using effect size (ES) is that it facilitates comparisons between different variables of interest within the same study, and between different studies, through the use of a common metric. It also facilitates comparisons between achievement differences and interventions that could be used to overcome them.[13] The achievement gap in initial reading scores between Latinos and whites represents an effect size of –.37, which can be considered small.[14] However, by the end of first grade, the achievement gap increases to a moderate size of –.50. In math, Latinos begin kindergarten more than 2 months behind white students, which represents an achievement gap of –.48. By the end of first grade, the achievement gap in math grew to –.63.

What accounts for this achievement gap? To address this question, we first estimated a statistical model to identify how much of the variation in achievement was because of differences among students and how much owed to differences among the schools they attended. We found that between 72 and 88 percent of the variation owed to differences among students, and 12 to 28 percent owed to differences among the schools they attended (see Rumberger and Arellano, 2004:tables 4 and 5). In other words, as virtually all previous studies have shown, most of the variation in student achievement can be explained by differences in the attributes of students and their families, rather than by differences in attributes of their schools.[15] Nonetheless, differences in schools still contribute to differences in student outcomes.

Next, we estimated a series of statistical models in order to identify which factors predicted achievement in reading and math, and the extent to which the Latino–white achievement gap was reduced after controlling for those factors. We focused first on achievement differences upon entry to kindergarten and then on differences in achievement growth during kindergarten, first grade, and the summer in between.

Differences in Initial Achievement

Our analysis revealed that differences in initial achievement in reading and math could be explained largely by two demographic factors: SES and language background. As shown in Table 3.1, Latino and white students vary widely with respect to these two factors. For example, mean SES for Latino students is about .94 points lower than for white students, which represents an effect size of –1.06 (or more than one standard deviation). And half of all Latino kindergartners in our sample come from non-English backgrounds, compared to only 4 percent for white students.[16] In order to determine the effects of language background on Latino achievement, we compared Latinos from English backgrounds with Latinos from non-English (Spanish) backgrounds.

We found that both SES and language background have significant effects on initial achievement. The effect size of SES is .40 on initial reading achievement and .39 on initial math achievement (see Figure 3.2). The effect size of coming from a home where English is not the dominant language is –.45 on initial reading and –.37 on initial math. This means that non-English background Latino children begin kindergarten at a sizable disadvantage compared to English background Latino children.

After controlling for the effects of SES and home language, the Latino–white achievement gap in reading is reduced to –.061, or by more than 80 percent,

Table 3.1. Differences in background characteristics of Latino and White kindergarten students

	Latino	White	Difference (Effect size)
Mean SES	–.44	.50	–1.13
Percent non-English background	.50	.04	.98

Note: Differences in values between Latino and White are all statistically significant at .1 level (ANOVA).

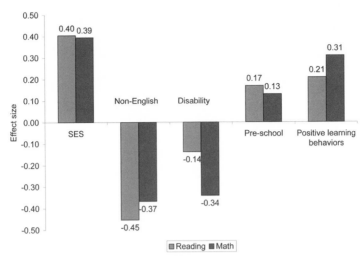

Figure 3.2. Effect sizes for selected predictors of initial reading and math achievement. Effect size represents the predicted change in reading or math performance, expressed in standard-deviation units, associated with a one unit (for dichotomous variables) or one standard deviation (for continuous variables) change in the predictor variable. The effects of SES and non-English were estimated only controlling for those variables; the effects of the other variables were estimated controlling for a larger set of predictors (see Rumberger and Arellano, 2004, table A4).

and is no longer statistically significant (see Figure 3.3). This means that Latino and white students with the same SES and language backgrounds would essentially have the same reading levels upon entry to kindergarten. Controlling for the effects of SES and home language reduces the achievement gap in math from –.48 to –.16, or by two-thirds, rendering it marginally insignificant.

Next we estimated the effects of a large number of additional predictors. We found a number of these factors had significant effects on initial reading and math achievement. Some of the more powerful factors are illustrated in Figure 3.2.[17] Students with disabilities had lower initial reading (ES = –.14) and math (ES = –.34) than students without disabilities; students who participated in preschool (excluding Head Start) had higher initial reading (ES = .17) and math (ES = .13) than students who did not participate in preschool. Finally, prolearning behaviors (for example attentiveness, eagerness, independence) had positive effects on initial reading (ES = .21) and math (ES = .31). Controlling for all these factors completely eliminated the initial achievement gap between Latino and white students in reading, and reduced the achievement gap in math by more than 80 percent.

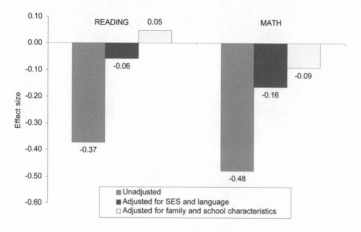

Figure 3.3. The Latino–white achievement gap in initial reading and
math achievement. Effect size represents the predicted change in
reading or math performance, expressed in standard-deviation units,
associated with a one unit or one standard deviation change in the
predictor variable.

After examining differences in initial achievement, we then examined differences in student learning during kindergarten and first grade. We found
that there were no significant differences in student learning between Latinos
and non-Latino whites during kindergarten, first grade, or the summer in between. In other words, although Latinos begin kindergarten with significantly
lower achievement levels than non-Latino white students, their achievement
increases at essentially the same rate during the first two years of school.
Nonetheless, as shown in Figure 1, by the end of first grade, the achievement
gap has increased slightly. This suggests that schools neither increase nor decrease the achievement gap during the first two years of elementary school.

Our analysis did identify a number of factors that predict student learning
during each of these periods. During kindergarten, we found: (1) prolearning behaviors increased student learning in reading (ES = .19) and in math
(ES = .12); (2) second-time kindergartners learned less than other students
in reading (ES = −.40) and in math (ES = −.47); and (3) students with disabilities learned less than nondisabled students in reading (ES = −.28), but
not in math.

During the summer between kindergarten and first grade, we did not find
any significant predictors of student learning.

During first grade, we found: (1) second-time kindergartners learned less
than other students in reading (ES = −.26), but not in math; (2) students

attending schools with a higher proportion of second-time kindergartners learned less than other students in reading (ES = –.12), but not in math; (3) students attending schools with a higher proportion of minority students learned less in reading (ES = –.18), but not in math; (4) students attending large schools (750 students or more) learned less in reading (ES = –.23), but not in math; and (5) students in private schools learned less than students in public schools in math (ES = –.34), but not in reading. This last finding is probably because twice as many students attending public schools had teachers who taught math more than sixty minutes a day (40 percent versus 20 percent). The emphasis on math in public schools could be a direct result of California's accountability system that measures math and reading performance beginning in second grade.

Summary and Policy Implications

This study examined the achievement gap between California Latino and white students in the first two years of elementary school. Because the data used in this study assessed students' performance in reading and math at the beginning and end of both kindergarten and first grade, it was possible to examine the extent of the achievement gap when students first began school, the achievement gap in learning during kindergarten and first grade, and the achievement gap in summer learning between kindergarten and first grade.

The analysis revealed that in California, Latino students begin kindergarten at a significant disadvantage to non-Latino white students: In the fall of 1998 the achievement gap at the beginning of kindergarten, as measured by the difference in average test scores, was –.37 of a standard deviation in reading and –.48 of a standard deviation in math. The analysis also revealed that the achievement gap changes very little over the first two years of school. By the end of first grade, the achievement gap grew to –.50 of a standard deviation in reading and to –.63 of a standard deviation in math. These results suggest that schools do little to either widen or close the sizable achievement gap that exists among students when they walk in the door.

Achievement data from other sources suggest that the achievement gap widens as students progress through school. For example, an analysis of data from the National Assessment of Educational Progress for California students in the fourth grade shows an achievement gap of –.84 in 1998 reading scores and –.85 in 2000 math scores.[18] Comparing those figures with the present findings suggests that about half of the achievement gap in fourth grade exists when students walk in the door at kindergarten. This means that efforts to close the gap must focus not just on schools, but also on opportunities outside of school, particularly before students begin school.

The analysis also revealed that most, but not all, of the initial achievement gap can be explained by two demographic characteristics of Latino students—socioeconomic status and language background. That is, Latinos as a group are disadvantaged in two ways, one related to language background and one related to socioeconomic background. As we suggest below, it is important to distinguish between these two disadvantages in formulating strategies to close the achievement gap. At the same time, the analysis suggests that English-background, middle-class Latino students are not disadvantaged relative to white students.

The study not only revealed the extent of the achievement gap, but also a number of factors that contribute to promote or impede the achievement of all students. Some of these factors reflect the practices of students and their families. Students who attended center-based preschool began kindergarten at a considerable advantage to students who attended Head Start or did not attend any preschool. Yet white students were twice as likely to participate in center-based preschool programs than Latino students. On the other hand, Latino students were more likely to participate in Head Start, the federally funded preschool program for disadvantaged students. Although earlier studies have found a positive benefit to students from participating in Head Start, including Latinos (Currie and Duncan, 1995; Currie and Thomas, 1999), the present study found no overall benefit to California students participating in Head Start.[19] Students with positive learning behaviors (for example attentiveness, eagerness, independence) learned more in school. Both parents and schools can encourage these behaviors that enhance learning.

Other factors reflect the policies and practices of schools. Retention had a large negative impact on learning. Not only did retained students learn less than other students the year they were retained, they also learned less the year after. This suggests that retention, by itself, is not an effective practice to overcome whatever difficulties students have that lead them to be retained in the first place.[20] Instead, parents and schools should address those difficulties before students are retained (Grisson and Shepard, 1989).

The social composition of schools also appears to affect learning. In particular, students experience slower reading development during first grade in schools with high concentrations of second-time kindergartners and high concentrations of minority students. Because the socioeconomic composition of schools and a number of school resource measures were not related to learning, this suggests that students improve their reading by being exposed to higher-achieving peers. Other research, including a recent study in San Diego, also demonstrates that student learning is affected by the achievement level of their classmates (Betts et al., 2000; Hanushek, Kain, Markman, and Rivkin, 2003; Rivkin, 2001; Ryan, 2000). Because California students are highly segregated by race, social class, and language (Betts et al., 2000:figure 3.1), all of which are related to student achievement, then segregation in California is probably contributing to the growth of the achievement gap.

The study also investigated whether a number of school structural features and resources impacted learning. For the most part, they did not. For instance, neither small schools nor private schools imparted any advantage on learning during the first two years of school (although students in elementary schools with more than 750 students had lower learning levels in reading). In fact, students who attended private schools actually learned less math in first grade than students attending public schools, probably because public schools spend more time teaching math. For the most part, class size also did not predict differences in learning, except in the case of math learning during first grade. This analysis raises questions about whether California's expensive investment in reduced classes during the first four years of elementary school is a worthwhile investment (Hanushek, 1999; Jepsen and Rivkin, 2002; Stecher and Bohrnstedt, 2002).

The achievement gap between Latino and white students in California is large, even in the first couple of years of schooling. In fact, it is sizable as soon as students enter school. Since the achievement gap is largely because of two types of disadvantages—language and socioeconomic status—it is important for educators to correctly identify and address the learning needs of Latino students associated with both disadvantages. That is, Latinos who are English-dominant but economically disadvantaged may have different needs and require different forms of support than Latinos who are from Spanish-speaking households and economically disadvantaged.

In general, the prospects of closing the achievement gap through educational policies alone are limited. Although a number of educational programs have been shown to produce sizable improvements in the educational outcomes of Latino students (Slavin and Calderón, 2001), statewide policies have shown much more modest effects. For example, what some observers consider to be a highly successful statewide school reform program—the Tennessee class size reduction experiment—produced a modest effect size of .25 over four years (Finn and Achilles, 1999). California's class size reduction program has had an even smaller impact (Jepsen and Rivkin, 2002; Stecher and Bohrnstedt, 2002). Even if statewide reform efforts were more successful at improving student achievement, they would do little to close the achievement gap unless they somehow were able to target Latino students and high-concentration Latino schools.

The present study finds that most of the disparities in achievement between Latino and white students can be traced to factors outside school. Therefore, to close the achievement gap will take concerted efforts not just in the educational arena but also in the larger arena of social policy.

Because Latino students start school behind other students and learn less when school is not in session, policy interventions should focus on closing the gap during these times. For example, the present study and other research document the effectiveness of preschool in improving early student achievement (Gorey, 2001). Because Latino families are less likely than white families to participate in center-based child care, at least in part because of their lower income levels (Liang, Fuller, and Singer, 2000), the provision of subsidized child care would likely reduce disparities in school readiness. Programs to increase the English literacy skills of parents may also be promising. With the passage of Proposition 227, California adopted the Community-Based English Tutoring (CBET) program, which provides $50 million to local education agencies to set up programs to provide adult English language instruction to parents and other community members, who then are supposed to provide tutoring to English learners.[21] Although no formal evaluation of the program's effectiveness has been conducted, anecdotal evidence suggests it is having a positive effect on parental involvement in children's schooling (Merickel et al., 2003:IV43–44.). Finally, targeted summer programs could also reduce disparities in summer learning (Cooper, Charlton, Valentine, and Muhlenbruck, 2000), although future studies will need to determine which programs are most effective.[22]

Yet these efforts, even if they are successful, may not be enough to overcome disparities in family income, employment opportunities, housing, and access to health care that all contribute to the welfare of families and their children (Reyes, 2001). Ultimately, eliminating disparities in educational opportunities and educational outcomes in California is such an immense challenge that it will require concerted efforts to overcome disparities in all areas of social policy.

Notes

This paper is a revised and condensed version of a report submitted to the University of California Latino Policy Institute (LPI) and presented at the Latinos in California II conference, September 11–13, 2003, Mission Inn, Riverside, California. The report was supported through a grant from the University of California Latino Policy Institute and through research funding from the University of California Linguistic Minority Research Institute. We would like to acknowledge the helpful comments of Jennifer Kuhn on the larger report. The views and opinions expressed do not necessarily represent those of LPI or the regents of the University of California.

1. Between 1994–95 and 2004–2005, Latino public school enrollment increased more than 50 percent, while white enrollment declined by 8 percent. Between 2001 and 2011, Latino public school enrollment is projected to increase by 18 percent, while white enrollment is projected to *decrease* by 18 percent (California Department of Finance, 2005).

2. For example, in the 2006 California Standards Tests, only 29 percent of fifth grade Latinos and 25 percent of eighth grade Latinos were proficient in English language arts, compared to 63 percent of fifth grade non-Latino whites and 62 percent of eighth grade non-Latino whites (California Department of Education, 2006).

3. To preserve space, the paper references a larger report that contains additional tables and a technical appendix (Rumberger and Arellano, 2004).

4. For example, poverty rates for children under the age of eighteen in 2004, were 14.4 percent for whites, 32.9 percent for blacks, and 28.6 percent for Latinos (U.S. Department of Education, National Center for Education Statistics, 2006:table 21).

5. For more information on how the sample was selected, see Rumberger and Arellano (2004). While there are a number of K-1 longitudinal weights in the dataset, we selected the sample associated weight, Y2COMW0, which provides child direct assessment data from fall-kindergarten, spring-kindergarten, and spring-first grade, in conjunction with parent and/or teacher data from spring-first grade, and one or more base year rounds of parent and/or teacher data (see U.S. Department of Education, 2002, p. 6).

6. Both outcomes were assessed using a computer-assisted interviewing methodology that included the use of a small easel with pictures, letters of the alphabet, words, short sentences, numbers, or number problems (see NCES, 2001, p. 2–6).

7. Only one-quarter of the students were assessed in the fall of first grade.

8. See U.S Department of Education (2001), 2–2 to 2–4, for more information.

9. As the ECLS-K user manual points out, gains at different points in the scale have different meanings in that they may connote qualitatively different reading activities (see U.S Department of Education, 2001, pp. 3–11).

10. See Rumberger and Arellano (2004), table A2, for a complete list of the variables and how they were constructed.

11. Although achievement differences exist among all major ethnic groups, we focused on comparisons with non-Latino white students because, historically, they have constituted the largest and most dominant racial/ethnic group in America.

12. Because the outcome variable in the HLM analysis has two standard deviations, one associated with students and one associated with schools, we estimated effect sizes using the standard deviation in achievement growth at the student level. This tends to overstate the actual effect sizes because it does not include the variance at the school level (Rosenthal, 1994), but we estimate that in this study the overstatement is only about 10 percent.

13. It should be pointed out that the term *effect* does not imply a causal relationship between the predictor and the outcome.

14. Cohen (1988) suggests that effect sizes larger than .8 should be considered as large, those above .5 should be considered as moderate, and those above .2 as small (pp. 24–27).

15. Rowan, Correnti, and Miller (2002) argue that more refined statistical models show the majority of the variability in student learning can be attributed to teachers.

16. The percentage of students from non-English backgrounds in the sample used in the multilevel analysis is somewhat smaller than the percentage in the full ECLS California subsample of 1,874 students (50 versus 56 percent) because non-English students who were not yet proficient in oral English by the end of first grade were not assessed in English reading and were excluded from our analysis.

17. The complete list of predictors is shown in Rumberger and Arellano (2004), tables 3 and 4.

18. Data retrieved February 1, 2003 from the NAEP Web site: http://nces.ed.gov/nationsreportcard/naepdata/.

19. A recent national study of preschool also found no overall benefit from students attending Head Start (Rumberger and Tran, 2006).

20. A study of retention among Latinos and whites in a southern California school district also found that kindergarten retention had an adverse effect on first-grade achievement (Cosden, Zimmer, Reyes, and Gutierrez, 1995). A recent review of the research literature found that retention also increases the likelihood of dropping out of high school (Jimerson, Anderson, and Whipple, 2002).

21. For more information, see the California Department of Education Web site: http://www.cde.ca.gov/sp/el/cb/.

22. Because only 30 percent of the ECLS participants were surveyed in the fall of first grade, we were unable to examine the impact of summer school and other activities on summer learning. However, another study using a smaller, national sample of the ECLS data found little impact of summer school on summer learning, although the study did find modest effects of home literacy activities (Lee and Burkam, 2003).

4. Reaffirming Affirmative Action

*An Equal Opportunity Analysis
of Advanced Placement Courses
and University Admissions*

ARMIDA ORNELAS AND
DANIEL G. SOLÓRZANO

Introduction

On December 1, 2003, Clark Kerr, the former president of the University of California, passed away. One of the legacies he left was the 1960 California Master Plan for Higher Education. The Master Plan set up California's three-tiered system of higher education that included the University of California admitting the top 12.5 percent of California high school graduates, the California State University system admitting the top 33 percent, and the California Community College system admitting anyone over the age of eighteen, or high school graduates. Despite this legacy of equal opportunity in higher education, in 2002 Clark Kerr expressed sadness about the direction and future of California higher education. In a May 16, 2002, interview with the *UCLA Daily Bruin* (Falcone, 2002), Kerr responded to a question about the future of the California Master Plan, and stated,

> The big thing that we were working on in 1960 was equality of opportunity. The big thing that we did—and nobody had done it anywhere else in the world—was to guarantee that there would be a place in higher education for every high school graduate who wanted to attend. That was just absolutely phenomenal. We did that by building up the community colleges, and provided that at the university we reserve half of our upper division places for transfers from the community colleges. We were really trying to build toward equal opportunity as had never been seen before in world history. In the mean time two sad things happened: One was that the good high schools developed advanced placement

classes and the UC began taking advanced placement classes into account in accepting students. The poor school districts had none at all. While we were trying to increase equality of opportunity, there was being built by this new system of advanced placement, inequality for those from low income areas.[1]

This chapter attempts to address Clark Kerr's concern by examining the opportunity of Latina/o students to access Advanced Placement courses in California's public high schools. Indeed, issues of access and inequality have long overwhelmed the educational experience of Latina/o students. If one examines the educational pipeline—irrespective of how educational outcomes are measured—Latina/o students do not perform as well as whites (Chapa and Valencia, 1993; Garcia, 2001; Moreno, 1999; Rumberger, 1991; Solórzano, 1994, 1995; Solórzano and Yosso, 2000; U.S. Bureau of the Census, 2000; Valencia, 2002). Although many factors shape this educational reality for Latina/o students, this chapter will consider one critical point in the educational pipeline—the role of Advanced Placement courses as one of the curricular options that impact college admissions. We begin by examining the Latina/o educational pipeline. Next, we give an overview of the current legal status of using race in the college admissions process and the role of AP courses in determining college admission eligibility. Then, we introduce critical race theory as a framework to help understand the educational experiences of Latina/o students. Finally, we examine one point in the educational pipeline that impacts Latina/o participation in college—access to Advanced Placement courses.

Latina/o Education: A Portrait

Using the 2000 U.S. census data, Figure 4.1 takes us through the national picture of the Latina/o educational pipeline (U.S. Bureau of the Census, 2000). The pipeline utilizes three U.S. census data points: (1) high school graduation rate, (2) baccalaureate attainment, and (3) graduate school attainment.[2] We use 2000 census data as estimates to hypothetically start with one hundred students and show the decline in the educational attainment of Latina/o students as they make their way through the educational pipeline.

Figure 4.1 begins with one hundred Latina and Latino students at the elementary level. Of those one hundred students, fifty-three are expected to drop out at some point in the K-12 educational pipeline, and only forty-seven will graduate from high school. Of the forty-seven who graduate from high school, only twenty-six will pursue some form of a postsecondary education.

Of those twenty-six, about seventeen continue on to community colleges and nine will go to a four-year institution. Hence, around 65 percent of Latina/o students who pursue a postsecondary education will enter at a community college. Unfortunately, of the seventeen students who begin at the community college, only one will transfer to a four-year institution. Next, whether their college experience began by transferring from a community college or at a four-year university, only eight Latina/o students will graduate with a baccalaureate degree. Finally, three students will continue and graduate from a graduate or professional school, and fewer than one will receive a doctorate degree. Figure 4.1 shows how the dramatic "leakages" throughout the Latina/o educational pipeline are affecting educational attainment for Latina/o students. When compared to other ethnic groups, Latina/o student educational outcomes are consistently lower (Chapa and Valencia, 1993; Rumberger, 1991; Solórzano, 1994, 1995; Solórzano and Solórzano, 1995; U.S. Bureau of the Census, 2000; Valencia, 2002).

In order to explain these low educational outcomes, many social scientists implicitly begin with the assumption that the educational opportunities and conditions are the same for all students, from the elementary through the postsecondary levels. This is not the case. At the elementary, secondary, and postsecondary levels, Latina/o students attend schools whose educational conditions are some of the most inadequate in the United States (see Garcia, 2001; Moreno, 1999; Oakes, 1985; Solórzano and Solórzano, 1995; Solórzano and Yosso, 2000; Valencia, 2002). Some of the educational inequalities Latina/o students face are the lack of enriched curricula in K-12 schools, tracking of students into remedial instruction, racial segregation, and lower-financed schools, which all contribute to fewer positive educational outcomes (Chapa and Valencia, 1993; Donato et al., 1991; Orfield and Monfort, 1992; Valenzuela, 1999; Vigil, 1997).

Additionally, at the postsecondary level, though there have been absolute or numerical increases in Latina/o college enrollment in the last twenty years, three patterns related to these gains become clear when examined closely: (1) the increase is not in proportion to the overall growth of the Latina/o population, (2) the increase is located in two-year community colleges from which the transfer rate to four-year institutions is low, and (3) there are a disproportionate number of part-time college students (Aguirre and Martinez, 1993; Astin, 1982; Wilds and Wilson, 2001). These conditions only partially begin to explain the educational inequalities that lead to poor educational outcomes for Latina/o students.

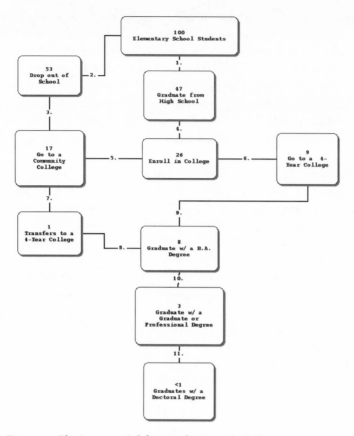

Figure 4.1. The Latina/o California educational pipeline.

The University of Michigan Affirmative Action Cases

On June 23, 2003, the U.S. Supreme Court reaffirmed in *Grutter v. Bollinger* (539 U.S. 306, 2003) that the University of Michigan Law School could consider race in its admissions. The Supreme Court reaffirmed the 1978 *Bakke v. Regents of the University of California* case (438 U.S. 265, 1978) by finding that having a racially diverse student body is a compelling state interest, and the University of Michigan Law School's use of race in the admissions process is narrowly tailored to meet those interests. As the Court's opinion indicated, "More important, for reasons set out below, today we endorse Justice Powell's view that a student body diversity is a compelling state interest that can justify the use of race in university admissions" (539 U.S. 13, 2003).

However, in a companion case—*Gratz v. Bollinger* (539 U.S. 244, 2003)—the undergraduate admissions policy at the University of Michigan's College of Literature, Science, and the Arts (LSA) was shown to be unconstitutional because its use of race in the admissions process was not narrowly tailored. Indeed, the Court found that the University's allocation of twenty points (in a 150 point undergraduate admissions system) for African American, Latina/o, or Native American students was too "mechanistic" and did not provide for "individualized consideration" in the admissions process—a practice the Court claimed was outlawed in university admissions in the 1978 *Bakke v. Regents of the University of California* case.

However, the Gratz case did not consider that an applicant could be given admission points in at least four other areas where "underrepresented "students of color"[3] might face various forms of discrimination. First, an applicant could be awarded up to sixteen points for being a Michigan resident and living in a Michigan county that was underrepresented at the university. These underrepresented counties tend to be in the northern part of the state, where few African Americans, Latina/os, or Native Americans reside. Second, if an applicant's parents graduated from the university, the student was given four points. In comparison to white applicants, fewer underrepresented students of color have graduated from the University of Michigan. Third, students were awarded from zero to ten points based on the quality of their high school. The research is clear that students of color attend schools of lesser quality than white students (see Solórzano and Ornelas, 2002, 2004a; Solórzano and Solórzano, 1995). Finally, students were awarded up to eight points based on the difficulty of the high school curriculum and whether or not they took the demanding college preparatory courses like Advanced Placement and honors. In fact, if the college preparatory curriculum was available and a student did not take the courses, she/he could lose up to four points. Again, in previous work, we have shown a "school within a school" effect. That is, attending a school with a challenging curriculum does not guarantee that students of color will be enrolled in the college preparatory curriculum (Solórzano and Ornelas, 2002, 2004a). In each of these four areas, students of color are put at a disadvantage in the University of Michigan's selection index. These four potential forms of discrimination were not addressed in the Supreme Court's 2003 ruling in *Gratz v. Bollinger*. Indeed, as colleges and universities develop *Grutter* type (and *Gratz* proof) affirmative action admissions programs, they must be aware of the potential to discriminate against the very students they are attempting to admit to "diversify" their incoming classes.

Critical Race Theory: A Lens for Research on Access and Enrollment in AP Courses

Critical race theory (CRT) provides a framework to address these issues and draws from a broad race and ethnic relations literature base in law, sociology, history, ethnic studies, and the field of education (see Ladson-Billings 1996; Ladson-Billings and Tate, 1995; Solórzano, 1997, 1998; Solórzano and Yosso, 2002; Solórzano and Ornelas, 2002, 2004a; Tate, 1997). CRT consists of basic insights, perspectives, methods, and pedagogies that seek to identify, analyze, and transform those structural and cultural aspects of education that maintain subordinate and dominant racial positions in and out of the classroom (see Matsuda, Lawrence, Delgado, and Crenshaw, 1993; Tierney, 1993). CRT in education includes the following five elements that form its basic model: (1) the centrality of race and racism and their intersectionality with other forms of subordination in education, (2) the challenge to dominant ideology around school failure, (3) the commitment to social justice in education, (4) the centrality of experiential knowledge, and (5) the transdisciplinary perspective (see Solórzano, 1997, 1998; Solórzano and Delgado Bernal, 2001; Solórzano and Yosso, 2000).

Though these themes are not new in and of themselves, together they represent a collective challenge to the existing methods of conducting and interpreting educational research on race and inequality. Indeed, using critical race theory in education is different from other critical frameworks because it simultaneously: (1) foregrounds race and racism in the research, (2) challenges the traditional paradigms, methods, texts, and separate discourse on race, gender, and class by showing how these social constructs intersect to impact on students of color, (3) helps us focus on the racialized, gendered, and classed experiences of students of color, (4) offers a liberatory and transformative approach when examining racial, gender, and class discrimination, and (5) utilizes the transdisciplinary knowledge and methodological base of ethnic studies, women's studies, sociology, history, and the law to better understand the various forms of discrimination (Solórzano 1997 and 1998).

In this chapter, we take the five CRT themes and, where applicable, apply them to the access and availability of AP courses for Latina/o students. CRT's centering of race and racism allows us to think critically about AP enrollment patterns. Using a CRT framework, we ask the following questions:

- How do school structures, practices, and discourses help maintain racial and ethnic discrimination in access to AP courses?

- How do Latina/o students and parents respond to the educational structures practices and discourses that help maintain racial and ethnic discrimination in access to AP courses?
- And, how can school reforms help end racial and ethnic discrimination in access to AP courses?

In order to answer these questions and to elaborate on how CRT can help examine the access and availability of AP classes and enrollment for Latina/o students, we examine both California high schools generally and the Los Angeles Unified School District (LAUSD) specifically.

Methodology

We address these questions by examining two levels of educational data—California and the Los Angeles Unified School District (LAUSD). Using 2000–2001 data from the California Department of Education, we were able to examine all of California's high schools. We looked at schools that had a minimum of five hundred students enrolled, for a total of 780 high schools. Because AP course availability and school size varied dramatically from school to school, we developed an AP Student Access Indicator (APSAI), which controls for both the size of the school and the number of AP courses offered. This indicator divided the overall high school student enrollment by the number of AP courses available at a high school.

High School Student Enrollment = APSAI

AP Classes

APSAI is an indicator that measures the number of students for each AP class. For instance, we calculated the APSAI score at Whitney High School in Cerritos, California, by dividing the 1,025 students by thirty-four AP courses, for a score of thirty. That is, for every thirty students, there is one AP class available. The lower the ratio of students to AP courses, the higher the ranking of the school.

Indeed, Whitney High had the lowest ratio of students to AP courses and was ranked first. From there we calculated an APSAI score and ranked each high school in the state. We then combined the top fifty public high schools and examined their collective racial make-up.

Our second layer of analysis used LAUSD data for the 2001–2002 academic year. With this data, we examined overall student enrollment in AP courses, student racial/ethnic enrollment in AP courses, and AP course availability for each high school in the district. Using the APSAI we were able to rank all of the LAUSD high schools.

Results: Access and Enrollment of AP Courses—
The Case for California

Latinas/os are one of the fastest growing ethnic groups in the state of California. According to the 2000 U.S. census, Latinas/os made up 32 percent of the state's population. Moreover, Latinas/os constituted 43 percent of the state of California's K-12 public school enrollment (California Department of Education, 2000–2001)—the largest and fastest growing ethnic group of California's K-12 public schools. Indeed, by the 2009–2010 academic year, Latina/o students are expected to reach 51 percent, or the majority of the state's K-12 student enrollment (California Department of Finance, Demographics Unit, 2000).

In this demographic context we begin to address the question of access and student enrollment in AP courses for Latina/o students. One place to begin addressing educational inequalities is to examine the negative consequences of the inequalities in access to and enrollment in high school AP courses. We begin this discussion by reaffirming that colleges and universities continue to focus on traditional indicators to determine the eligibility of students. Hence, high school grade point averages (GPAs), standardized tests (SAT and ACT), and AP courses weigh heavily in determining eligibility for college admission. Therefore, one could argue that, to be equitable, all California comprehensive high schools should offer a full array, or at least an adequate number, of AP courses and ensure proportionate ethnic student enrollment as one factor in preparing competitive applicants for university admission. When examining the top-performing schools in California (as measured by the AP Student Access Indicator), we find that students do in fact benefit from a demanding college preparatory curricula in addition to other factors, which all contribute to preparing a competitive applicant for university admission. For instance, Table 4.1 profiles the top three AP enrollment high schools in California.

Not only do these top three California high schools have numerous AP classes available to their students, but they also enjoy low overall enrollment, have high UC/CSU-eligible graduates, employ an extremely high percentage of fully credentialed teachers, and they tend to serve higher socioeconomic communities.

Table 4.1. California's top advanced placement schools, 2000–2001

	Whitney High School	Saratoga High School	Vallejo High School
Enrollment	1025	1255	2137
Number of AP classes	34	32	53
APSAI	1/30	1/39	1/40
State rank	1	2	3
UC/CSU eligible graduates	157	209	112
Percent fully credentialed teachers	93%	93%	91%
Percent free and reduced price meals	3%	0.4%	16%

Source: California Department of Education, Educational Demographics Office, 2000–2001.

When we take the APSAI and examine the ethnic make-up of California's top fifty AP high schools, Figure 4.2 reveals that in 2000–2001, while Latina/o students made up 38 percent of California's overall high school enrollment, they made up only 16 percent of the student population in these top fifty high schools.

Compared to their overall California state enrollment, Latina/o students are less likely to be in the top fifty AP public high schools. Students who do not have access to these courses are not afforded the extra GPA points and other college admissions benefits for taking AP courses, and thus reduce their chances of becoming competitively eligible for university admissions. While this inequality exists in California's fifty most competitive high schools,

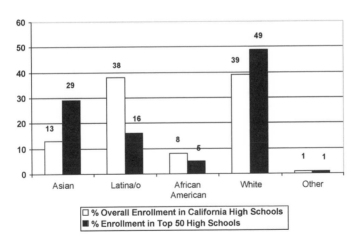

Figure 4.2. Percentage of enrollment by ethnicity in California's top 50 AP high schools, 2000–2001. Source: California Department of Education, 2000–2001.

the phenomenon of underenrollment of Latina/o students continues to increase across the remainder of California public high schools (California
Department of Education, 2000–2001). Furthermore, the lack of access and
availability of AP classes may be an indicator of a school's lack of a "college-
going culture," making college enrollment for students less likely (see Oakes,
Rogers, McDonough, Solórzano, Mehan, and Noguera, 2000).

In this context, we must pose this question: Do Latina/o students have
equal access to AP courses at their high schools? To best answer this question, we examine a specific school district in California—the Los Angeles
Unified School District.

Access and Enrollment of AP Courses:
The Los Angeles Unified School District

In this section we analyze AP enrollment in the Los Angeles Unified School
District (LAUSD), California's largest school district. The district serves predominantly urban, low-income communities of color. Like many districts
across the country, the LAUSD has an underrepresentation of Latina/o students enrolled in AP courses. For example, in the 2001–2002 academic year
(Figure 4.3), Latina/o students were 71 percent of the LAUSD's high school
enrollment, while they comprised only 49 percent of districtwide AP enrollment (LAUSD, 2001). Similarly, African Americans were 12 percent of the
overall high school population and 8 percent of the AP student enrollment.
This is clearly disproportionate to their districtwide enrollment. In contrast,
Asian and white students show the opposite trend. As Figure 4.3 points out,
whites comprised 10 percent of the overall student population and 22 percent
of AP enrollment, and Asians comprised 6 percent of the district's student
population and 21 percent of AP enrollment (LAUSD, 2001).

This finding invites us to ask: How does this data get played out in specific schools within LAUSD? To answer this question, we profiled the three
high schools within the district with the lowest AP Student Access Indicator
(APSAI).

The first school we examined was Belmont High School. We chose this
school because in 2001–2002, it was the largest high school in LAUSD. This
high school is located in the predominantly low-income, Latina/o community
adjacent to downtown Los Angeles, and had an enrollment of 5,447 students.
Using the APSAI, Belmont High School ranked fifty-second (out of fifty-four
high schools) in the LAUSD. Its APSAI was 195. That is, for every 195 students,
there was only one AP class available. Despite the size of this campus, only

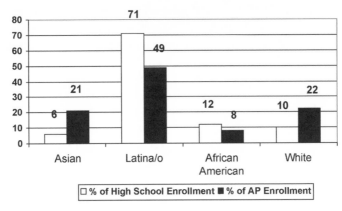

Figure 4.3. LAUSD percentage of enrollment by ethnicity in AP courses, 2001–2002. Source: LAUSD, 2001–2002.

twenty-eight AP classes were offered at Belmont High School. Furthermore, only 680 students (12 percent) were enrolled in AP classes and 481 graduates met UC/CSU admission eligibility. At Belmont High School, 79 percent of teachers were fully credentialed and 74 percent of its students were enrolled in the free and reduced-price meals program. According to Figure 4.4, during the 2001–2002 academic year, Latina/o students comprised 89 percent of the student population at Belmont High School. However, Latina/o students made up 80 percent of students enrolled in AP classes. Asian Americans made up 9 percent of the student population and 18 percent of AP enrollment.

Our second school is Gardena High School, which is located in the South Bay area of Los Angeles County. We chose this school because of the ethnic student diversity of the campus. In the 2001–2002 academic year, Gardena

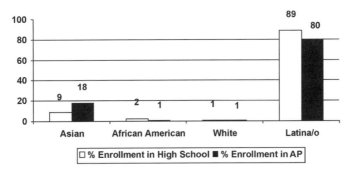

Figure 4.4. Belmont High School, AP enrollment, 2001–2002. Source: LAUSD, 2001–2002.

High School's enrollment totaled 2,955 students. Using the AP Student Population Indicator, Gardena High School ranked fifty-third (out of fifty-four schools) in the LAUSD. Its APSAI was two hundred, so for every two hundred students, there was only one AP class available. Although Gardena High School is a relatively large campus, only sixteen AP classes were offered. Furthermore, only 428 students (13 percent) were enrolled in AP classes and only thirty-nine graduates met UC/CSU admission eligibility requirements. At Gardena High School, 71 percent of teachers were fully credentialed and 61 percent of its students received free or reduced-price meals. According to Figure 4.5, during the 2001–2002 academic year, Latina/o students comprised 46 percent of the population at Gardena High School and 45 percent of AP classes. African Americans made up 44 percent of the student population and 33 percent of AP enrollment. In contrast, Asians comprised 8 percent of the student population and 20 percent of AP enrollment.

The last school we examined was Huntington Park High School. This high school is located in the predominantly low-income, Latina/o immigrant community in southeast Los Angeles. In the 2001–2002 academic year, Huntington Park High School's enrollment totaled 4,324 students. Using the AP Student Population Indicator, Huntington Park High School ranked fifty-fourth (out of fifty-four schools) in the LAUSD. With an APSAI score of 206, Huntington Park High School ranked the lowest in the LAUSD when measuring AP programs. That is, for every 206 students, there was only one AP class available. Despite the size of this campus, only twenty-one AP classes were offered at Huntington Park High School. Furthermore, only 387 students (9 percent) were enrolled in AP classes and only 213 graduates met UC/CSU admission eligibility. At Huntington Park High School, 82 percent

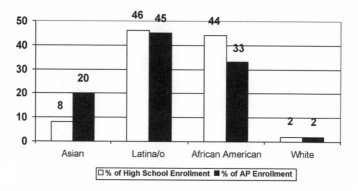

Figure 4.5. Gardenia High School, AP enrollment, 2001–2002. Source: LAUSD, 2001–2002.

of teachers were fully credentialed and 79 percent of its students received free or reduced-price meals. According to Figure 4.6, during the 2001–2002 academic year, Latina/o students comprised 98 percent of the student population. For Huntington Park High School, we stress different conditions for measuring educational outcomes. For instance, this school continues to be one of the most segregated and impoverished in the state of California, with almost no ethnic diversity.

The three schools described above have significant similarities that all contribute to low educational outcomes for Latina/o students. For instance, compared to the top three high schools in the state of California (Whitney, Saratoga, and Vallejo), these LAUSD schools are large campuses in very low-income and predominantly Latina/o communities, offer a minimal number of AP classes for their students, have an overall low number of students enrolled in AP classes, and send relatively few students to the UC or CSU. For these schools, and others like them throughout the state and the nation, the educational playing field is far from level.

Discussion: Responses to Unequal Access and Enrollment for AP Courses

We have discussed three different patterns that emerged at the district level: (1) Latina/o students are disproportionately underrepresented in AP enrollment in the top AP high schools in the state and the LAUSD (See Figures 4.2 and 4.3); (2) schools that serve urban, low-income Latina/o communities have a limited number of AP classes available for their students; and (3) schools that serve urban, low-income Latina/o communities have an overall low number of students enrolled in AP classes. Such educational disparities

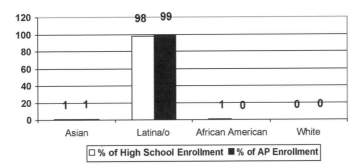

Figure 4.6. Huntington Park High School, AP enrollment, 2001–2002.
Source: LAUSD, 2001–2002.

place Latina/o students at a significant disadvantage when preparing and applying for university admission. Hence, the majority of Latina/o students are ineligible for university admission. Therefore, many turn to the community college to access a postsecondary education or opt out of postsecondary education altogether. Unfortunately, as Figure 4.1 indicates, only one of every seventeen Latina/o community college students will transfer to a four-year college (see Solórzano and Ornelas, 2004b). Indeed, this finding reinforces a second concern mentioned by Clark Kerr in the May 16, 2002, *UCLA Daily Bruin* interview (Falcone, 2002). When discussing the unequal opportunities for transfer to four-year colleges from California's community colleges, Kerr declared: "Second, the good community colleges will have college preparatory courses there that you can then transfer your credits (to the UC) and the poor community colleges will have no transfer courses whatsoever. So if you want to transfer and you haven't taken any transfer courses, you can't."

In response to unequal access and enrollment in AP courses in California high schools, two court cases have emerged. The first is a California Superior Court case titled *Daniel et al. v. State of California* (1999). This civil rights class-action suit was filed on behalf of California public high school students who were being denied equal and adequate access to Advanced Placement courses by the state's local school districts. In this case, the four student of color plaintiffs (along with their parents) argued that there was a lack of availability of AP courses at their high school and there was little encouragement and support from the high school for them to enroll in AP courses and take AP exams (*Daniel et al. v. State of California,* 1999). The student plaintiffs argued that this lack of access to AP courses and exams placed them at a disadvantage vis-à-vis other California high school students when competing for admission to California public universities. Before the Daniel case went to trial, the parties agreed to a consent decree that in part culminated in state legislation that gave financial support for California public high schools to build otherwise weak AP programs—the AP Challenge Grant Program.

The second court case is *Castaneda et al. v. University of California Regents* (1999). This is a United States federal civil rights class-action lawsuit that claims the UC Regents and UC Berkeley have violated and continue to violate the civil rights of students of color, who, in part, were denied equal access to AP courses at their high schools. Specifically, this occurs when the University of California adopts and implements admissions policies and procedures that disproportionately deny to otherwise qualified minority applicants an equal opportunity to compete for admission to undergraduate studies. The case argued that the University of California at Berkeley used admissions criteria that have a disparate impact on African American, Latina/o, and Pilipino applicants because it uses and gives added weight to AP course enrollment, AP grades, and AP exams in its admissions process. Indeed, AP programs serve at least three benefits in the admissions process to those who have access: (1) AP courses are an indication of a school's high-quality curriculum; (2) students who take AP courses receive an extra grade point in their GPA; and (3) AP courses usually lead to students taking AP exams. In many cases, if they score a "3 or better" on the AP exam, they receive college course credit. As a result, students who do not have access to such AP programs are at a distinct disadvantage when applying for university admissions. Many colleges and universities throughout the state, and indeed the nation, provide similar benefits to students who have access to and take AP courses.

Both of these legal cases are important because they illuminate the unequal educational conditions and opportunities across California high schools. We would predict this unequal pattern of access to AP would hold in most school districts across the country (U.S. Department of Education, Office of Civil Rights, 2000). This is why we argue that as colleges and universities develop admissions programs in a post–*Grutter* and *Gratz* legal environment, they must take into consideration the lack of AP and other educational opportunities that exist in public high schools throughout the state. Equally important is that these legal cases demonstrate how students and parents are resistant to educational structures and practices that maintain unequal conditions and outcomes in these schools. Students and their parents are not only critical of these educational inequalities, but by using the legal system, they are proactive in challenging these inequalities (*Castaneda et al. v. The Regents of the University of California, 1999* and *Daniel et al. v. The State of California, 1999*). A critical race framework suggests, and these cases illustrate, that marginalized groups can be agents of their own transformation. In these and other cases, students and parents are demanding equal educational access and opportunity through the state and federal courts and state and local legislation.

Recommendations

Although many steps must be taken in order to remedy the unequal access and enrollment for AP courses, we recommend the following as a starting point:

K-12 RECOMMENDATIONS

- K-12 institutions must develop a college-going culture that includes at minimum the following six conditions (see Oakes, Rogers, McDonough, Solórzano, Mehan, and Noguera, 2000):

1. A school culture supportive of advanced study and college going.
2. Student participation in rigorous academic courses (that is, college preparatory courses and AP programs); schools must ensure that all students have equal access to and consider ethnic proportions in AP enrollment and other college preparatory programs. Indeed, states and/or districts might consider that the default curriculum in all high schools be the college preparatory curriculum.
3. Student access to qualified teachers.
4. Student access to intensive academic support.
5. The school developing a multicultural college-going identity.
6. The school's connections with parents and community around advanced study.

UNIVERSITY ADMISSIONS RECOMMENDATIONS

- Colleges and universities must apply pressure on states and their local school districts to offer a rigorous academic curriculum for all students regardless of race or ethnicity, gender, or social class.
- Eliminate the extra grade point allocated to AP courses.
- Develop more accurate measures for student academic success, such as the student's GPA in college preparatory courses (see UC Latino Eligibility Task Force, 1997).
- Develop and implement the AP Student Admissions Index. This Index is calculated as the ratio between the number of AP courses the student takes divided by the number of AP courses her/his school offers. For example, using the index score, students are given a higher weight if a school offers five AP courses and a student takes all five compared to a school that offers twenty AP courses and a student takes only five.
- Develop and implement an AP School Equity Index. This School Equity Index would equal the number of specific students of color enrolled in AP courses divided by the number of those specific students of color enrolled in the school. For example, at a particular school you would calculate the number of Latino/a students enrolled in AP courses divided by the number of Latina/o students enrolled in the school. The School Equity Index could identify schools with high underrepresented students of color participation in AP courses, equal participation, and low participation. Implementation of this policy could also begin to address the "school within a school" phenomenon.

Conclusion

"The gains we thought we'd made in 1960, leading the
world, have now been taken away in very large part by the
two things I just mentioned. That's where I think the new
Master Plan ought to concentrate—to bring back this greater
emphasis on equality of opportunity."
—Clark Kerr, 2002

This final quote from Clark Kerr's 2002 interview (Falcone, 2002) sums up
both his and our major concerns. California public schools are unequal and
the University of California and California State University systems use
measures (AP courses, grades, and tests) in their admissions process that
discriminate against a large number of students in urban and rural schools
in predominantly low-income communities of color.

As researchers and policy makers, we must address the educational inequalities that exist for underrepresented students of color. We must ensure
that all students are afforded an equal educational opportunity to learn. Although this study has looked at the unequal access and enrollment in AP
classes for Latina/o students, we must keep in mind that access to AP classes
is one example of many educational inequalities that occur throughout the
educational pipeline, and it helps explain the dismal educational outcomes
for Latina/o students illustrated in Figure 4.1. Disparities in AP course enrollment should be used as a window that offers a glimpse into other educational
inequalities that exist in schools. Furthermore, using a critical race framework
allows us to specifically place race and racism at the center of the analysis
and focus on those educational inequalities that impact students of color and
poor students inside and outside the schools.

Notes

1. See: http://dailybruin.ucla.edu/news/printable.asp?id=19827&date=5/16/2002, retrieved on December 18, 2006.

2. The doctorate attainment data is taken from the Doctorates Records Project of the
National Research Council (see Sanderson et al., 2000).

3. In this chapter, the term "underrepresented students of color" is defined as persons
of African American, Latina/o, or Native American ancestry. It should be noted that
certain Asian American students continue to be underrepresented in some educational
outcomes. However, the data reported is not disaggregated by Asian subgroups.

5. Chicano Struggles for Racial Justice

The Movement's Contribution to Social Theory

RAMÓN A. GUTIÉRREZ

Forty years after the beginnings of the Chicano movement in the late 1960s, it is not unusual to hear this question asked: What were the movement's lasting results? One can easily point to greater access to employment, to education, to housing, and to health care in answer. There have been advances in political representation and public visibility, albeit largely spurred by demographic growth. One legacy of the Chicano movement that rarely gets mentioned is its contribution to social theory, which is the topic of this essay.

Since the late eighteenth century, when thinkers first began elaborating complex theories about the nature, organization, and functions of society, those theories have been largely the products of European facts or inspired by European presence or observations in other parts of the globe. Theories of European immigrant assimilation in the United States are an excellent example of this pattern. Marxism, psychoanalysis, structuralism, postmodernism, to name but a few theories, all were products of experiences and thought gener-ated in Europe, and only after the fact inflected by the particularities of life in other places. As far as I can ascertain, only three exceptions to this pattern exist. Internal colonialism, a theory of racial domination and subordination elaborated by African American and Chicano and Chicana activists in the United States during the mid-1960s and 1970s, liberation theology, which hailed from Latin America in the 1980s (Gutiérrez, 1984), and much more recently, subaltern studies theorized by Indian scholars (Chaturvedi, 2000).

The goal of this essay is to provide a historical genealogy for the theory of internal colonialism that blacks and Chicanos first articulated in the United

States, exploring its origins in Latin American theories of dependency and underdevelopment, and finally its extension, diffusion, and transformation among African Americans and Chicanos.

The belief that there were "domestic" or "internal" forms of colonialism operant within nation-states was an idea that initially emerged among Latin American development economists eager to understand the unequal terms of trade between the third world and the first, and between dominant and subordinate groups in these societies. Racial minorities in the United States found these theoretical formulations particularly compelling, and quickly adapted them to their own particular needs. Internal colonialism offered minorities an explanation for their territorial concentration, spatial segregation, external administration, the disparity between their legal citizenship and de facto second-class standing, their brutalization by the police, and the toxic effects of racism in their lives.

Internal colonialism represented a radical break in thinking about race in the United States after the Second World War. For far from seeking an understanding of racism in psychic structures, in an irrational fear of the "Other," or in the putatively predictable course of race relations cycles, blacks and Chicanos reasoned that their oppression was not only personal but structural, not only individual but institutional. Racism was deeply historical, rooted in the legacies of conquest and colonialism, and in personal and systemic effects of poverty, segregation, and white skin privilege.

In the early 1960s, motivated primarily by their poverty, by their exploitation as laborers, by their low levels of educational achievement, by their occupational and residential segregation, and by their constant police harassment, a massive grass-roots movement emerged in the United States among minorities that questioned the country's rhetoric of democracy and equality. In the American South, African Americans fought racism and segregation. In the Southwest, Mexican Americans, Native Americans, and citizens of Asian origin voiced similar grievances, drawing liberal and religious allies along the way, demanding equal access to better education, to fair housing and employment, and to full membership in American society. It was out of the confluence of these diverse interests and experiences that the civil rights movement gained its vibrancy.

In the early 1960s the movement's protests began peacefully, appealing to the country's conscience through sit-ins and boycotts, through prayers, pilgrimages, and marches, through freedom rides and voter registration drives, simultaneously litigating in the courts and offering nonviolent resistance, even to death. Faced with massive civil unrest, with a worldwide television audience daily observing and judging the harsh realities of America's rhetoric of equality, the state responded legislatively to quell protest. In January 1964 the U.S. Congress ratified the Twenty-fourth Amendment to the Constitution, outlawing those arbitrary poll taxes that historically had kept blacks from voting in the South. Later that year, on July 2, the Civil Rights Act was passed and signed into law by President Lyndon B. Johnson, guaranteeing citizens protection against discrimination in voting, education, and the use of public facilities. On August 6, 1965, President Johnson signed the Voting Rights Act, banning poll taxes, literacy tests, and all restrictions that might impede citizens from exercising their right to vote in federal elections.

Despite this legislation and the government's rapid infusion of funds into antipoverty programs, into labor force training, and into housing development, "optimism gave way to pessimism and even cynicism," explain historians John Hope Franklin and Alfred A. Moss Jr. (1988:458). Violence erupted, particularly in cities. Some of it was undoubtedly provoked by white anger at the rapid pace of desegregation and legal reform, but much of it was undoubtedly born of minority misery and hopelessness. Rioting erupted in Harlem while the ink was still wet on the newly signed Civil Rights Act. The following summer, five days after the Voting Right Act was signed into law, Watts, a minority neighborhood in Los Angeles, California, went up in flames, making it then the most destructive riot the nation had ever seen.

While civil rights activists were chalking up legislative victories in Washington, D.C., on the streets of Los Angeles, New York, and Chicago, and in the fields of California, Texas, and Florida, the realities of minority life were as bleak as they had been at the beginning of the decade. For many of the young, for those who expected a faster pace of change, the nonviolent integrationist politics of the Southern Christian Leadership Conference (SCLC), of the League of Latin American Citizens (LULAC), and of the American G.I. Forum offered more symbolic than material hope. The appeal of nationalism and separatism first articulated by men such as Malcolm X, before his 1965 death, increasingly sank deep roots in minority communities, nurtured as they were by much older nationalist ideals and sentiments.

For a number of African American radicals, the slogan that quickly came to symbolize their separatist aspirations and nationalist dreams was "Black Power." Voiced first by Stokely Carmichael, then chairman of the Student Nonviolent Coordinating Committee (SNCC) in the summer of 1966, Black Power crystallized the complex grievances that were fueling black resentment toward whites. In replacing the slogan "Freedom Now," which Martin Luther King and the SCLC had long espoused, King confronted Carmichael, explaining that "the words 'black' and 'power' together give the impression that we are talking about black domination rather than black equality" (King,

1968:31). King preferred "black equality" or "black consciousness" to Black Power, and correctly predicted that the slogan would unleash a torrent of white prejudice that up to that point many whites had been too timid to express openly.

The tide of African American radicalism in the form of Black Power proved impossible to contain, particularly as the war in Vietnam intensified in late 1966 and minorities were disproportionately among those drafted and increasingly among the dead. Like a rapidly spreading wildfire, young Mexican American men increasingly began to imagine what Brown Power and Chicano Power could mean. Among the first to gather to articulate such a dream were a group of Mexican American students that gathered on the UCLA campus in Los Angeles in 1967 and again in 1968. Celebrating their Mexican culture and Spanish language, they declared that they sought ways to "strive for power as a group, in the manner of militant Negro Black Power groups" (Haney-López, 2003:18).

These young Mexican Americans, who by 1967 were increasingly calling themselves Chicanas and Chicanos, much as blacks began insisting that they were not negroes, engaged in fierce intellectual debates to define what Brown Power meant. Typical were the discussions of La Junta, a group of East Los Angeles Chicanos committed to community empowerment. In 1968 they defined Brown Power thus: "Brown power has to be our cultural heritage. So we can get those values that were inherent in the Indians of ancient Mexico. And we can take those same values and same culture and use it in our lives and our movement. The way an Indian would relate to his family, to his tribe; the pride he had in his Indian nation. Brown power is first of all nationalism . . . that we know existed among our people thousands of years ago. It was true then, today, and it will be true a hundred years from now. . . . Brown power means liberation . . ." (Steiner, 1969:214–15).

For high school students such as David Sanchez, Carlos Montez, and Ralph Ramirez, who in 1967 founded the Young Citizens for Community Action under the sponsorship of Los Angeles Mayor Sam Yorty, the times called for more radical alternatives. Their own radicalization was reflected in their organization's name, which quickly became Young Chicanos for Community Action, before finally fixing on Brown Berets. Sporting paramilitary uniforms, topped with brown berets that bore a cross crisscrossed by bayonets, their motto was "To Serve, Observe and Protect," openly lampooning the motto of the Los Angeles Police Department, which was "To Protect and Serve."

Mimicking the Black Panther Party in ideology, dress, and demeanor, the Brown Berets engaged in military discipline and drills, in the prohibition of alcohol and drugs, demanding utmost cleanliness of their members, and adopting hierarchical titles for themselves: Gilbert Cruz Olmeda was the chairman, David Sanchez was the prime minister, Carlos Montez the minister of information, and Ralph Ramirez the minister of discipline. "The Brown Berets recruit from the rebels without a cause and make them rebels with a cause," explained David Sanchez in 1969, as chapters of his group mushroomed throughout the Southwest. He continued, "I wear the Brown Beret because it signifies my dignity and pride in the color of my skin and race" (Salazar, 1995:217). Serving the community in East Los Angeles with the establishment of a free clinic, constantly spouting quotations from Malcolm X, the Brown Berets issued a ten-point program demanding bilingual education, an end to urban renewal programs, and extensive community control over the police (Haney-López, 2003:178–90).

Just as Martin Luther King had himself been radicalized by the war in Vietnam, moving from earlier integrationist goals to broader issues of economic justice for all, the civil rights coalition fractured into two major camps in the late 1960s. At one end remained the integrationists, who favored slow legislative change through coalitions with liberal whites and other minorities. At the other end were the separatist and cultural nationalists, cognizant of their racial oppression, celebrating blackness and brownness, and seeking solidarity with anticolonial movements in the third world.

The theory of internal colonialism was born during this search for radical solutions to urban poverty and hopelessness. Colonial domination, in whatever its guise, required a nationalist movement for liberation. Internal colonialism became the model that was quickly heralded as holding the most potential for the liberation of minorities in the United States.

Internal colonialism as a theory grew out of the brutal urban conditions minorities faced in the United States. Seeking a theory of historical development that better explained their circumstances and offered tangible political strategies on which to act, radicals were clearly influenced by the militant third worldism then rampant on college campuses. Revolution, colonialism, and imperialism were constant themes of debate. Given the near iconic importance of the Chinese Revolution at the time, activist blacks and Chicanos naturally sought inspiration in the writing of Mao Tse Tung. "We read Mao," explained sociologist Tomás Almaguer, "the writings of Franz Fanon on the Algerian Revolution and Ernesto 'Che' Guevara on the Cuba Revolution; we read about American imperialism and about anticolonial liberation struggles around the globe" (Almaguer, 2003).[1] Indeed, in October 1966, when Huey P. Newton and Bobby Seale announced the formation of the Black Panther Party for Self-Defense in Oakland, California, they posed for pictures prominently displaying their rifles in honor of Mao's motto that "power flows from the barrel of a gun" (Van Deburg, 1992). This was a theme David Sanchez and the Brown Berets emulated, brandishing rifles, their breasts festooned with strings of bullets.

By studying national liberation struggles, blacks and Chicanos began to imagine themselves as oppressed nations that soon would be liberated through overt revolutionary struggle as part of the larger worldwide decolonization movements. Urban ghettos and Chicano *barrios* had the structure of domestic colonies, they asserted. They were isolated and segregated. Racism daily constrained the lives of residents in these domestic colonies. Like the wretched of the earth elsewhere, the residents of these domestic colonies had few opportunities or means to improve their material conditions. They wanted independence. Participants at the Black Power Conference of 1967, held in Newark, New Jersey, called for the "partitioning of the United States into two separate independent nations, one to be a homeland for whites and the other to be a homeland for black Americans" (Franklin and Moss, 1988:459). Chicanos in 1969 likewise demanded independence for Aztlán, the legendary homeland of the Aztecs, which they claimed as their putative land of ethnogenesis.

The Latin American Origins of Internal Colonialism

The existence of "domestic" or "internal" forms of colonialism was not a new idea. Latin American development economists had first postulated it in the 1950s as a corollary to the larger body of thought known as dependency theory. Though many names are historically associated with Latin American dependency theory, André Gunder Frank, then a professor of economics at the National University of Mexico in Mexico City, was critical to its elaboration and diffusion. His postulates about the "development of underdevelopment" became dogma (Frank, 1969, 1972). Though Frank's writings were far from original and were largely derivative, he did manage to crystallize into a number of theorems what dependency meant historically and how the theory could be tested empirically. Parenthetically, in the African context, and almost simultaneously, similar theoretical advances were being made. Walter Rodney wrote *How Europe Underdeveloped Africa* (1972), drawing largely on the works of African scholars such as Samir Amin.

To Latin American dependency theorists the central question of economic life was: Why, in the prosperity of the post–World War II era, had Latin American, Asian, and African economies not experienced sustained development and growth? The success of the Chinese and Cuban Revolutions and the rise of nationalist movements in the colonial world brought into serious question the cold war evolutionary theory of economic development.

The Latin American developmental wisdom of the day, preached by men such as Raúl Prebisch, the chief economist of the United Nations Economic Council on Latin America, was that industrialization and prosperity would be achieved in Latin America through economic nationalism (Prebisch, 1950). By restricting the level of foreign imports, practicing import substitution, and supporting nascent national industries, states eventually would experience economic growth. In fact, Latin American prosperity historically had been greatest in periods of isolation, such as during the Great Depression, when the region had to depend on its own resources to survive.

By the 1960s it had become clear to many Latin American economists that development strategies based solely on import substitution had not and could not succeed. Economic underdevelopment had a distinct and particular morphology. National markets were too small to support the establishment of intermediate and heavy industry. Income distribution was too skewed to promote large-scale national consumption markets. And land concentration was too profound to spur the consumption of manufactured goods by the rural masses.

André Gunder Frank saw these inequalities not as temporary blockages in the developmental trajectory toward industrial capitalism, but as permanent and systemic barriers. Historically, Latin American economies had been systematically plundered to fuel the industrialization of the metropolitan core economies. Frank coined the phrase "the development of underdevelopment" to explain how this relationship of colonial exploitation had progressed. So long as Latin American nations participated in the capitalist world's division of labor, this legacy would not be erased easily. It would be changed only when Latin Americans "destroy the capitalist class structure through revolution and replace it with socialist development," Frank opined (1972:19).

Latin America's underdevelopment was a historic product of its satellite relationship to the metropolitan economies of Europe and the United States, explained Frank. The areas of greatest underdevelopment and feudal-like institutions were precisely those regions that once had been tied to export booms in raw materials. The areas of most sustained autonomous development were those that had been isolated preceding their incorporation into the world capitalist system as satellites. Latin America's most substantive growth had occurred when ties to the world economy were weakest—the depression of the seventeenth century, the Napoleonic Wars, the First World War, the Great Depression of the 1930s, and the Second World War. When the metropolitan economies recovered and reestablished ties to their satellites, these ties immediately choked off what autonomous growth had transpired (Frank, 1969:1–27).

The idea that forms of "domestic" or "internal" colonialism existed within states emerged in the dependency literature primarily as a way to critique the then-dominant view that Latin American economies were dualistic, composed of modern and backward sectors. Instead, the theorists asserted, internal colonies composed the mass of Latin America's poor population, providing wealth to the metropolises. These internal colonies had a "racial dimension of being dominated . . . as well as an economic one; and more clearly lack social mobility (because of racism and their economic role as cheap labor)" (Cockcroft, Frank, and Johnson, 1972:xix).

Mexican sociologist Pablo González Casanova appears to have been the first dependency theorist to actually use the term "internal colonialism" (1963). He used it to describe the racialized economic dimension of relations between the dominant Mexican *mestizo* (mixed race) class and subordinated Indians. Several years later, in 1965, this analysis was deepened by the Mexican anthropologist Rodolfo Stavenhagen, depicting race relations between Ladinos and the Maya Indians of Chiapas and northern Guatemala as a case of "internal colonialism." Indians here had lost their lands, been forced to work for outsiders, been coerced into a monetary economy, and had been politically dominated by Ladinos (1965:271). Such relationships were a "function of the structural development-underdevelopment dichotomy" and would persist for the Indians as heightened racism, rigid social stratification, cultural isolation, and their use as cheap, disposable labor (1965:277).

Julio Cotler, a Peruvian political economist, offered a very similar reading of race relations between Ladinos and Indians in Peru, arguing in 1967 that the discrimination Indians suffered was owed not only to cultural differences but also to long-standing economic forces that dictated the very ways they had been incorporated into the international capitalist order (1970).

U.S. Ghettos as Domestic Colonies

That race relations between blacks and whites in the United States could also be characterized as "domestic colonialism" was first proposed by African American scholar Harold Cruse in 1962. Writing in *Studies on the Left*, a then newly established academic journal, Cruse argued that "the Negro is the American problem of underdevelopment" produced by the domestic colonialism in which they lived. Like the poor in underdeveloped countries, the lives of American blacks were characterized by "hunger, illiteracy, disease, ties to the land, urban and semi-urban slums, cultural starvation, and the psychological reactions to being ruled over by others not of his kind" (Cruse,

1968:74, 76). Celebrating the Cuban Revolution as a fundamental challenge to Western Marxist theory, Cruse maintained that what blacks needed in the United States was a revolutionary nationalist movement to extend anticolonial victories from the third world to the first.

The colonial metaphor was used repeatedly, but only in passing and quite superficially, to describe the condition of American blacks in the years that followed. In the book *Youth in the Ghetto* (Harlem Youth Opportunities Unlimited, 1964), Kenneth Clark argued that the sociopolitical and economic structure of Harlem was that of a colony. John Lindsay, the mayor of New York City, did not mention internal colonialism explicitly when he described Harlem, but he nevertheless seems to have accepted the fundamental premises of the nascent theory when, in 1966, he surmised: "Harlem has many of the features of underdeveloped countries. . . . The basic similarity between Harlem and an underdeveloped nation is that the local population does not control the area's economy, and therefore most of the internally generated income is rapidly drained out. That money is not returned or applied to any local community improvement" (Johnson, 1966:74). Writing several months later in the *New York Review of Books*, I. F. Stone concurred that "In an age of decolonization, it may be fruitful to regard the problem of the American Negro as a unique case of colonialism, an instance of internal imperialism, an underdeveloped people in our very midst" (1966:10). By 1968 even presidential candidate Eugene McCarthy began routinely referring to American blacks as colonized people in his campaign speeches (Blauner, 2001:65).

The fullest elaboration of internal colonialism as refracted through the African American experience appeared in Stokely Carmichael's and Charles V. Hamilton's 1967 book, *Black Power*. Offering a "framework" for black political, economic, and psychological empowerment in the United States, they began their searing critique of "white power" by differentiating between individual and institutional racism, locating the foundation of the latter in colonialism, and concluding that only by imagining Black Power as a global libratory movement of the colonized would American blacks become active agents in forging their own freedom (p. xi).

Conceding that the colonial analogy was not perfect, Carmichael and Hamilton nevertheless maintained that it well enough described the way colonizers enriched themselves while furthering the "economic dependency of the 'colonized.'" Reciting the ways black ghetto residents were denied mortgages and loans yet paid more for the items they bought in white-owned stores, they explained how "exploiters come into the ghetto from outside, bleed it dry, and leave it economically dependent on the larger society" (p. 17).

Blacks had to develop among themselves a sense of community to fight white racism. They had to question the values and institutions of society and gain economic change through their own political engagement and empowerment (p. 39). The ghetto's "colonial patterns" would only be shattered when blacks took community control over their schools and made them accountable, organized tenants' unions, demanded that merchants create reinvestment programs in the form of jobs and scholarships, and created independent political parties attuned to their own needs. This was what was necessary "to achieve dignity, to achieve their share of power, indeed, to become their own men and women . . ." (p. 185).

Chicanos as a Colonized Minority

The Chicano quest for a theory that explained their own colonial oppression in the U.S. Southwest dates to 1964. That summer Luis Valdez and Roberto Rubalcava, two students active in the establishment of Mexican American studies at San José State College in California, traveled to Cuba as members of the first Venceremos Brigade (Huerta, 1982:13–14). Eager to demonstrate their solidarity with Latin America's poor and with the Cuban Revolution, young Americans gave up their summer vacations to harvest sugar cane in Cuba. On their arrival on the island, Valdez and Rubalcava read a statement entitled "Venceremos! Mexican-American Statement on Travel to Cuba," in which they decried the condition of Mexican Americans in the United States as born of colonialism. "The Mexican in the United States has been . . . no less a victim of American imperialism than his impoverished brothers in Latin America . . . tell him of misery, feudalism, exploitation, illiteracy, starvation wages, and he will tell you that you speak of Texas; tell him of unemployment, the policy of repression against workers, discrimination . . . oppression by the oligarchies, and he will tell you that you speak of California . . ." (Valdez and Rubalcava, 1972:215–16). Valdez's and Rubalcava's analysis clearly tied Mexican American marginality in the United States to the hemisphere's colonial legacy. As colonial subjects, they believed that Mexican Americans would only be emancipated through a nationalist, anticolonial revolt.

This theme—the need for a nationalist, anticolonial revolt—was repeated over and over again, particularly among college students. Addressing students at the University of Colorado in 1967, Rodolfo "Corky" Gonzales, one of the more radical Chicano nationalists, called to revolution: "[R]ealize that the Southwest is very much like one of the colonies that have been colonized by England, by some of the European countries and those places that are economically colonized or militarily taken over by the United States. We have the same economic problems of those underdeveloped countries, and we suffer from the same type of exploitation and political strangulation. And because of this, you have a new cry for militancy . . ." (Rosales, 2000:339).

Speaking to those gathered in Washington, D.C., for the Poor People's March in May 1968, Reies López Tijerina, leader of the New Mexican Alianza Federal de Mercedes, and Rodolfo "Corky" Gonzales of the Crusade for Justice, a Denver civil rights organization, again emphatically declared: "Robbed of our land, our people were driven to the migrant labor fields and the cities. Poverty and city living under the colonial system of the Anglo has castrated our people's culture, consciousness of our heritage, and language" (Gonzales, 2001:32). Invoking the U.S. Constitution, they articulated a development plan for decent housing, free, community-controlled, and culturally relevant educational institutions, an end to police surveillance and violence, job training, and the restitution of lands fraudulently stolen by Anglos (Rosales, 2000:306–7).

The analysis Tijerina and Gonzales offered was quickly assimilated and echoed by students more broadly. This outcome was virtually guaranteed by the fact that Corky Gonzales, under the auspices of the Crusade for Justice, convened the first National Chicano Liberation Youth Conference in Denver on March 27–31, 1969. The conference brought together some 1,500 students who had previously thought of themselves as Mexican Americans. These students emerged from the conference proclaiming themselves a brown race, demanding Chicano Power, and calling themselves Chicanas and Chicanos. *El Plan Espiritual de Aztlán,* the conference manifesto, gave substance to Chicano/a as a political identity by declaring Aztlán as the lost Chicano homeland in need of liberation. "With our heart in our hands and our hands in the soil," *El Plan* stated, "we declare the independence of our *mestizo* nation. We are a bronze people with a bronze culture. Before the world, before all of North America, before all our brothers in the bronze continent, we are a nation, we are a union of free pueblos, we are Aztlán." Decrying the "gringo" invasion of their territories and the need to regain the natural riches stolen by outsiders, those gathered proclaimed, "Aztlán belongs to those who plant the seeds, water the fields, and gather the crops and not to the foreign Europeans." Aztlán as a physical and psychic space would only be reclaimed by driving exploiters "out of our community and a welding together of our people's combined resources to control their own production through cooperative effort." That effort included political, cultural, social, and economic activities, or demands similar to those articulated earlier by Tijerina and Gonzales at the 1968 Poor People's March (*El Plan de Espiritual de Aztlán* in Rosales, 2000:361–63).

Later that year, in April 1969, when faculty, students, and staff of institutions of higher learning met at the University of California, Santa Barbara to discuss their educational needs, they gathered not as Mexican Americans but as colonized Chicanos. In *El Plan de Santa Bárbara,* this conference's manifesto, attendees described Chicano *barrios* (ghettos) and *colonias* (neighborhoods) as "exploited, impoverished, and marginal. . . . The result of this domestic colonialism is that the *barrios* and *colonias* are dependent communities with no institutional power base of their own" (*Plan de Santa Barbara* in Rosales, 2000:191, 193).

The ideas articulated in the streets by activists and students soon enough began to receive formal academic analysis. Internal colonialism as an analytic model for understanding the condition of Chicanos/as was elaborated most extensively by Berkeley sociologist Robert Blauner and by his then–graduate student, Tomás Almaguer. Blauner maintained that while the United States was never a "colonizer" in the nineteenth-century European sense, it had nonetheless been economically developed through the conquest and seizure of indigenous lands, the enslavement of Africans, and the usurpation of Mexican territory through war. "Western colonialism," wrote Blauner, "brought into existence the present-day pattern of racial stratification; in the United States, as elsewhere, it was a colonial experience that generated the lineup of ethnic and racial divisions" (1972:51–81).

Blauner admitted that race relations and social change in the United States could not be explained entirely through internal colonialism because the country was a combination of colonial-racial and capitalist class realities. Internal colonialism was a modern capitalist practice of oppression and exploitation of racial and ethnic minorities within the borders of the state characterized by relationships of domination, oppression, and exploitation. Such relationships were apparent as forced entry, cultural destruction, external administration, and racism (1972:51–81). White skin racial privilege was at the heart of the colonial relationship, manifested as an "unfair advantage, a preferential situation or systemic 'head start' in the pursuit of social values, whether they be money, power, position, learning, or whatever," maintained Blauner. White people had historically advanced at the expense of blacks, Chicanos, and other third world peoples, particularly in the structure of dual labor markets and occupational hierarchies. Given these material facts, racism was far from a purely psychic phenomenon or a form of false consciousness; it was a structural and material reality that resulted in concrete benefits for whites.

Sociologist Tomás Almaguer went on to give these ideas their fullest scholarly elaboration as applied to Chicanos in a series of essays that appeared between 1971 and 1975. Others in the academy followed on Almaguer's heels, offering emendations to his and Blauner's basic theoretical framework. Historian Rodolfo Acuña embraced the model in his sweeping survey of the Chicano experience entitled *Occupied America: The Chicano's Struggle Toward Libera-*

tion (1972). Herein he contended that the experiences of Chicanos were quite akin to patterns of exploitation common in the third world. "The conquest of the [U.S.] Southwest created a colonial situation in the traditional sense—with the Mexican land and population being controlled by an imperialistic United States . . . colonization—with variations—is still with us today. Thus, I refer to the colony initially, in the traditional definition of the term, and later (taking into account the variations) as an internal colony" (1972:3).

Embracing internal colonialism as the theory for empirical studies, Richard Griswold del Castillo's *The Los Angeles Barrio, 1850–1890: A Social History* (1979) and Albert Camarillo's *Chicanos in a Changing Society: From Mexican Pueblos to American Barrios in Santa Barbara and Southern California, 1848–1930* (1979) looked at the aftermath of U.S. military conquest of former Mexican territories and found that it explained the political marginalization of Mexicans and their segregation in *barrios*. Ramón A. Gutiérrez described the mobilization and manipulation, the recruitment and repatriation of Mexican labor between 1880 and 1930, also as a case of internal colonialism (1976).

Just as internal colonialism gained vogue among Chicano/a scholars as a searing critique of social science theories that rationalized Chicano marginality as self-generated and rooted in cultural deficiencies, sociologist Joan Moore gently cautioned about its use. She understood well the model's appeal but wondered about its validity and rigor (1970). The Mexican-origin population of the Southwest was complexly stratified geographically, economically, and politically, she argued, such that the social order in New Mexico was a case of "classic colonialism," Texas "conflict colonialism," and California "economic colonialism." If internal colonialism as a political concept was to spur Chicanos/as to militant action, it would have to elaborate an ideology capable of reducing such differences. Marveling at the 1969 *Plan Espiritual de Aztlán,* she noted: "[T]he ideology reaches out to a time before even Spanish colonialism to describe the Southwestern United States as 'Aztlán'—an Aztec term. 'Aztlán' is a generality so sweeping that it can include all Mexican Americans. . . . That the young ideologues or the 'cultural nationalists' (as they call themselves) should utilize the symbols of the first of these colonists, the Aztecs (along with Emiliano Zapata, the most 'Indian' of Mexican revolutionaries from the past), is unquestionably of great symbolic significance to the participants themselves" (1970:471). Whether nationalists would ultimately succeed in elevating the symbols of despised lower-class Mexican Americans to popular use as "colonialist" Moore thought more unlikely.

Internal Colonialism and Its Political Legacy

Among Chicanas/os, internal colonialism was widely utilized by activists and intellectuals as an analytic tool to understand their structural location in American society from roughly 1965 to 1990. Why after nearly twenty-five years of use the theory was abandoned is more difficult to explain. One can easily offer a number of hypotheses, all of an internalist nature, the product of the Chicano movement's splintering and implosion. One of the strongest critiques of the Chicano nation-building project came from Chicanas, from feminists who protested the movement's elision of their issues and concerns. Chicanismo was a masculinist project seeking the return of a homeland called Aztlán, they argued (Garcia, 1997; Gutiérrez, 1993). This nation-building project was misogynist and exclusionary of women and sexual minorities. It was from this and other vantage points that critiques of Chicanismo emerged. A number of activist scholars who were committed to materialist and class-based analyses of racial oppression pointed to the deepening of class inequality in the shadow of civil rights legislation. They lamented how state-sponsored programs of government beneficence had swelled the Mexican American middle class, and how calls to nationalism only intensified racial/class oppression.

In the 1980s and early 1990s, four highly influential books appeared that moved the study of the Mexican American experience away from structural explanations to personal history, elevating individual experience to global theory. This move broadened the gap between scholars and activists committed to building grass-roots community organizations and self-help institutions as essential for national liberation. Though this university/community dichotomy is undoubtedly too stark and deserving of more complex hues of gray, it nevertheless captures some of the tug of war that masculinist Chicano nationalism provoked. Starting with Richard Rodriguez's *Hunger of Memory: The Education of Richard Rodriguez* (1982), and followed by Cherríe Moraga's *Loving in the War Years: Lo que Nunca Pasó por Sus Labios* (1983), Gloria Anzaldúa's *Borderlands/La Frontera: The New Mestiza* (1987), and Tomás Almaguer's *Racial Fault Lines: The Historical Origins of White Supremacy in California* (1994), these works asked fundamental questions about membership in the Chicana/o political community. All of these authors were political subjects who had been largely excluded as lesbian and gay and branded as counterrevolutionaries.

In his autobiography, Richard Rodriguez refused inclusion in the Chicano community, decried affirmative action and bilingual education, expressed his erotic desires for dark-skinned Mexican working-class men, and wanted nothing more than to become Americanized. Born to Mexican American parents in California, he desired above all else a slice of the white American middle-class dream. Cherríe Moraga in her narrative ruminated on her mixed racial ancestry. A white Anglo father and a Mexican mother had given her a blond *güera* look, which racial purists deemed sufficient reason for exclusion, only compounded by the fact that she was a lesbian. As Moraga wrote, "I am the daughter of a Chicana and anglo. I think most days I am an embarrassment to both groups. I sometimes hate the white in me so viciously that I long to forget the commitment my skin has imposed upon my life. To speak two tongues. I must. But I will not double-talk and I refuse to let anybody's movement determine for me what is safe and fair to say. . . . Any movement built on the fear and loathing of anyone is a failed movement. The Chicano movement is no different (1983:vi, 140)." Gloria Anzaldúa's *Borderlands/La Frontera* (1987) was undoubtedly the most influential of these books challenging Chicano nationalism. Anzaldúa exploded the simplistic notion of a Chicano space-based identity, claiming instead multiple identities as a Jewish, lesbian, working-class *Tejana* who had grown up along the porous U.S.-Mexico border speaking multiple dialects of Spanish. She counted herself among those living at the margins of society, those called *los atravesados,* "the squint-eyed, the perverse, the queer, the troublesome, the mongrel, the mulatto, the half-breed, the half dead; in short, those who cross over, pass over, or go through the confines of the 'normal'" (1987:3).

Years after his own articles on internal colonialism had reached canonical status, Tomás Almaguer, now writing as an openly gay scholar, recanted much of what he had written previously (1989). Internal colonialism's emergence among Chicano scholars had been an exaggerated overcompensation, he explained, but a necessary break from assimilation and Marxist class-based theories that viewed Mexicans as simply another European immigrant group that would eventually experience upward mobility. Chicanos in the 1960s needed a theory that accounted for their experiences of racial oppression and domination. Internal colonialism was wrong, but an expedient fix. Mexicans in the United States were complexly stratified not only by race, but also by class. In *Racial Fault Lines* (1994) Almaguer showed how in comparison to Asians and blacks, Mexicans in nineteenth-century California had enjoyed an intermediate racial status. Marked as they were by their Christianity, by their European-origin language, and their European national descent, they were, after all, almost white. "The claim that Chicanos were victims of colonial systems based on racial domination is also seriously open to question," Almaguer proposed, "given the racial status actually accorded Mexicans after United States annexation and the modest advantages they held over other minority groups" (1989:11). There were simply too many historic disjunctures between the nineteenth- and early twentieth-century experiences of Mexicans in the United States for "colonial" to be a particularly usefully adjective.

There is today considerable contestation among Chicano/a studies scholars about what precisely the Chicano movement was, what its tangible results were, and how its theoretical concerns live on. "Chicano movement" is now increasingly deemed a misnomer for several loosely allied grass-roots political organizations that per chance occurred simultaneously and haphazardly coalesced, as part of the larger worldwide egalitarian impulse to eradicate the most egregious forms of racial discrimination that emerged in the 1960s.

In the American Southwest, four quite distinct organizations tried to better the lives of their largely Mexican American members in different ways. Though they each scored initial successes, in the end their efforts were thwarted and their results short lived. Cesar Chavez, the champion of agricultural workers, employed union-organizing strategies to win wage contracts and better working conditions for the multiethnic members of the United Farm Workers of America (UFW). In 1967 the UFW signed labor contracts with many California growers, only to see those gains evaporate in the face of opposition from the government, growers, and organized labor.

The firebrand evangelical Baptist minister Reies López Tijerina, likewise during the 1960s, led a small organization in northern New Mexico, the Alianza Federal de Mercedes, which sought to regain the lands fraudulently stolen from New Mexico's longtime Hispano residents after U.S. conquest in 1848. While Tijerina agitated against the federal government, "illegally" seized federal lands, and spent the late 1960s in a jail cell, his organization was discredited and its members surveilled by the government, their poverty only intensified (López Tijerina, 2000).

Following an electoral strategy akin to that employed by blacks in Mississippi with the 1964 founding of the Freedom Party, so José Angel Gutiérrez launched La Raza Unida Party in Texas in 1970. Though able to seize control of the city government of Crystal City, Texas, white capital flight left factions squabbling over the morsels of poverty their control of the city had wrought (Gutiérrez, 1998; Navarro, 2000; García, 1989).

If any person can be considered the genitor of what remains of the "Chicano movement," it was "Corky" Gonzales, the former boxing champion whose bellicose in-your-face machismo rabidly challenged American racism. He gave the movement its name, mobilized Chicana/o students to demand control over their curriculum and schools and to resist police harassment, to protest the war in Vietnam, and to assert their national autonomy through his self-help programs, manpower development, and consumer cooperatives (Vigil, 1999; Gonzales, 2001).

The utopian nationalist ideals embedded in the theory of internal colonialism—territorial autonomy, self-determination, community control, an end to racism—were advanced largely by the students Corky Gonzales radicalized as Chicanos and Chicanas. Cries for community control quickly became student demands for university-based Chicano/a studies programs, for curricular reform, for identity-based syllabi, and for majors, minors, and all the infrastructure associated with academic programs (for example, Chicano studies libraries, student services, theme houses). The gulf between those engaged in grass-roots community politics and scholars based in the academy grew. For such scholars, cultural nationalism easily translated into a textual nationalism waged in the university through scholarly resistance to white racial hegemony, rather than in the streets with sticks and stones, or in the courts.

For African Americans, the dreams that internal colonialism ignited in the hearts of men also resonated more like tin in the ears of women. "The only position for women in SNCC is prone," Stokely Carmichael announced in 1964, and though slightly less openly misogynist as a prophet of Black Power, the legacy of militant machismo lived on unrepentant (Brown, 1992; Wallace, 1991). Jail sentences, FBI surveillance, provocations, and assignations decimated the leaders of the Black Power movement and accordingly left their programs of economic development and political empowerment in ruins, much as had been the case with Chicanos/as. White backlash weakened the will of liberal politicians for further legislative change, and with the election of Richard Nixon as president in 1968, the federal government's commitment to equality and access to housing, education, and work rapidly slackened and retrenched. Faced with racial hostility, what allies the Black Power movement had maintained moved on to mobilize against the war in Vietnam, and at the war's end, to comfortable middle-class suburban homes.

The tangible results of the civil rights movement remain evident through heightened levels of political representation, patterns of voting participation, and economic upward mobility for some, increasing the ranks of the black and Mexican American rich and middle class. Left behind was a much larger class of poor and working poor who have continued to fall further and further behind. The theory of internal colonialism was elaborated in the United States for them. Whether it be blacks in Harlem or Chicanos/as in East Los Angeles, the theory that promised to better their lives migrated elsewhere. And what remained were the *barrios* and ghettos, their conditions largely unchanged.

Note

1. Personal interview with Tomás Almaguer, San Francisco, December 15, 2003.

6. "Lifting As We Climb"

Educated Chicanas' Social Identities and Commitment to Social Action

AÍDA HURTADO

A recurrent debate in the social sciences is whether the increased social and educational mobility experienced by Chicanos/as, however limited, results in cultural and structural assimilation. In the 1970–80s, as the affirmative action movement transpired, a presumed tenet of the initiative was that, if given opportunities to obtain educational degrees, individuals from economically depressed and ethnic communities would return to their constituencies and labor on behalf of those left behind (Lawrence III and Matsuda, 1997). A classic contribution confirming this view is Bowen's and Bok's *The Shape of the River* (1998), which demonstrates systematically that affirmative action recipients from Ivy League schools did indeed contribute to ethnic and racial communities and exhibited a greater commitment to civic citizenship through public service than did their white counterparts. The focus of this pathbreaking study, however, was on African Americans; too few Latinos were included for an in-depth analysis of this population, a fact the researchers fully acknowledged and regretted. Furthermore, the Bowen and Bok study used large-scale survey data from "academically selective colleges and universities" (p. xxvi), which provided a high degree of explanatory power for group trends, but was limited to a narrow band of institutions. In addition, the respondents' perspectives—how they felt and made sense of their political commitment to civic participation—were absent from the study.

The question lingers: what of the recently educated Chicana population and the rising call to social activism? In this chapter, I examine Chicanas' identification with their ethnicity, race, sexuality, class, and gender to see if their affinities toward these social formations generate a political consciousness that leads to social action on behalf of these communities. In this case, "social action" is broadly defined to include political activism, civic participation, promotion of educational reforms to increase underrepresented students, environmental activism, and activities designed to end sexism, homophobia, and classism. I begin this examination by reviewing well-accepted concepts in social psychology used to understand social and personal identities and the connections between social identities and political consciousness. I then link these concepts to emerging theories on intersectionality. I present data from a national study of a nonrepresentative sample of educated Chicanas to demonstrate how these social psychological concepts come into play in the lives of these young women. Finally, I propose several policy recommendations derived directly from the study. The implementation of these policies (such as mentoring programs) at critical stages of young adult lives—from high school to entrance in a professional career—can help establish a pattern of educational and professional success among Chicanas and Chicanos as well as for other underrepresented students.

Social Identities and Political Consciousness

To probe the origin of commitment to social action, I look first to the social psychological literature on the construction of social identities. Within this framework are several theoretical distinctions that help us understand an individual's social identities. The foremost distinction, as held by most social psychologists, is between *personal* and *social identity,* which together form a person's total sense of self (Baumeister, 1998). Social psychologist Henri Tajfel (1981) posits that personal identity is that aspect of self composed of psychological traits and dispositions that give rise to personal uniqueness. Personal identity is derived from intrapsychic influences, many of which are socialized within family units (however they are defined) (Hurtado, 1997:309). From this perspective, human beings have a great deal in common precisely because their personal identities are comprised of universal processes, such as loving, mating, doing productive work—activities that are considered universal components of self. Personal identity is much more stable and coherent over time than social identity. Most individuals do not have multiple personal identities, nor do their personal identities change from one social context to another (Hurtado, 1996).

On the other hand, *social identity* is that aspect of self derived from the knowledge of being part of social categories and groups, together with the value and emotional significance attached to those group formations (Hurtado, 1997:309). Tajfel argues that the formation of social identities is the consequence of three social psychological processes. The first is *social catego-*

rization. Nationality, language, race and ethnicity, skin color, or other social or physical characteristics that are meaningful in particular social contexts can be the basis for social categorization and thus the foundation for the creation of social identities. For example, Mexicans immigrating to the United States are surprised to be categorized as "ethnic minorities"; in Mexico they enjoyed full citizenship and membership within a national culture, a notably different social category.

Another process underlying the construction of social identities is *social comparison.* In this process a group's status, degree of affluence, or other characteristic achieves significance *in relation to* perceived differences, and their value connotations, from other social formations. For example, Chicana students may see themselves as "middle class" when they are in their predominantly working-class communities; upon entering institutions of higher education attended largely by white students, they shift the comparison from neighborhood to college peers and reassess their class identification, most often from middle class to poor (Hurtado, 2003:116–20).

The third process involves *psychological work,* both cognitive and emotional, that is prompted by what Tajfel assumes is a universal motive—the achievement of a positive sense of self. The social groups that present the greatest obstacles to a positive sense of self are those that are disparaged, whose memberships have to be negotiated frequently because of their visibility, that have become politicized by social movements, and so on. They are the most likely to become problematic social identities for individuals. Moreover, these social identities become especially powerful psychologically; they are easily accessible and dwelt upon, apt to be salient across situations, and likely to function as schema, frameworks, or social scripts (Gurin, Hurtado, and Peng, 1994). For example, a poor African American woman with a physical disability is more likely to reflect on her social identities than is a wealthy white heterosexual male with no physical impediments. Unproblematic group memberships— ones that are socially valued or accorded privilege and are not obvious to others—may not even become social identities. Until very recently, being white was not the subject of inquiry, and it is still not widely thought of as a social identity (Fine et al., 1997; Hurtado and Stewart, 2004; Phinney, 1996).

Individuals belong to multiple groups and therefore possess multiple social identities. How identities generate a commitment to social action is largely explained through the ensuing process, *consciousness.* Social identities gain particular significance when they represent "master statuses" and when they are stigmatized. Race, social class, gender, ethnicity, physical challenges, and sexuality are the social identities assigned master statuses, because individuals must psychologically negotiate their potentially stigmatizing effects.

In the United States, as in many other countries, master statuses are used to make value judgments about group affiliations. Tajfel's theory of social identity, which has been elaborated upon by others, provides a sophisticated framework for understanding how individuals make sense of their group affiliations—both unproblematic and stigmatized ones. However, Tajfel does not elaborate on the individual's awareness of other social formations in the environment and on what basis judgments are made about inferiority or superiority of the individual's group affiliations. Patricia Gurin and her colleagues (1980) provide the theoretical bridge between group affiliations and awareness of the values attached to the groups' status by making a distinction between *identification* and *consciousness*. According to their elaboration, most people are aware of their social identities. For example, individuals can almost universally tell if they are female or male, Chicana or white, poor, middle class, or wealthy, or physically challenged or not. But according to Gurin and her colleagues, individuals are less likely to be aware of how the entire group of individuals in that category rate in relation to other social formations in the same life space (Lewin, 1948)—that is, the individuals may be highly identified but not at all *conscious* of their entire stratum or social formations. According to Gurin et al. (1980), "Identification and consciousness both denote cognitions: the former about a person's relation to others within a stratum, the latter about a stratum's position within a society. Identification refers to the awareness of having ideas, feelings, and interests similar to others who share the same stratum characteristics. Consciousness refers to a set of political beliefs and action orientations arising out of this awareness of similarity" (p. 143). Through identification, then, individuals see themselves belonging to certain social formations, say, for example, ethnic, gender, and class groups. Through consciousness, individuals become aware that the social formations they belong to hold a certain status (either powerful or not powerful) in society, and they can decide (or possibly feel compelled) to take action to change this status, not just for their own benefit but for others in the group as well.

Thus social identity, which consists of an individual's group affiliations and emotional attachments to those group memberships, is largely derived through social comparison. The meaning of an individual's group affiliation—its value and significance—is largely based on the presence and significance of other social formations in the environment. When different values are attached to different group affiliations, individuals have to do psychological work to come to terms with their social identities. As Tajfel posits, individuals strive not only to be different from other groups, but the difference has to be positive.

The Significance of Social Identities for Intersectionality

Looking beyond the theory of social identity, the concept of *intersectionality* facilitates an understanding of the social and economic conditions of women of color in general and of Chicanas specifically (traditionally considered problematic social categories) (Anzaldúa, 1987; Castillo, 1995; Sandoval, 2000; Collins, 2002; B. Pesquera and D. A. Segura, 1996). Sociologist Patricia Hill Collins (2002) broadly describes several components of intersectionality:

> The very notion of the intersections of race, class, and gender as an area worthy of study emerged from the recognition of practitioners of each distinctive theoretical tradition that inequality could not be explained, let alone challenged, via a race-only, or gender-only framework. No one had all of the answers and no one was going to get all of the answers without attention to two things. First, the notion of interlocking oppressions refers to the macro-level connections linking systems of oppression such as race, class, and gender. This is a model describing the social structures that create social positions. Second, the notion of intersectionality describes micro-level processes—namely, how each individual and group occupies a social position within interlocking structures of oppression described by the metaphor of intersectionality. Together they shape oppression. (p. 82)

More concretely, theories of intersectionality developed as a reaction to primarily white feminist analyses that privileged gender as the cornerstone of oppression that united women worldwide (Nesiah, 2000). Intersectionality theorists like Collins argue that "gender-only" or "race-only" analyses do not lead to an understanding of the position of all women, nor to a dismantling of the structures that oppress them. Intersectionality theorists also refuse to "rank the oppressions" (Moraga, 1981:29) and instead argue that membership in oppressed groups (such as being poor, of color, or lesbian) intersects in significant ways that affect women's experiences of oppression. Theories of intersectionality have also been applied to understand categorical differences between women in different nation-states (ibid.). For example, Rosa-Linda Fregoso (2003) problematizes the human rights paradigm applied by "First World Feminists" to women worldwide by stating: "Claiming a singular transnational identity for women ignores the profound differences among women across the globe, but especially within specific localities. . . . Although First World Feminists have contributed significantly to 'the theoretical and practical revision of international rights law,' especially in their redefinition of women's rights as human rights, the challenge today involves framing women's international human rights within very complex and specific cultural contexts" (p. 23). By applying the concept of intersectionality, Fregoso avoids homogenizing all Mexican women; thus she can analyze more specifically why young, working-class, dark-skinned Mexican women rather than wealthy, light-skinned Mexican women were the victims of "feminicide" in the border city of Ciudad Juarez (across from El Paso, Texas). For Fregoso, intersectionality provides a theoretical bridge for identifying variations based on class and race among different Mexican women, giving rise to a more penetrating analysis of the murders than the one provided by human rights discourse.

Although some social scientists have challenged theories of intersectionality as too abstract and not addressing the concreteness of social interaction (Fenstermaker and West, 2002), the theories have nonetheless had an enormous influence in the fields of political science (Kosambi, 1995), sociology (Browne and Joya, 2003), psychology (Stewart and McDermott, 2004), and literature (Saldívar-Hull, 2000). In my own work, I have linked the theories of social identity, as first proposed by Henri Tajfel, the extension of identification to consciousness (Gurin et al.), and the theories of intersectionality.

As discussed earlier, in social psychology the stigmatized social identities of sexuality, class, gender, race, ethnicity, and physical ableness are the ones that influence an individuals' construction of self (see Figure 6.1).

Which stigmatized social identities gain significance is largely context dependent. As noted, Mexican immigrants do not think frequently about being Mexican in Mexico. In fact, having a Mexican national identity does not carry negative connotations and therefore may not even be a social identity in the

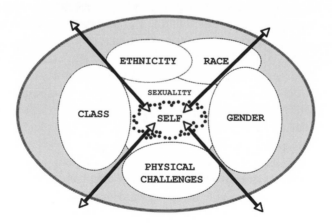

Figure 6.1. An individual's creation of self through intersectionality.

strictest use of the Tajfelian definition. However, upon entering the United States, the category of Mexican becomes salient and requires negotiation because of its negative implications within the U.S. context. Therefore Figure 6.1 can be conceptualized as a moving, fluid, amorphic "amoeba" that changes shape, making one (or more) social identities especially salient depending on the context. From a social psychological point of view, intersectionality refers to this particular constellation of social identities that is the primary basis for stigmatization: class, race, sexuality, gender, ethnicity, and physical ableness.

Chicanas can belong to several social categories that are devalued—being female, coming from working-class backgrounds, being immigrants, speaking Spanish, looking racially nonwhite, having nonwhite cultural backgrounds, and being lesbians—all of which contribute to experiencing racism, ethnocentrism, classism, heterosexism, and sexism. The experience of multiple oppressions, which varies based on social context, may theoretically facilitate the development of a *consciousness* about the position of all the Chicanas' denigrated group affiliations in society. In other words, according to the concept of *intersectionality* I have adopted here, Chicanas in the United States are more likely to see social injustice based not only on their class, their race, their ethnicity, their sexuality, but on all of these categories *simultaneously.* The experience of intersectionality therefore also leads to a multilayered, complicated sense of self (Hurtado, 2003).

In this chapter I address several research questions based on a study of educated, young Chicanas interviewed across the country (Hurtado, 2003). Do highly educated women identify with their ethnic background, gender, race, sexuality, and class? Does identification with different social formations lead to consciousness such that the women express a commitment to social action on behalf of Chicano/a and Latino/a issues? Do respondents ascribe their social and civic commitments to ethnic, racial, women's, sexuality, *and* class issues to the notion of intersectionality proposed by feminists of color? Do respondents report what influenced their development of a political consciousness? Based on the respondents' accounts, what policy recommendations can be implemented to increase the social and civic engagement of young, educated Chicanas/os and Latinas/os?

The Study

I interviewed 101 Chicanas in focus groups of two to three members. Respondents in the study had at least one parent of Mexican descent. (Of the 101, fourteen respondents came from mixed-heritage families. Ten respondents were the product of intermarriage between Mexican and white parents, the most common interracial coupling.) The respondents were between the ages of twenty and thirty, the average age being twenty-four, and were attending or had attended an institution of higher education.

I interviewed respondents living in five southwestern states—California, Colorado, New Mexico, Texas, and Arizona—as well as in Chicago, Cambridge, Ann Arbor, New York, and Washington, D.C. I contacted the majority of the respondents through counselors, professors, student organizations, and personnel or student affairs offices. I usually sent an electronic message describing the study and outlining the age and ethnic requirements for potential respondents. I had no difficulty obtaining responses and setting up interviews, which took place mostly in hotel rooms and occasionally in conference rooms at various universities. Focus groups had two or three respondents, although occasionally I interviewed respondents individually. The interviews took between two and three hours, depending on the number of respondents in each focus group, and were audio- and videotaped. The audiotapes were transcribed by bilingual, bicultural research assistants and crosschecked with the videotapes. The transcripts were coded and bivariate data analyses were conducted on the respondents' social identifications and commitment to future social action.

In addition to the interviews, I mailed a questionnaire to each of the respondents and shadowed thirty-five of them, spending one or more days in their company. As part of the shadowing activity, I met their parents, siblings, and other relatives. I attended respondents' graduations, weddings, baptisms, and professional presentations. I received notes, letters, electronic mail, pictures, cards, and books from many of the respondents.

A total of twenty-seven respondents had already graduated from colleges or professional schools and were employed. The remaining seventy-four respondents were attending institutions of higher education such as the University of California (Berkeley, Los Angeles, Santa Cruz); California State University, San Diego; Harvard University; New York University; University of Michigan; Columbia University; University of Texas; University of Texas–Pan American; University of New Mexico; and Arizona State University, among others.

Almost all (ninety-two) of the respondents were born in the United States; eight were born in Mexico but raised in the United States. Although most respondents were single, fifteen were married, and of those, seven had children. Five respondents had children when they were teenagers and remained single. Only one respondent was divorced and had a child. The majority of respondents represented the first generation in their families to graduate from high school and attend an institution of higher education.

Lifting as We Climb or Leaving Ethnic Ties Behind?

Consistent with the definition of identification provided by Gurin and colleagues, all of the respondents identified with their significant social groups, which included ethnicity, race, gender, sexuality, and class background. Although all respondents identified as Mexican descendents, they applied different ethnic labels to themselves (for example, Hispanic, Chicana, Latina, Mexican American, and so on). Almost all of the respondents used multiple ethnic labels to name their ethnicity and chose different ethnic labels depending on the context. For example, several respondents mentioned using "Mexican" while in their family's company but "Chicana" in university settings. Ethnic labeling also varied regionally, with many respondents in Texas and Arizona using the label "Hispanic," a rare occurrence among respondents in California.

The majority of the respondents identified their class background as poor or working class (see Table 6.1). They were aware of the economic struggles their families had endured as they were growing up. At the same time, their class assessments were made in *social comparison* to the communities around them. Many of the respondents mentioned thinking they were "middle class" until they attended institutions of higher education, at which time they realized that their parents' income was not high in comparison to the wealth they encountered at college.

All of the respondents were aware that Latinos in general and Chicanas/os specifically are *mestizos*—that is, racially mixed. They talked extensively about being racialized by their families, communities, and society in general depending on their phenotype—that is, whether they were light- or dark-skinned and whether they looked "indigenous" or "European" to others. Again, these judgments were highly dependent on social context; in certain settings, for example, respondents from East Los Angeles were judged as not looking "very Mexican," but in predominantly white institutions of higher

Table 6.1. Respondents' views of their social class background

Class Identification	Number of Respondents
Poor	18
Working class	32
Lower middle class	16
Middle class	30
Upper middle class	4
Rich	1
Total	101

education, their "Mexicanness" was the primary way in which they were socially categorized.

Of the 101 respondents, six identified as lesbian or bisexual. Five of the six had come out to their families in late adolescence. Each of the five reported that their families accepted their sexuality, although for some there had been a period of tension and even estrangement until the families finally accepted their sexual orientation. The one respondent who had not come out to her family was afraid of the consequences should she make the disclosure.

With regard to consciousness (a la Gurin et al.), respondents were highly aware of their stratum's position in society and had developed a commitment to working for social justice for their various communities. Ninety-three percent of the respondents were committed to working on behalf of Latino issues, and 92 percent were committed to working on behalf of ethnic and race issues in general because they felt that Latinos and other people of color were treated unfairly in society.

Respondents were also deeply aware of gender issues within their own communities and families as well as in society. The majority of the respondents identified themselves as feminists with no qualifications (51 percent). An additional 33 percent identified as feminists with reservations. Respondents gave several common reasons for not fully embracing the feminist label. Some felt they could not adhere to feminist prescriptions for appearance, which they believed included not wearing makeup or shaving legs and underarms. Others were concerned that feminism was associated with white, middle-class women, and they did not feel completely comfortable ascribing the label to themselves. Still others, like Felisa, a twenty-year-old undergraduate majoring in neuroscience at Colorado College, did not feel she was a "staunch" feminist and therefore had reservations about fully embracing the feminist label. However, she fully embraced gender equality in society, as well as in her future marriage. As Felisa stated: "I think of myself as a feminist. I'm not like a staunch feminist, where I'm out in the battlefield, but I definitely believe in equality for women and believe that we are just as capable as men in performing in the workplace. And that we are just as deserving of promotions and equal wages and all that. . . . For myself I want a marriage that is equal. Like I think my [future] husband is going to have to cook because I can't cook. (laughter). . . . My idea of having a successful marriage would entail having the male and female performing equal roles inside and outside the house. I definitely plan to have a career so I am not going to stay home with the kids."

Only 17 percent of the respondents explicitly rejected the feminist label. Several of these respondents recounted incidents in which they had initially embraced feminism but had negative experiences in white feminist organizations and concluded that, until the feminist movement was more ethnically and racially integrated, they could not claim the label. A total of 78 percent of the respondents were pro-choice and felt the government should not legislate what women can or cannot do with their bodies. Many of the respondents who were pro-choice mentioned an important caveat to their position. Even though they would vote to safeguard women's right to choose an abortion, if faced with the decision, they would opt against having one.

Most respondents also felt solidarity with the political struggles for gay and lesbian rights. Many of the respondents had relatives and friends who were gay or lesbian. They perceived the struggle for sexual freedom to be as important as other political issues. Respondents also tried to intercede with their families on behalf of their gay relatives in an effort to decrease the family's tension around issues of sexuality. As Gisela Hernández-Martínez, a twenty-four-year-old recent graduate of Indiana University Northwest with a bachelor's degree in business administration, explained: "I have a cousin who we [her family] all know he's gay, and I think it would be easier for him to just come out of the closet and just tell us all. Because he tried to commit suicide one time [because] his father always called him *maricon* [fag]." Gisela loved her cousin and socialized with him: "I go to clubs with him, and I know he's gay and I have a lot of fun with him. He's one of the people I'm closest to in my family." Gisela thought her family knew he was gay and they still "loved him as he is." She tried to make the transition easier for her cousin by asking her parents, "What if he came out? It would be easier for us and for him just to accept him." Gisela's consciousness about gay issues allowed her to advocate for her cousin within her family, hoping to make his life easier and countervail the negative reactions her uncle had toward his son.

As predicted by Gurin and colleagues' definition of consciousness, an essential component of the respondents' consciousness of group stratum was their commitment to take social action on behalf of the group's issues. Most respondents did not distance themselves from their political insights by claiming they did not apply to them or that they held no responsibility for remedying them. On the contrary, as a group, the respondents felt very privileged to have triumphed over the challenges they faced as members of stigmatized groups and were eager to effect change for others within their communities.

As noted earlier, Gurin and her colleagues' original position on consciousness only considered one social formation at a time. Based on this study, I find that respondents' consciousness was closer to the concept of intersectionality adopted here—that is, most respondents were aware that they experienced *multiple oppressions* as a result of their denigrated group affiliations that operated simultaneously but varied from context to context. They articulated that Mexican descendants were not treated equally because of their class status, lack of access to education, and cultural differences from white mainstream society, and because they were *mestizos,* they were subject to race discrimination. As such, respondents did not end up "ranking the oppressions" but rather "acknowledge[d] the specificity of the oppression[s]" (Moraga, 1981:29).

For example, the respondents' views on gender issues were entwined with their views on issues of poverty and social justice in general. Respondents' identification as feminists did not mean abandoning their concerns for their communities of origin. In fact, their intentions appeared to be the opposite— they wanted to bring their gender consciousness to their communities and hoped their feminist views might have an influence on ethnic issues. Most respondents had a high level of gender consciousness and were committed to working for gender equity in all contexts—professionally, in their various communities, and in their personal relationships.

Respondents' political mobilization took many avenues. Several respondents created recruitment programs at elite colleges to increase the number of underrepresented students. For example, Sofia had obtained her undergraduate degree at Williams College, located in western Massachusetts. At the time of the interview, she was twenty-six years old and enrolled in the master's program in education at Harvard University. Sofia grew up in a predominantly Mexican neighborhood in Chicago and, on entering college, had been shocked to find very few students of color at Williams College. "I started out with volunteer work in the admissions office and found out that I was the only Mexicana from the city of Chicago who had ever been enrolled at Williams. From the beginning we were told you are the bicentennial class, two hundred years of Williams College. I started thinking that is a tragedy that they've never had Mexicanas from Chicago." She and three other women became the core of an organization that instituted an enormous amount of change at the college. "[The organization] was called VISTA. It was an umbrella group because we didn't have enough people to make a Mexican group and a Puerto Rican group. But I was one of the coordinators and I was very actively involved. I went to Williams from '89 to '93, which was a time when, in the larger society, issues of multiculturalism and diversity were being played out. We coined the term 'Latina' on that campus because they always called people 'Hispanics' or 'Spanish.' So we did a lot of things. We instituted a lot of firsts—the Annual Latino Heritage Month and the First Annual Chicano Conference—first time this, first that. I personally worked a lot."

Sofia found it very gratifying that, years later, Latina students from Williams College would approach her to thank her for all the changes she had helped formulate. "I just saw someone at an event. She came up to me and said, 'Did you go to Williams?' I said, 'Yes, how did you know?' She's a senior there now. She saw me in pictures of the Latino group we formed. Then I met somebody else who said, 'Oh, I know you from Williams.' She worked in Admissions. She said Williams was known for recruiting people of color. I was like, 'Oh really?' I never knew but now that I think about it, the first time I was there was almost ten years ago. I didn't fully realize the significance of what we did in those four years. People tell me all the time, 'We have to thank you guys for doing this.' But I left before I really got to see the fruits of what we had done. So I can't say I regret my time there."

Other respondents refused prestigious corporate job offers to take positions that allowed them to serve predominantly poor communities of color. Many respondents felt that succeeding economically did not necessarily entail leaving their working-class communities behind. Instead, economic success enabled them to do "heart work," a phenomenon that journalist Christine Granados, one of the respondents, writes about in an issue of *Latina Magazine* (2001). In her article, Granados explores the development of a recently identified trend—educated Latinas leaving high-pressured careers to follow their passion. Granados writes: "Lupe Castañeda, a 55–year-old baby boomer, chose the career track as a young woman, working her way up the ladder to become a human resources manager at Levi Strauss & Co. It wasn't until she turned 53—after decades in corporate America and just two and a half years shy of a retirement package—that she gave up her nearly six-figure salary for a job in social work. 'I realized at that point in my life that there were more important things than being an executive,' Castañeda says. Today she is a licensed social worker for the project ELLA in El Paso, Texas, helping victims of domestic abuse make their way back into society. Her job is what she calls *heart work* [emphasis added]" (p. 103).

Lupe, Christine, and Sofia's deeds were not isolated demonstrations of commitment to social action. Many other respondents were equally committed to using their educational training to help others—to "lift as they climbed."

Pathways from Identification to Consciousness

A central question that emerges from these interviews is, how did so many of the respondents progress from simply identifying with their multiple "stigmatized" groups to developing a feeling of empowerment and commitment to political mobilization? When asked, many of the respondents saw several pathways contributing to their political transformation. Although their over-all consciousness was informed by lived experience, respondents noted two particular paths that facilitated the "jolt" of recognition of previously unde-tected discriminatory treatment. One jolt was their exposure to knowledge as they entered higher education; the other was exposure to political activism as enacted by women (and some men) in their lives.

Higher Education as Transformation: The Importance of Ethnic Studies, Women's Studies, and Student Organizations

The transformative power of higher education, with its intrinsic exposure to ethnic and women's studies and student organizations, cannot be overstated. A total of 77 percent of respondents belonged to ethnic organizations during their college years (only two belonged to ethnic organizations during high school). A total of 24 percent of respondents belonged to women's organizations during college (none belonged to women's organizations during high school). Very few respondents participated in gay organizations. Many of the 101 respon-dents felt they and their communities were not represented in the academic curriculum while they were in high school. In fact, many of the respondents knew little about their history and did not gain an intellectual framework for understanding their cultural and linguistic practices until they attended col-lege. Once in college, 56 percent of these high-achieving Chicanas took at least one course (and many times more than one) in Chicana/o studies. Similarly, a majority of the respondents had taken courses in women's studies.

Respondents' Parents as Models for Political Activism

The second most often mentioned pathway leading to political transforma-tion was the political activity undertaken by the respondents' parents. Several of their parents were civic minded and highly interested in electoral politics, both at the local and national levels. Others were interested in union politics and had their children participate with them in union meetings and strikes, or had openly discussed the importance of boycotts as a political mobilizing tool. Bianca, a twenty-six-year-old doctoral student in political science, explained that her father taught her the intricacies of verbal argument by watching news shows together, such as *Sixty Minutes,* and discussing the issues presented. As a child, Bianca's father took her to union meetings, where she watched heated debates taking place and took away powerful lessons for organizing workers.

A smaller number of respondents experienced another type of political mobilization. Several had mothers (no fathers were mentioned in this regard) who were active members in their churches; most were Catholic, but not all. These mothers participated in charitable activities such as providing food for homeless individuals, facilitating access for poor people to health clinics, and even working across the U.S./Mexican border helping poor people in neighboring Mexican communities obtain expensive medical procedures in the United States, in addition to food, clothes, and medicine.

From their mothers' examples, these respondents learned the importance of compassion, as well as the value of working collectively to help others less fortunate than themselves. This economic comparison, however, was at times precarious, as many of the mothers participating in these activities were not middle class by any measure. They lived in extremely poor communities, but a number of them were not employed outside the home and felt they "had time" to help others. In several instances, the mothers worked in factories, often laboring long hours for little pay, but they used their weekends and a few hours after work to help others they perceived as "less well off."

A small number of respondents had parents who had been actively involved in the Chicano movement for civil rights. These respondents had been socialized by their parents to attend rallies and walk picket lines, and they were well aware of the history of Chicanos' political struggles. Because political involvement was a normal part of these respondents' socialization as they were growing up, they did not see themselves as separate from these historical experiences. Their commitment to social action following their college years was a continuation of their earlier dedication to their communities.

Intersectionality in Understanding Political Transformations

To heighten an understanding of Chicanas' political transformation from consciousness to commitment (Gurin, Miller, and Gurin, 1980), I analyze the social identification of Chicanas from the perspective of intersectionality. I find it particularly noteworthy that respondents did not choose to "rank the oppressions"; rather they focused on social issues that were most relevant to their lived experience. For some respondents, promoting educational issues became a focus, others fought for environmental causes, some were committed to providing better health care in their communities, and still others saw art and cultural production as the area where they could make a difference. Although they focused on specific issues, they had a deep respect for the political commitment of others. Accordingly, they did not feel their ethnic and racial group should be the only ones with claims to public funding; most saw themselves in coalition with other similarly situated groups in the United States and internationally. Many respondents' consciousness about oppression extended to a global view of social justice.

The application of intersectionality also encouraged the examination of *multiple* stigmatized social identities simultaneously rather than artificially constraining respondents to consider only one social identity at a time—say, gender at the expense of ethnicity, race, class, and sexuality. Respondents integrated all of their group affiliations into their consciousness, creating a view of self that was accordingly complex.

The concept of intersectionality can also explain the respondents' adoption of additional group affiliations throughout their lives. Many respondents were invested in *crossing group borders* (Anzaldúa, 1987) to broaden who they were and to cultivate their critical consciousness about oppression. The borderlands as a metaphor was further reinforced as many of the respondents regularly traveled to Mexico, other parts of Latin America, and Europe. As bilingual, multicultural subjects, they were socialized into multilayered social meanings that gave them insight into the constructed nature of all social categories. Furthermore, respondents saw themselves as members of multiple communities, as exemplified through their social identities, and saw the endeavor to "bridge" (Moraga and Anzaldúa, 1981) their multiple worlds as part of their mission in life. On returning home from college, many respondents harbored political ideas about social inequality and feminism and struggled to make their families understand their newfound transformation. Instead of disengaging themselves from their families, they brought home books to share what they had learned in college.

Policy Recommendations

Through the theoretical frames of social identity, social categorization, political consciousness, intersectionality, and border crossing, many lessons from this study become apparent. The respondents' views on their identification and consciousness can be translated into specific policy recommendations that may lead to a heightened awareness of the numerous denigrated groups Chicanas/os belong to, as well as an increase in their commitment to social action. Furthermore, the policy recommendations that follow, although specifically derived from the experiences of Chicanas, are potentially applicable to other Latinas/os as well, and to underrepresented students in general.

Policy Recommendation Number One

BECAUSE POLITICAL SOCIALIZATION IS A DEVELOPMENTAL PROGRESSION, INCREASE THE NUMBER OF STUDENT ORGANIZATIONS IN HIGH SCHOOL TO EDUCATE STUDENTS ON THE POLITICAL PROCESS, THEIR OWN HISTORY, WOMEN'S ISSUES, AND SEXUALITY.   It is commonly assumed that young people's political consciousness is an issue of individual will and choice, and that they should automatically have a critical view of the inequalities in society and apply a political analysis to solutions for social problems. Young people of color are especially held accountable to this logic, and if they have not developed a consciousness, it is perceived as an individual choice and, at times, labeled as a failure to think critically. From the respondents' accounts, high schools in general, even private ones, are not geared toward teaching a critical perspective on racial, ethnic, sexuality, or women's issues. There were no political organizations in high school akin to those found in higher education, where students were exposed to critical discourse about race, ethnicity, sexuality, class, and gender.

In conjunction with this absence in socialization to critical perspectives, the curriculum in most high schools excluded writings by people of color and issues of sexuality. Many respondents spoke eloquently about the transformative power of higher education at institutions where they were exposed to history, literature, writers, and analyses that they had no clue existed while attending high school. Many of the respondents had been academic "stars" in their high schools, often graduating at the top of their class; their earlier ignorance felt especially poignant, because they had considered themselves "well educated" and had seen their high school curriculum as rigorous and challenging.

Consciousness is a developmental process in which students have to be exposed to critical perspectives throughout their schooling. Through exposure to the history and analyses of ethnic and racial groups, gender, and sexuality during high school, and perhaps even middle school, young people's involvement in civic affairs should increase. Waiting until college for students to become politically engaged is not an efficient way to socialize the next generation of voters and public servants.

Policy Recommendation Number Two

INCREASE THE OPPORTUNITIES FOR CHICANA/O AND OTHER LATINO/A STUDENTS AT ALL ACADEMIC LEVELS TO PARTICIPATE IN THE POLITICAL PROCESS.   In addition to established courses and student organizations, the respondents mentioned participation in internships and conferences as transformative in terms of their intellectual and political engagement. Several respondents participated in summer internships, often outside their home states. These experiences inspired them to attend universities away from home. High school and college students would greatly benefit from working side-by-side with legislators and with social and political organizations, as well as educational programs abroad. All of these experiences should increase intellectual and civic engagement.

Policy Recommendation Number Three

DEVELOP LEADERSHIP PROGRAMS, SPECIFICALLY TARGETED AT PUBLIC SERVICE, FOR EDUCATED CHICANAS/OS AND OTHER LATINOS/AS.   Financial aid in institutions of higher education is predicted to decrease in the near future. At the same time, all public universities are predicted to raise their tuition and fees fairly dramatically. One possible avenue for young Chicana/o students to obtain financial assistance would be to link undergraduate and graduate training to public service occupations upon graduation. Many of the respondents were unaware of public service jobs or professions while they were in high school and college. If they made a connection with public service employment, it was usually through a fortuitous encounter with a faculty mentor, special program, or fellow student who alerted them to the possibility. Leadership and other programs that are coordinated and actively recruit Chicana/o students are likely to increase their participation in the public sector.

Policy Recommendation Number Four

PROFESSIONALS SHOULD TARGET YOUNG CHICANOS/AS AND LATINOS/AS FOR MENTORING.   Finally, it is important for Chicana/o professionals to actively seek young people to mentor to produce the next generation of academics, politicians, legislators, social activists, artists, doctors, and lawyers, among other professions. Many respondents lamented never having had a mentor at all. Many times these respondents had graduated from the most demanding colleges and universities in the country, but they did not continue on to graduate or professional schools because no one had encouraged them to pursue their education, in spite of sterling academic records. Similarly, many of the respondents had graduated from the most demanding graduate and professional schools, but had not been guided in the next steps of their professional careers. Even when Latina/o students have successfully overcome enormous academic obstacles, some do not progress to the next level of achievement because of the lack of guidance. Any intervention that increases mentoring among Chicana/o students throughout the academic pipeline, from high school through higher education, is likely to increase Chicana/o educational achievement and successful entry into professional and academic fields.

"Lifting as we climb" is the motto of one of the oldest African American service organizations in the United States, the National Association of Colored Women's Clubs (NACWC), whose mission is "to promote racial understanding, justice and peace among all people . . . and help to improve the quality of life for all people, especially those in the African American community" (<http://www.nacwc.org>). NACWC was established in 1896 and continues to advocate and organize on behalf of young people, helping them find a productive place in this society. The young women in this study were carrying on the tradition established by NACWC of not forgetting or distancing themselves from the less fortunate members of their communities as they climbed up the ladder of educational and economic success. It is a fine tradition, one in which policy makers can play an active role.

PART III

Culture and Self-Representation

7. The Quebec Metaphor, Invasion, and Reconquest in Public Discourse on Mexican Immigration

LEO R. CHAVEZ

Harvard professor Samuel P. Huntington caused quite a stir when he raised the alarm about Mexican immigration in a 2004 article in *Foreign Policy*: "In this new era, the single most immediate and most serious challenge to America's traditional identity comes from the immense and continuing immigration from Latin America, especially from Mexico, and the fertility rates of those immigrants compared to black and white American natives" (Huntington, 2004).

Huntington's statement is all the more remarkable given the historical context in which it was made. At the time, the United States was waging war in Iraq, deeply involved in the war on terrorism in Afghanistan, and still searching for bin Laden and al Qaeda operatives worldwide. And yet amid all these crises, Huntington chose Mexican immigration to single out as America's most serious challenge. But this was not the first time Huntington had made such pronouncements. In an article in *American Enterprise* magazine, Huntington (2000) warned about the threat to the nation posed by Mexican immigration to the United States: "The invasion of over 1 million Mexican civilians is a comparable threat [as one million Mexican soldiers] to American societal security, and Americans should react against it with comparable vigor. Mexican immigration looms as a unique and disturbing challenge to our cultural integrity, our national identity, and potentially to our future as a country."

The cover image of the *American Enterprise* magazine complements Huntington's message but in more iconic terms. The headline reads: "Fixing Our Immigration Predicament." To the right is a photograph of two young Latinos, who look like gang members, in front of a wall covered in graffiti. Below the

Figure 7.1. *The American
Enterprise*, 2000.

photograph is the text: "This is the problem." Another photograph sits below
this one, and features six young people of various backgrounds, all of whom
look clean-cut, with one woman holding a book with "SAT" in big letters
across the cover. None of the individuals in the photograph appear to be
Latino, although the woman may be. Below this photograph is written: "This
is the solution." Because the young Latino males in the first photograph are
no longer represented in the second photograph, their absence or removal
is suggested as the solution.

Huntington is not alone in singling out Mexican immigration as a particularly insidious threat to the nation. In 1994, Patrick Buchanan (1994), a
nationally recognized conservative commentator, wrote an opinion article
in the *Los Angeles Times* in which he expressed a deep concern for the future
of the American nation. His concern was with the very real possibility that,
sometime in the near future, the majority of Americans would trace their
roots not to Europe but to Africa, Asia, Latin America, the Middle East, or
the Pacific islands. He thus asked: What would it mean for "America" if, for
example, south Texas and southern California became almost exclusively
Latino? He provided the following answer: "Each will have tens of millions of
people whose linguistic, historic and cultural roots are in Mexico," and thus

"like Eastern Ukraine, where 10 million Russian-speaking 'Ukrainians' now look impatiently to Moscow, not Kiev, as their cultural capital, America could see, in a decade, demands for Quebec-like status for Southern California" (Buchanan, 1994:B11).

Echoes of Buchanan's and Huntington's discourse are found in many places (Chavez 2008). Indeed, a veritable publishing industry has emerged to play to the public's fears of immigration, especially Mexican immigration. Among the many books on the topic that have appeared since the early 1990s are Peter Brimelow's (1995) *Alien Nation;* Arthur Schlesinger's (1992) *The Disuniting of America;* Georgie Anne Geyer's (1996) *Americans No More;* Patrick J. Buchanan's (2002) *The Death of the West: How Dying Populations and Immigrant Invasions Imperil Our Country and Civilization;* Victor Davis Hanson's (2003) *Mexifornia: A State of Becoming;* Tom Tancredo's (2006) *In Mortal Danger;* Jim Gilchrist's and Jerome R. Corsi's (2006) *The Minutemen;* and Buchanan's (2006) second book on the topic, *State of Siege.* These works often explicitly refer to the Quebec metaphor and the reconquest of the U.S. Southwest by Mexican immigrants.

In this chapter, I trace, in genealogical fashion, the development of the Quebec metaphor as a "lesson" for the threat of Mexican immigration, and the related ideas of invasion and reconquest. I will examine how these ideas become repeated and elaborated upon over time so that, in essence, they become "true." Representations of Mexican immigration are, as Foucault (1980) suggests, embedded in a discursive regime, by which is meant that these authors and these representations do not exist in isolation. They can be found in works by a number of authors and various media, often self-referencing, that construct knowledge and truth about Mexican immigration. Edward Said (1978:20) referred to this as a "strategic formation." I begin this analysis by focusing on a sample of magazine covers, and their related articles, that referenced immigration to the United States beginning in 1965 and to the end of 1999 (Chavez, 2001). These magazines are "popular" (rather than obscure), national in distribution, and varied as to their place in the political spectrum. Extensive library searches resulted in a sample of seventy-six magazines that explicitly referenced, through text or image, immigration, often in relation to race, multiculturalism, and national identity. Covers and related articles were copied for analysis. Mexican immigration was referenced on sixteen of the magazine covers. Although the analysis is based on these magazines, their covers, and on related articles, examples after 1999, such as the Huntington examples above, reflect how the patterns extend into the present (Chavez, 2008).

Mexican Exceptionalism:
Alarmist and Affirmative Representations

Before examining the Quebec metaphor and the related themes of invasion and reconquest, it is important to provide an overview of the representation of immigration presented by the magazines, and how Mexican immigration proved to be an exceptional case when compared to the general pattern. Magazine covers were classified based upon their use of images that were affirmative, alarmist, or neutral toward immigration.

Affirmative covers used images and text in a way that celebrated immigrants, typically tying them to the nation's identity (for example, America as a "nation of immigrants") or presented images that appealed for compassion for immigrants. Affirmative images often emphasized America's willingness to accept immigrants into its fold. The grand narrative of a "nation of immigrants" is central to the telling of this story. For example, On July 5, 1976, *Time* magazine published an issue celebrating the nation's bicentennial. The cover image was a mosaic of words printed in red, white, and blue. The capstone to the image is the bold text THE PROMISED LAND, which forms a protective semicircle above the text AMERICA'S NEW IMMIGRANTS. Symbolically, the "new immigrants" were contained within the protective structure of the nation. The cover for *Time*'s 1976 birthday issue was an affirmative rendition of "the nation of immigrants" theme that is a central part of the story America tells about its history and national identity.

Inside the magazine was another mosaic of images made up from photographs of immigrants from different periods in U.S. history and from different countries, along with a series of profiles on "America's new immigrants" from various countries, including Italy, Cuba, Lebanon, England, China, and Mexico. The theme underlying the immigrants' stories was the desire for economic opportunities and "a better life" for themselves and their families. A strong immigrant work ethic also permeated the stories. Interestingly, *Time* felt that it was important to let its readers know that immigration was not only part of America's past but also an important part of its present. As the article notes (p. 16): "Though many people think of mass immigration as a closed chapter in the nation's history, more than 1,000 newcomers now arrive in the U.S. every day. Since American birth rates are declining, that influx from abroad represents about one-fifth of the nation's annual increase in population. . . . All in all, the 400,000 new immigrants arriving every year represent, after decades of discriminatory national quotas, a comparatively enlightened policy that admits more people from poorer countries, particularly more Orientals."

Figure 7.2. *Time,* July 5, 1976.

The article and the cover both celebrated the "nation of immigrants" birthday by representing immigrants as central to the nation's history and identity. *Time* characterized as "enlightening" changes to the nation's immigration policy that allowed a wider diversity of immigrants.

Covers raising an alarm about immigration typically used images and text to suggest problems, fears, or dangers raised by immigration, such as population growth, demographic changes, a lack of assimilation, a breakup of the nation, or the death of the nation. Alarmist covers may also have featured words such as "invasion," "crisis," or "time bomb" that characterized immigration as a threat to the nation, or that appealed to fears and anxieties about immigration. Neutral covers did not make an obvious statement of affirmation or alarm, or were seemingly balanced in their message. Whenever it was not obvious if a cover was affirmative or alarmist, it was assigned to the neutral category.

Nineteen magazine covers (25 percent) used affirmative images and text to present issues related to immigration, and fifty (66 percent) covers used alarmist imagery, metaphors, adjectives, or other symbols. Seven magazine covers (9 percent) conveyed neutral or balanced messages about immigration. Alarmist covers, in this sense, were two-and-a-half times as common as affirmative covers. Even if neutral covers were included with affirmative ones, alarmist covers would still total about double their number. The majority of magazines published covers that at times were affirmative and at other times were alarmist. The use of alarmist and affirmative imagery did not generally follow a pattern based on perceived "conservative" or "liberal" ideology of the magazine. *Atlantic Monthly, The New Republic, The Nation,* and *The Progressive* more often used alarmist rather than affirmative or neutral images and text on their covers dealing with immigration. *The Progressive* and *The Nation* used alarmist imagery as a way of raising critiques of existing anti-immigrant attitudes and policies.

Alarmist images of immigration became more prevalent during the 1980s and 1990s, and affirmative images became relatively less frequent. This coincides with major economic recessions in the early 1980s and early 1990s. As the economy experienced downturns, the number of alarmist images of immigration came to the fore in public debate. Nor surprisingly, the U.S. Congress passed major legislation—the Immigration Reform and Control Act of 1986 and the immigration law of 1996—designed to restrict immigration in the aftermath of these recessions and increases in alarmist discourse.

A general pattern of representation can be discerned from this review of the magazine covers. Over the entire thirty-five-year period under examination, both alarmist and affirmative images have appeared on magazine covers. However, if we select just the covers that referenced Mexican immigration, we find a pattern at great variance from the general one. The first magazine covers referencing Mexican immigration appeared in 1975 with alarmist images, and they maintained that perspective during the entire thirty-five-year period. Of the sixteen covers referencing Mexican immigration, all but one are alarmist, and that one is neutral. I refer to this as Mexican exceptionalism when it comes to representations of immigration. This pattern of accentuating the alarmist view of Mexican immigration is not random or arbitrary, nor does it mean that an affirmative image of Mexican immigration is impossible to construct. For example, California's $27 billion agricultural industry is based largely on the labor of Mexican immigrants. It is not inconceivable that a magazine cover could represent this positive contribution to the nation's economy. But the point is that in the thirty-five-year period examined here, none of these magazines chose to present an image of Mexican immigration in such positive and affirmative terms.

Developing the Quebec Metaphor and the Themes of Invasion and Reconquest

French-speaking Canadians who sought separation from English-speaking Canada provided the basis for what is called here the Quebec metaphor for the threat posed by Mexican immigration. As the Quebec metaphor develops over succeeding years, what gives it its urgency is the concomitant representation of Mexican immigration as a looming crisis for American society, especially in terms of the growing numbers and fertility rates of Mexican immigrants and their offspring (Chavez, 2004; Inda, 2000; Inda, 2002). What emerges from these trends is the idea that what is occurring is a Mexican "invasion" of the United States, which is tantamount to a "reconquest" of territory once held by Mexico but lost as an aftermath of the U.S.–Mexican War. The Quebec metaphor is a reminder of just how politically volatile and dangerous such a situation can be for a nation. As will become apparent, *U.S. News & World Report* helped establish the contours of this discourse beginning in the 1970s, elements of which soon thereafter began appearing on the covers and in articles of other magazines in the 1980s and beyond.

The Quebec metaphor first surfaced on the cover of *U.S. News & World Report*'s December 13, 1976, issue, which featured the headline, "Crisis Across The Borders: Meaning to U.S." The cover's image is a map of North America with two arrows, both beginning in the United States, with one pointing to Mexico and the other to Canada. The problem in Canada was Quebec, where many French-speaking residents were pushing for greater sovereignty and even separation from the English-speaking provinces. The crisis from Mexico was the potential for increased migration to the United States. The "Quebec problem" would come to serve as a metaphor, or civics lesson, for the "Mexican problem" in later years.

The following year, *U.S. News & World Report*'s April 25, 1977, issue featured the cover headline: "Border Crisis: Illegal Aliens Out of Control?" The specific "out of control" behavior referred to on the cover is clarified in the accompanying article, which outlined how Mexican immigrants' use of welfare, medical, and related social services threatened the economic security of the nation. Also at issues was whether they abused the welfare system, displaced citizens from jobs, and turned to crime (p. 33).

The militaristic or warlike cover imagery is reinforced in the article when undocumented immigrants are referred to as "invaders." Invaders are, of course, unwelcome and hostile in their intentions. A nation that is invaded suffers an incursion into its sovereign territory, which could be interpreted as a hostile act, even an act of war. The metaphor of invasion leads easily to the next level of severity for a nation, which is to succumb to the invasion. "On one point there seems little argument: The U.S. has lost control of its borders" (p. 33). The siege mentality is further emphasized by the following statement: "In some communities along the Mexican–U.S. border, residents are so angry about crime committed by border crossers that they are arming themselves and fortifying their homes" (p. 33). The "fort" image is one that resonates well with the overall "at war" image that is developed. Finally, the U.S.–Mexico border is likened to the Maginot Line the French built between themselves and the Germans before World War II. According to Representative Lester L. Wolff, a Democrat from New York who toured the border, "We really have a Maginot Line. It is outflanked, overflown, and infiltrated. And you know what happened to the French" (p. 33). Such discourse characterizes the U.S.–Mexico border as a war zone that is "under siege," "invaded," "defended," and "lost" because of Mexican immigration.

Three months later, on July 4, 1977, *U.S. News & World Report*'s cover again focused attention on Mexican immigration. The cover's text reads: "TIME BOMB IN MEXICO: Why There'll Be No End to the Invasion of 'Illegals.'" The image is of a group of men standing, most with their hands in the air or behind their heads. The scene is taking place at night, a strong light making the men visible. The individuals all have dark hair and appear Latino. A lone Border Patrol agent, barely visible in the background, helps establish the scene's location: the U.S.–Mexico border. The men's stance, the officer, and the word "illegals" tell us this is an apprehension scene. The image uses the visual technique of the infinity line—detained border crossers are strewn haphazardly across the cover from left to right—to suggest that the line of men continues in one or both directions beyond the cover's physical border.

This is the first instance of the word "invasion" being used on one of the magazine covers under examination. This is a noteworthy escalation in the alarmist discourse on Mexican immigration. Invasion is a word that carries with it many connotations, none of them friendly or indicating mutual benefit. Friends do not invade; enemies invade. The invasion metaphor on this cover builds upon the visual imagery of *USN&WR*'s previous cover, which suggested a militarized U.S.–Mexico border. Escalating the militarized image, this metaphor evokes a sense of crisis. Invasion puts the nation and its people at great risk. Exactly what the nation risks by this invasion is not articulated in the image's message. The war metaphor is enhanced by the prominence of the words "Time Bomb." The text conjures up an image of Mexico as a bomb that, when it explodes, will damage the United States. The damage, the message makes clear, will be the unstoppable flow of illegal immigrants.

Although in hindsight the time bomb has had a rather long fuse, the image is disconcerting. It suggests that the bomb will go unnoticed and unprepared for, which adds to its destructive force.

The accompanying article clarified that the "time bomb" was Mexico's population (p. 27). The article cites predictions that Mexico's population, then at about sixty-four million, could grow to as many as 132 million by 1997. The yearly population increase at the time was somewhere between 3.2 and 3.5 percent. In addition to population pressures, Mexico had to confront high levels of unemployment and underemployment (then affecting about 40 percent of the working-age population), rapid urbanization that further strained a limited infrastructure, a level of agricultural production that failed to meet the needs of the country, growing inequality between rich and poor, and political corruption at all levels of government. Added to these problems was the political consideration of America's interest in maintaining political stability in Mexico. In this sense, immigration was an "escape hatch" for Mexicans who might otherwise stay and foment political unrest. Finally, from Mexico's viewpoint, the emigration of some of its population was not a problem but a "natural" response to limited economic opportunities at home and available jobs in the United States.

In short, the "invasion by illegals" was being propelled by forces in Mexico that was, the information suggested, getting worse. Importantly, however, this magazine and its cover drew attention to the external threat posed by the reproductive capacity of Mexican women, a threat that was also internal because Latinas' fertility levels were implicated in the nation's changing demographic profile.

Eighteen months later, on January 29, 1979, *U.S. News & World Report* published another cover on undocumented immigration. The cover's text read: "ILLEGAL ALIENS: Invasion Out of Control?" The image is a photograph of three Latino men being arrested by a Border Patrol agent. The setting is dry, hilly land. The inside article, by the same title as the cover text, examined illegal immigration and the difficulties involved in reducing it. "The guardians of America's borders, handcuffed by policy disputes at home and diplomatic hazards abroad, are falling steadily behind in their struggle to close the door to thousands of illegal aliens sneaking into the U.S. every day" (p. 38). The article noted that "up to 12 million" undocumented immigrants may have been in the United States at the time and that they could account for 10 percent of the population by the year 2025. But controlling immigration, according to *USN&WR*, was hampered by a lack of funding for the INS and the unwillingness of politicians to upset Mexico, whose sudden oil wealth raised the possibility of Mexico supplying the United States with 30 percent

Figure 7.3. *U.S. News & World Report,* January 29, 1979.

of its oil needs. In addition, Mexico's population was once again cited as a problem, as was the wage differential between the two countries (menial jobs were said to pay ten times as much in the United States as in Mexico).

The negative implications of undocumented immigration raised by the magazine include displacing U.S. citizens from jobs, the use of welfare, and crime. But even more important was the internal threat posed by the children of immigrants, which was central to the reconquest theme and Quebec metaphor. As Labor Secretary Ray Marshall was quoted as saying: illegal immigration "sows the seeds of a bitter civil-rights struggle in the 1990s by the children of today's illegal aliens" (p. 41).

The invasion metaphor is underscored in an article titled "Mexicanization of Los Angeles: A Trend That Is Spreading." As the article asserted, through a quote attributed to an unnamed official: "For all intents and purposes parts of Los Angeles are colonies of Mexico" (p. 42). Claiming that parts of Los Angeles are "colonies" of Mexico suggests that Mexico has not only invaded California but has managed to establish political control over territory. How did this come about? Los Angeles' growing Latino population, "swollen" by undocumented immigration, has "inherited" portions of the downtown area. The article goes on to argue that the influence of Latinos was magnified because "the traditions of Mexican Americans remain undiluted, refreshed daily by an influx of illegal immigrants from the mother country" (p. 42). "Undiluted traditions" is another way of saying that Mexican Americans do not assimilate into American society and culture. They remain separate and apart. So separate and apart, in fact, that there is no mixture, no dilution. Are we to interpret from this that Mexican Americans only speak Spanish, no matter how long or for how many generations they have lived in Los Angeles? Are Mexican Americans really so impervious to influences other than that of "illegal immigrants," such as the behavior and beliefs of the many other people in Los Angeles, the school system, the media, that their "traditions" remain undiluted? Characterizing Mexican Americans as foreigners who remain foreign (undiluted) gave added urgency to the invasion metaphor of the article and the cover.

U.S. News & World Report's March 9, 1981, issue featured an illustrated map of the North American continent, including Mexico. The United States is the focal point of the map and the stars and stripes of the U.S. flag cover it. To the north is Canada, with the image of a Mountie holding the Canadian flag and a French Canadian holding the Quebec flag in one hand and raising his other hand in a defiant, closed-fisted gesture toward the Mountie.

Figure 7.4. *U.S. News & World Report,* March, 1981.

To the south is Mexico, also with symbols of the nation and its people, animals, and economic strengths. There is the colonial cathedral representing the nation and its religious and colonial history. A modern tourist hotel on the Pacific Coast, oil wells and an oil worker on the East Coast, and cattle on the Yucatan Peninsula represent Mexico's economic strengths. Mexico's people are represented by a man wearing white peasant clothes, sitting in a stereotypical resting pose—usually he is found under a cactus—with legs bent at the knee, arms on knees, head resting on one hand. The sleepy peasant sits in the southern mountain area and he is perhaps meant to represent Mexico's Indian populations in the southern states of Oaxaca and Chiapas. A line of men (all individuals in the image appear to be male) emerge from the mountains and walk in a single file toward California. The man in front actually has his left foot ready to step on the red and white of California, at about San Diego. The text tells us that the image is about "OUR TROUBLED NEIGHBORS—Dangers for U.S." The cover's image places both the Quebec "problem" and the Mexican "problem" in the same symbolic space, thus merging them into one unified problem for the United States.

In the accompanying article, we learn about the problems posed for the United States by its neighbors. To the north was the possible political turmoil resulting from the French-speaking Canadians' movement for political independence from English-speaking Canadians. Western provinces also posed a separatist threat should the federal government usurp power at the expense of the provinces. For the United States, economic stability under such political pressures was a concern (p. 38). On the Mexican side, a familiar litany of problems included poverty, lagging farm production, an "explosive" birth rate, and illegal immigration.

Time's June 13, 1983, issue featured a cover with the headline "Los Angeles: America's Uneasy New Melting Pot." Los Angeles, as the title of the accompanying article informed, was "The New Ellis Island." The metaphor of Ellis Island was used to bestow on Los Angeles the title of the most important port of entry for immigrants coming to the United States. The report uses various phrases throughout to give a sense that immigration was high. Such phrases include: "Los Angeles is being invaded" (p. 18); "The statistical evidence of the immigrant tide is stark" (p. 19); and "Even before the staggering influx of foreign settlers" (p. 20). The report focuses on how immigration, particularly from Asia and Latin America, was resulting in dramatic changes in the city's ethnic composition. Mexicans, however, were distinctive, according to the article, in that the Southwest was once part of Mexico, and so Mexicans arrive "feeling as much like a migrant as an immigrant, not an illegal alien but a *reconquistador,*" or a reconquerer (p. 24). The reconquest metaphor refers to the separatist sentiments that were attributed to Mexican-origin people in the United States as part of the Quebec narrative.

Another example appeared on *U.S. News & World Report*'s March 7, 1983, cover, which announced: "Invasion from Mexico: It Just Keeps Growing." The image on the cover is a photograph of a line of men and women being carried by men across a canal. At the head of the line is a woman being carried to the United States on the shoulders of a man. This cover is momentous in that not only is a metaphor of war—invasion—foregrounded, but the foreign country—Mexico—accused of invading U.S. national territory is named. This is the first instance in this sample of magazine covers that the words "Mexico" and "invasion" have been directly linked together, and as such signaled a new level in the discourse on undocumented immigration. Mexico was now explicitly placed in the role of aggressor and the United States was the nation whose sovereign territory was under attack by this hostile country and its people.

Newsweek's June 25, 1984, cover relies on many of the same basic visual elements to tell its story as *USN&WR*'s cover, above. Once again we have a photographic image of a man carrying someone—a woman—across a shallow body of water. The woman is wearing a headscarf and a long shawl. The man carries the woman's handbag, which suggests she is traveling somewhere,

Figure 7.5. *Newsweek,* June 25, 1984.

moving with a purpose and for an extended amount of time. She holds a walking cane. The text states: "Closing the Door? The Angry Debate over Illegal Immigration. Crossing the Rio Grande." This is *Newsweek*'s first cover to explicitly reference Mexican immigrants.

Featuring women so prominently on the covers of these two national magazines while warning of an "invasion" sent a clear message about fertility and reproduction. Rather than an invading army, or even the stereotypical male migrant worker, the images suggested a more insidious invasion, one that included the capacity of the invaders to reproduce themselves. The women being carried into U.S. territory carry with them the seeds of future generations. The images signaled not simply a concern over undocumented workers, but a concern with immigrants who stay and reproduce families and, by extension, communities in the United States. These images, and their accompanying articles, alluded to issues of population growth, use of prenatal care, children's health services, education, and other social services.

Importantly, fertility rates of women in Mexico actually fell in subsequent years, contrary to the dire predictions found in this discourse on Mexican immigration. In 2002, Mexico's fertility rate had dropped to 2.9 children born to a woman during her lifetime (compared to 2.1 for U.S. women) according to the Population Reference Bureau.[1] Mexico's Consejo Nacional de Poblacion put the fertility rate lower, at 2.4 children per Mexican woman in 2000.[2] Clearly, Mexico has experienced dramatic declines in fertility rates over the last few decades. Also, the average size of Mexican American families, which was about 4.4 persons, or about one person larger than for all Americans (3.5 persons per family) in 1970, became significantly smaller since that time (Alvirez and Bean, 1976). As Bean, Swicegood, and Berg (2000) note, the mean number of children born to Mexican-origin women has decreased dramatically since 1970. Mexican-origin women in the United States between eighteen and forty-four years of age had an average of 1.81 children, well below zero population growth. Non-Hispanic white women between the same ages, however, only had 1.27 children, according to these data (June 1996 to June 1998 Current Population Surveys), so there still exists a difference, or "gap," of 42 percent (Chavez, 2004).

Almost a year later, on April 1, 1985, the liberal *New Republic* entered the debate over immigration. The editors of *The New Republic* staked out a position diametrically opposed to those who would like to restrict immigration (pp. 7–8). They viewed the immigration debate as one over "who deserves the highest distinction in the world—to be an American, with all the rights of American citizenship." The editors sided with advocates of an open door for immigrants escaping poverty and oppression. Relevant here is that the position against which the *New Republic* stands is one that argues the Quebec metaphor for Mexican immigration, or another way of putting it, Balkanization. For example, Senator Lawton Chiles of Florida was quoted as saying, "I think we would not recognize the United States as we see the United States today within a period of ten years if we do not regain control of our borders." House Majority Leader Jim Wright worried about "a Balkanization of American society into little subcultures." Richard Lamm feared that immigration would result in "a vast cultural separatism" and that the children of Latino immigrants would grow up not as loyal Americans but might lead "secessionist" riots in the Southwest to "express their outrage at this country."

Reproduction, immigration, and the Quebec threat, or "reconquest," came together in *U.S. News & World Report*'s August 19, 1985, cover. Its headline announces: "The Disappearing Border: Will the Mexican Migration Create a New Nation?" The cover's image renders the two nations, the U.S. and Mexico, through the strategic use of colors. Central to the image are large-block letters U and S, and their color is white. The U.S. letters sit in a field of green, and rest atop the smaller letters forming the word MEXICO. These letters are in red and sit on a field of yellow. The red of MEXICO is bleeding into

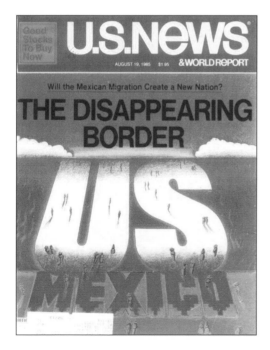

Figure 7.6. *U.S. News & World Report,* August 19, 1985.

the white of the U.S. letters, made possible by the disappearance of the lines (borders) between the letters. Without the borders, a one-way flow moves up (north) in the image. Little people are drawn in stereotypical fashion to suggest Mexicans migrating north. The accompanying article, titled "The Disappearing Border," establishes a "reconquest" theme:

> Now sounds the march of new conquistadors in the American Southwest. The heirs of Cortés and Coronado are rising again in the land their forebears took from the Indians and lost to the Americans. By might of numbers and strength of culture, Hispanics are changing the politics, economy and language in the U.S. states that border Mexico.
>
> Their movement is, despite its quiet and largely peaceful nature, both an invasion and a revolt. At the vanguard are those born here, whose roots are generations deep, who long endured Anglo dominance and rule and who are ascending within the U.S. system to take power they consider their birthright. Behind them comes an unstoppable mass—their kin from below the border who also claim ancestral homelands in the Southwest, which was the northern half of Mexico until the U.S. took it away in the mid-1800s. Like conquistadors of centuries past, they come in quest of fabled cities of gold. America's riches are pulling people all along the continent's Hispanic horn on a great migration to the place they call El Norte. (p. 30)

The *National Review*'s June 22, 1992, issue featured a cover with the Statue of Liberty standing with her arm outstretched, hand up, palm out, indicating STOP. The text read: "Tired, Poor, Tempest-Tossed? Try Australia." In the accompanying article, Peter Brimelow argues that Hispanics are particularly troublesome, going so far as to claim that they are "Symptomatic of the American Anti-Idea," which is neither defined nor clarified. But Brimelow leaves no doubt what he means: "Symptomatic of the American Anti-Idea is the emergence of a strange anti-nation inside the U.S.—the so-called 'Hispanics.' The various groups of Spanish-speaking immigrants are now much less encouraged to assimilate to American culture. Instead, as a result of ethnic lobbying in Washington, they are treated by U.S. government agencies as a homogenous 'protected class,' even though many of them have little in common with one another. . . . In effect, Spanish-speakers are still being encouraged to assimilate. But not to America" (p. 45).

The "anti-nation" Brimelow refers to is not located geographically, nor is its contours figured in any descriptive sense. But the "anti-nation" is a clear manifestation of what by this point has become "truth," the Quebec metaphor for understanding Mexican immigration and the conspiracy of Mexican Americans to keep themselves from integrating into U.S. society and culture.

Two years later, in 1996, David M. Kennedy, writing in the November issue of *The Atlantic Monthly,* again raises the Quebec metaphor and "The Reconquista." Despite the seeming interdependence between Mexico and the United States, Kennedy argues that Mexican immigration does not follow the pattern of pluralism supposedly exhibited by European immigrants. Mexicans are from a single cultural, linguistic, religious, and national source, and they concentrate in one geographical region, the Southwest. The United States, according to Kennedy, has had no experience comparable to this regional concentration of Mexican Americans. According to Kennedy, the possibilities of this trend are that Mexican Americans can, if they choose,

> preserve their distinctive culture indefinitely. They can challenge the existing cultural, political, legal, commercial, and educational systems to change fundamentally not only the language but also the very institutions in which they do business. . . . In the process, Americans could be pitched into a soul-searching redefinition of fundamental ideas such as the meaning of citizenship and national identity. . . . If we seek historical guidance, the closest example we have to hand is in the diagonally opposite corner of the North American continent, in Quebec. The possibility looms, that in the next generation or so we will see a kind of Chicano Quebec take shape in the American Southwest, as a group emerges with strong cultural cohesiveness and sufficient economic and political strength to insist on changes in the overall society's ways of organizing itself and conducting its affairs. (p. 68)

The Quebec narrative surfaced yet again in the *National Review*'s December 31, 1997, issue. The cover subtly referenced Mexican immigration. An illustration of Uncle Sam standing in a radiant but empty desert fills the cover. Uncle Sam's red, white, and blue hat sits on the arm of a cactus just behind him, to his right. His right hand holds a beige Mexican sombrero as he stares at the reader with an odd, slightly bemused look. The relevant cover text states: "De-Assimilation California Style." The heading and subheadings of the accompanying feature article by Scott McConnell emphasize the cover's message: "North of the Border, Down Mexico Way: Americans No More? Can assimilation operate today as it did a century ago? Or is it going into reverse?"

The author is identified as a writer based in New York City. The article provides an overview of writings, some academic and some ideological, about attitudes toward assimilation among Mexicans and Mexican Americans, many of whom do not live in southern California. McConnell begins with the assumption that "traditional" assimilation processes are not working in California, and therefore must be "revived" primarily because 38 percent of the foreign-born are from Latin America, and well more than half of those are from Mexico. "If assimilation can be revived it has to be revived among

Latinos," the author states, but he suggests that the "obstacles are daunting" (p. 32). The problems, according to McConnell, are both economic and attitudinal. Economically, he believes that Latinos face blocked upward mobility because of their high dropout and high poverty rates that will continue for generations, although virtually no academic research to support these assumptions was presented.

More problematic is the history of the Southwest. McConnell notes that "The Latino sense of the United States has always been different" (p. 33), and to prove this point he focuses on the terms "Aztlan," "Reconquista," and "Chicanismo" (Chicano nationalism). The author explains that Mexican American writers, especially during the 1960s and early 1970s, expressed the attitudes of contemporary Latinos who have not forgotten that the Southwest was once part of Mexico (their mythical "Aztlan" homeland). These writers also believed, according to McConnell, that they did not have to assimilate into American culture but instead were "reconquering" the land they lost through immigration. No evidence is provided on how widespread such views are among multigenerational Americans of Mexican descent. Assimilation, the author concludes, was reversing itself in Los Angeles, where neighborhoods were being "re-Mexicanized," a process he does not define other than to say people spoke Spanish in public and Mexican music was played in the streets. The author concludes that assimilation requires that immigrants and their children use English as their primary language, are politically loyal to the United States, and embrace the ideals of the Founding Fathers as their own. Importantly, no evidence or studies are provided on the use of English by Mexican immigrants and their children, or to examine issues of loyalty to the United States (for example, military service, acts of espionage), or on what they think about the ideals of American democracy and its economic systems.

The final image comes from *Time* magazine's June 11, 2001, issue. This cover appeared three months before the tragic events of September 11, 2001. Although this example takes us beyond our sample, it is illustrative of just how subtly the idea of reconquest, or a Mexican takeover of the United States, can be evoked. Here you have two smiling Latino children, dressed like American children anywhere might be dressed. Although the image may evoke a sense of pleasantness, the text raises an alarm about Mexican immigration: "Welcome to AMEXICA: The border is vanishing before our eyes, creating a new world for all of us." AMEXICA is a word made up of parts of AMERICA and MEXICO. But because this new word is framed by the "vanishing border" statement, it is MEXICO that is intruding on AMERICA, slowly obliterating, or taking over, AMERICA. Suddenly, the rather pleasant-looking children

Figure 7.7. *Time*, June 11, 2001.

are revealed as part of a reconquest of America, which is occurring because the "vanishing border" is letting them, and others like them, into the country and as a result creating a "new world."

Concluding Observations

The Quebec narrative powerfully encapsulates the threat to national security allegedly posed by the growing Mexican-origin population in the United States. The Quebec metaphor turns Benedict Anderson's (1983) notions of an "Imagined Community" on its head. Mexican immigrants and their children, and even their grandchildren, are imagined in this scenario as never becoming part of the community. Indeed, they are characterized as actively engaged in not becoming part of the community, imagined or otherwise. The narrative questions the Mexican-origin population's loyalty in that they are represented as possible enemy agents who wish to redefine U.S. territory as Mexican territory. Mexican immigrants, and Mexican Americans, are cast as perpetual foreigners, as outside the "we" of the "imagined community" of the nation (Anderson, 1983; Chavez, 1991). Leti Volpp (2002:1596) refers to such representations as "perpetual extraterritorialization," the idea that certain groups "are always already assumed to come from elsewhere, and to belong elsewhere when their behavior affronts."

Such imaginings have real political implications. For example, the Quebec metaphor played a central role in the debate over Proposition 187, the initiative on the 1994 California ballot to "Save Our State" from undocumented immigration. According to Linda B. Hayes, the Proposition 187 media director for southern California, the loss of U.S. territory can occur as a result of the rapid demographic shifts caused by Mexican immigration and, implicitly, the threat of reproduction in the growth of the Mexican-origin population. As she wrote in a letter to the *New York Times,* "By flooding the state with 2 million illegal aliens to date, and increasing that figure each of the following 10 years, Mexicans in California would number 15 million to 20 million by 2004. During those 10 years about 5 million to 8 million [non-Mexican] Californians would have emigrated to other states. If these trends continued, a Mexico-controlled California could vote to establish Spanish as the sole language of California, 10 million more English-speaking Californians could flee, and there could be a statewide vote to leave the Union and annex California to Mexico" (Hayes, 1994).

Despite such alarmist rhetoric, it should be noted that undocumented immigrants are not only from Mexico. Indeed, Suarez-Orozco and Paez (2002:10) note that only about 40 percent of undocumented immigrants in the U.S. are Mexicans, while Jeffrey Passel (2004) puts it at 57 percent. Moreover, Hayes does not explain why people who left a country in search of economic opportunity and a better life would vote to return California to the country they left. Nor is it clear why the children and grandchildren of immigrants—all U.S. citizens who did not grow up in Mexico and who will not have the same nostalgia for Mexico as their parents or grandparents— would vote to annex California to Mexico. However, the logic of the argument builds upon the Quebec metaphor so common in the discourse on Mexican immigration.

A final example of the Quebec narrative underscores its power in the political arena. In the 2003 race for governor of California, candidate Cruz Bustamante, the lieutenant governor, ran against Arnold Schwarzenegger, the actor. As the world knows, Schwarzenegger won. One of the key issues raised about Bustamante was his participation in MEChA (Movimiento Estudiantil Chicano de Aztlan), a college student organization, when he was a student. Opponents characterized MEChA, and thus Bustamante by association, as an organization that advocates taking over of the American Southwest by Chicanos because it was the mythical homeland of the Aztecs (Arellano, 2003:16). Thus, Cruz Bustamante, despite his protestations, became an Aztec warrior, a separatist, a member of the "Brown Klan," and a militant intent on "reconquering" the American Southwest. (Arellano, 2003). The image on the cover the *OC* [Orange County] *Weekly* (Vol. 9, No. 1, September 5–11, 2003) captures in satirical form the representation of Cruz Bustamante as an Aztec warrior, a representation the magazine was critiquing, not advocating.

As this reconstruction of the Quebec metaphor's development over the last forty years indicates, ideas have organic-like lives of their own. Once given birth, they grow and take on ever more elaborate and refined characteristics until they are able to stand on their own as taken-for-granted "truth." The Quebec metaphor is now easily invoked when necessary to call up the most dire fears, conspiracies, and imminent destruction of the American way of life by Mexican immigrants and their U.S.-born descendants. The problem, of course, is how difficult it is to uproot such a myth once it becomes well entrenched in public discourse. The task of the social scientist, however, is to provide information and reasoned analysis, even when such efforts may seem like fighting windmills.

As social scientists, we can point out that there is little, if any, empirical evidence of a Quebec-like separatist movement among Mexican Americans or Chicanos. We can point to alternative representations of Mexican immigrants and U.S. Mexican Americans, Chicanos, and other Latinos found in academic publications, ethnic magazines and newspapers, and sometimes even on television and in the movies, although the latter imagery often goes further

Figure 7.8. Bustamante in *Orange County Weekly.*

than the alarmist and often negative representations discussed here. We can also point out that during the mid to late 1990s, an expanding economy created a hyper-demand for immigrant labor, pulling Mexican immigrants to ever more "exotic" locations in the midwestern and southeastern United States (Grieco, 2003). Interestingly, during that time of economic expansion and need for immigrant labor, the alarmist discourse was superseded, if only for a few years, by more moderate views on immigration. George Will (2001), in *Newsweek,* argued that today's immigrants, including Mexicans, were no different from Italians and other earlier waves of immigrants. The AFL-CIO suddenly changed its policy to one that favored legalizing and unionizing undocumented immigrants (Cleeland, 2000). Federal Reserve chairman Alan Greenspan noted that immigrants were good for the economy (Scheer, 2000). And George W. Bush, shortly after assuming the presidency, put forward an ambitious immigration reform plan that would have legalized Mexican undocumented immigrants and created a new guest-worker program for Mexican workers (Smith and Chen, 2001). Finally, we can point to the historical foundations and social realities of United States–Mexico interdependence that will continue into the foreseeable future.

However, such pronouncements will not refute the "truths" in the Quebec metaphor, and the rhetoric of invasions and reconquests so prevalent in popular discourse. Such "truths" fueled the Minuteman Project's spectacle of surveillance at the Arizona-Mexico border in April 2005 (Chavez, 2007). In December of that year, the U.S. House of Representatives passed a punishment-only immigration reform bill (H.R. 4437) that sought to control undocumented immigration through greater surveillance and criminalizing the very act of being an undocumented immigrant (Curtius, 2005). In response to the House's draconian bill, in the spring of 2006, immigrants and their supporters marched throughout the country, asserting their right to belong to the nation (Miller, 2006). Then in October 2006, President Bush signed into law a bill authorizing the building of a seven-hundred-mile fence along the U.S.–Mexico border in a show of "getting tough" on undocumented immigration and increasing security against terrorism (Gaouette, 2006). All of these events occurred in a context in which the Quebec metaphor and reconquest scenarios were rampant in the popular imagination, and we are thus reminded just how powerful are the myths we construct.

Notes

1. Source: Population Reference Bureau 2003, www.prb.org. (July 30, 2003).
2. Source: www.conapo.gob.mx/m_en_cifras/principal/html. (July 30, 2003).

8. Prime-Time Protest

Latinos and Network Television

CHON A. NORIEGA

Introduction

Despite the well-documented growth of the Latino community as a political and market force within California and nationally, Latinos entered the twenty-first century with a lower level of media access and representation than when protests first raised the issue in the 1960s. After all, since 1970, Latinos have grown by roughly two and a half times relative to the national population, but they still receive the same small percentage of the jobs and on-screen representation (Noriega, 2002, 2003). In effect, employment opportunity for the Latino community has *decreased* in the entertainment industry to nearly one-third the level of the 1970s.

Given that Latinos constitute the plurality of Los Angeles (47 percent), their virtual absence within Hollywood is all the more shocking. This essay will focus on a single case study—that of the National Hispanic Media Coalition, established in 1986—which exemplifies the range of media reform activities over the past two decades, but especially since the Telecommunications Act of 1996.[1] While the act focused on the deregulation of competing business interests across media platforms (television, cable, Internet, phone), it also ended or eroded those regulatory policies focused on the social consequences of telecommunications that had emerged out of the civil rights era.[2] Following the case study, I will consider the current issues facing media reform and the most viable strategies.

Before turning to the National Hispanic Media Coalition, however, I would like to consider two examples of a shift in "image" advocacy for Latinos over the past decade, because it informs the context for media reform since the

1996 act. This shift is one from the articulation of a social agenda within a commercial context to the naming of an ethnic market through cultural nationalist rhetoric. The first incident involves a little-noted change in strategy for the Mexican American Legal Defense and Education Fund (MALDEF), and the second a recent controversy around a popular Spanish-language Los Angeles television station.

In February 1998, MALDEF began running a television ad in southern California just prior to the statewide vote on Proposition 227 (eliminating bilingual education). What was unusual about this ad is that it did not address the proposition or even the underlying issues about educational access, language use, and immigration. Instead, the ad focused on improving the Latino image, specifically addressing the 54 percent of whites who held negative views of Latinos as a group unconcerned with the quality of *American* life. Though primarily known for its precedent-setting cases related to voting rights and educational access, MALDEF had also played a crucial role in the media reform efforts of the 1970s. Now, facing an initiative that pitted white voters against Latino students, MALDEF turned from earlier legal and regulatory strategies and produced "the first-ever image ad for an ethnic group" (Gellene, 1998:D4). Even more telling, the image ad ran during the evening news.

The premise for this ad was that the evening news—and the press more generally—had played a role in shaping the negative views that white voters held about Latinos.[3] Thus, the ad was designed to counteract the biases of the mass media in an effort to reframe active political debates focused on immigration and affirmative action. But if the ad attempted to counteract the biases of the evening news, it also associated itself with journalistic notions of objectivity, acting as a supplement to the very same evening news it implicitly critiqued. Ironically, the press covered the image ad as an "advertising and marketing" story in the business section, which, in many ways, was all too true. The fact that access to the public sphere—as well as to the press that claimed to provide objective and balanced news based on both sides of the story—now had to be purchased raised no eyebrows.[4]

In spring of 2005, a local Spanish-language newscast leased billboard space from Clear Channel Communications for seventy-five posters around Los Angeles that heralded its newscast in the following terms: "Los Angeles, ~~CA~~ *Mexico*/Tu Ciudad. Tu Equipo." For the station, KCRA-TV Channel 62, the billboards merely addressed a local audience: "All we are saying is, 'It's your city, your town, your team.' We are a team that's educating and informing the Spanish-language marketplace" (Gorman and Enriquez, 2005:B3). The ad quickly became the target of the political action group Americans for Legal

Immigration, which called the billboards an example of "irresponsible corporate citizenship" because the message might "make illegal immigrants feel welcome" (ibid.).[5] By the end of the week, Governor Arnold Schwarzenegger called for the removal of the billboards, while also voicing support for a vigilante "Minuteman" campaign then active along the Arizona–Mexico border (Nicholas and Salladay, 2005:B1, B10).[6]

The billboards clearly reference the fact that Los Angeles was once part of Mexico, and that in recent decades the Mexican-descent population has become the largest single demographic *and* broadcast market in the region. What is of note here is how each side expressed a different focus with respect to this public statement. KCRA-TV engaged a marketplace through an ironic Mexican transnationalism. But it also continued a tradition in the U.S. Spanish-language press that goes back to the nineteenth century in such newspapers as *Eco de la patria* in Los Angeles: it placed the local news in a hemispheric context. Meanwhile, Americans for Legal Immigration focused on a strict and punitive definition of citizenship (including "corporate citizenship"). In the press coverage, the uproar over the KCRA-TV billboards revealed two groups of mostly non-Latinos fighting with each other over what to do with "Mexicans": broadcast marketing executives and politically active nativist groups. Spanish-language television stations are not necessarily owned and operated by those who speak Spanish, let alone by Latinos. In this case, however, KCRA-TV is Mexican American owned, by Liberman Broadcasting. Station general manager Lenard Liberman—a first-generation Mexican American who is also Jewish—not only cocreated the ad but also developed the controversial reality show "Gana la Verde" in which contestants vie for a green card (Morrison, 2005).[7] Thus, while publicly articulated in us-versus-them terms, this controversy actually proved much harder to map in social or even racial terms. Instead, it evidenced a much more fundamental conflict in our society: not between immigrants and citizens, but between the business sector and social conservatives. This conflict has been at the root of immigration debates throughout the twentieth century, and it continues full force into the twenty-first century. If MALDEF purchased access to the public sphere for a social message aimed at changing political views, thereby signaling the end of nearly three decades of media reform efforts predicated on creating access for "public interest" groups, less than a decade later Spanish-language television stations found their marketing efforts challenged on social and moral grounds. The ironies are perverse. Since at least the late 1980s, deregulation required social issues to be presented primarily in economic terms (hence MALDEF's revised strategy, but also that of most other Latino advocacy groups). But even that is now challenged *politically* when those economic terms do not reinforce a nativist Americanism. Perhaps no group better exemplifies reform efforts during this changing regulatory and political environment than the Los Angeles–based National Hispanic Media Coalition.

Deregulated Protest

In the 1970s, the telecommunications regulatory process limited the scope of reform, but it also facilitated the ability of social movements and professional groups to pressure the industry for minority public affairs series and employment. Since the 1980s, media reform efforts within a deregulated industry have had neither the active support of the state nor the benefit of an active social movement on the streets. Thus, by the mid-1980s, not only did Latino and other ethnic public affairs shows go off the air, but Latino broadcast journalists started to lose their jobs, as well. In response, the National Hispanic Media Coalition developed a new twist on old strategies to pressure the television industry in an era of FCC deregulation and media mergers. The coalition came together during 1986 as the end result of "a brilliant thought that all these different people had at the same time."[8] Armando Durón was finishing his term as president of the Mexican American Bar Association, looking for something more consequential than "press conference" advocacy; Esther Rentería—an associate producer of such early public affairs series as *¡Ahora!, Bienvenidos,* and *The Siesta is Over*—operated a public relations firm and had just founded the Hispanic Public Relations Association in 1984; and Alex Nogales, then a producer at KCBS–Los Angeles, served as president of the Hispanic Academy of Media Arts and Sciences (HAMAS), which was then in the midst of a contentious struggle between traditional advocates and an influx of actors concerned with their profile within the industry.[9] These three principal members would alternate four-year terms as chair: Durón (1987–91), Rentería (1991–94), and Nogales (1995–98). Nogales continues now as president; Rentería and Durón are no longer associated with the coalition.

The "brilliant thought" that brought these and other Chicano professionals together was based on a historical understanding of Chicano media activism, recounted for them in part by veteran activist Bert Corona, who had helped secure initial funding for Justicia, which was perhaps the most aggressive Chicano media reform groups in the 1970s. The coalition studied media reform history and its successes and failures, developing not just a viable strategy but a general theory about the nature of power—namely, that power has as much to do with perception as it does with coercion. By having no professional involvement with the media and by accepting no cash settlements, the coalition could avoid the blacklisting and cooptation that brought an end to earlier advocacy efforts. As Rentería explained, "We designed the coalition to be a group that could speak for those in the industry without having to go back the next day and say, 'We need a job.' We could be the battering ram!"[10] Thus, the coalition involved mostly nonmedia Latino groups, while Rentería and Nogales would quit their media-related jobs in order to pursue media activism.[11] Durón specialized in family law. This autonomy produced the appearance of "incredible strength" in the way theorized by Saul D. Alinksy: "Power is not only what you have but what the enemy thinks you have."[12]

In addition to its autonomy, the coalition understood the peculiar way in which the "petition to deny" a station's broadcast license—the so-called "heavy artillery" of the media reform movement in the 1970s—became increasingly viable in the midst of deregulation (Cole and Oettinger, 1978; Krasnow, Longley, and Terry, 1982:55). Though petitions to deny are almost never upheld, a transfer of license cannot be approved until all pending petitions have been resolved. Because the FCC is understaffed (and has been subject to repeated cutbacks), "the wheels grind very, very slowly," producing an economic incentive to enter into a settlement agreement to remove the petition.[13] One of the defining features of deregulation—and the move toward global media—has been the intensified rate of mergers and acquisitions. In other words, deregulation not only increased the opportunities for media reform groups to intervene, it produced the very time-based pressures that made settlement preferable to waiting for the FCC to reject a petition.

The coalition focused on employment figures derived from Form 395, following FCC guidelines established in 1978 that stations should employ women and minorities at no less than half-parity with the civilian labor force for their market area. With one exception, network stations in Los Angeles and New York were not in compliance (and public television and radio were the worst offenders). Starting in 1986, the coalition met with general managers of the local stations, working out an agreement with KCBS. When the new general manager refused to honor the agreement, he made the mistake of writing to the coalition on corporate letterhead informing them that "CBS Inc. and the station do not subscribe" to the concept of "goals and timetables for Hispanic employment at KCBS-TV"—even though affirmative action and equal opportunity policies were FCC license requirements at the time.[14] Rentería faxed the letter to a friend in Washington, D.C., who specialized in FCC law. Bob Thompson, who would thereafter serve as the coalition's pro bono lawyer, informed her that the general manager, as an officer of the corporation, had placed the entire CBS network in jeopardy. In a carefully orchestrated move that played off the time difference between the two coasts, Thompson faxed the letter to CBS in New York at 8:00 A.M. eastern time, so that when the coalition arrived to set up a picket line in front of KCBS in Los Angeles at 9:00 A.M., they were promptly informed that the manager had been fired four hours earlier and that the network was prepared to meet with them. The coalition would play similar roles in removing several other biased station managers and news directors in Los Angeles.[15] In addition, the coalition teamed with local groups in other cities across the nation, filing more than fifty petitions by 1995.[16] Many petitions resulted in "reporting conditions" that shortened the license renewal period, requiring the station to report on its EEO efforts on a quarterly basis. The coalition also negotiated affirmative action agreements with the ABC and CBS stations in Los Angeles (1988) and New York (1989). By 1995, after nearly a decade of coalition efforts, only two television stations were *not* in compliance in Los Angeles and New York: KCAL (owned by Disney) and WWOR.

Between 1989 and 1992, the coalition became involved in Spanish-language television, negotiating agreements with Telemundo (1990) and Univisión (1992). Telemundo agreed to increase Latino representation within its seven owned and operated stations as well as on the network's board, create local news and public affairs programming, and solicit community participation (from advisory boards to procurements from Hispanic-owned vendors and suppliers). Univisión, in the process of being sold by Hallmark Card, Inc. to two major media magnates in Latin America, agreed to develop children's educational programming in exchange for the coalition dropping its appeal of the FCC decision to deny its petition. Both agreements included benchmark dates that required contributions to scholarship funds if the networks did not meet certain deadlines—$100,000 for each missed deadline in the case of Univisión.[17]

The occasion for these negotiations grew out of internal conflicts at two Los Angeles stations: KMEX (Univisión) and KVEA (Telemundo).[18] In May 1989, eighty of 150 employees at KMEX signed a vaguely worded petition than nonetheless inferred that Mexican Americans were losing senior management positions at the station and within the network. The next month, KVEA fired its news director, Bob Navarro, who was the sole Mexican American within the station's senior management. Navarro, a veteran reporter who covered the Patty Hearst case and Robert Kennedy assassination for CBS, had joined KVEA ten months earlier with the goal of improving local news coverage on Spanish-language television. At the time, both networks were owned by U.S. holding companies and often filled management positions with non-Latinos who did not even speak Spanish. For the Spanish-language newspaper *La*

Opinión, however, the primary concern had to do with what it called the "cubanización" of the networks.[19] Univisión had announced that it would consolidate its production operations in Miami, even though Los Angeles accounted for half its revenues.[20] At KVEA, Navarro was replaced by a Cuban American, while two other management positions held by Chicanos—the general manager and the executive producer—were filled by a non-Latino and a Spaniard. For Frank del Olmo, writing in *La Opinión* and the *Los Angeles Times,* the "Chicano-Cuban rivalry" revealed the myth of "Hispanic" unity (del Olmo, 1989a, 1989b, 1989c). But the rivalry itself was a myth, a reenactment through identity politics of a more structural conflict, one between corporate networks importing Latin American product for national broadcast and U.S. Latino urban populations that had just developed a political and economic presence at the local level. Latino demands upon these networks were no different than those upon the English-language media, although in this case Latinos were not a minority audience, they were *the* audience, and still they found themselves excluded.

In 1993, the coalition focused its efforts on one network: ABC. The strategy reflected the coalition's limited resources, but it also dovetailed with increased media hearings and reports in advance of the planned overhaul of the Communications Act of 1934. Rentería herself testified before the U.S. Civil Rights Commission (June 17, 1993) and the National Telecommunications and Information Administration (February 16, 1994). The first hearing coincided with dismal minority employment reports from the guilds, generating considerable press (O'Steen, 1993a, 1993b, 1993c, 1993d; Benson, 1993; Robb, 1993a, 1993b; Pristin, 1993; Braxton, 1993a, 1994, 1996, 1993b; Varela, 1994; Snow, 1995).[21] In September 1994, the National Council of La Raza sponsored a study that showed Latino portrayals on prime-time programming had declined from 3 percent in 1955 to 1 percent in the 1990s (Lichter and Amundson, 1994; Puig, 1994; Du Brow, 1994; Rivera, 1994; Braxton, 1996; Del Zamora, 1996; Rivera, 1996).[22] Unlike local stations, television networks are not licensed by the FCC and are therefore outside direct regulation, limiting reform efforts to an economic approach that correlated audience size and spending power to improvements in employment and portrayals. But writing to production companies and holding meetings with network presidents and division heads resulted in empty promises: CBS Entertainment Division agreed to hire a Latino writer for each of its shows (which fell apart when Jeff Sagansky left the network); and Capital Cities/ABC president Robert Iger promised a Latino-themed program for fall 1994, as well as increased walk-on and supporting roles for Latino actors (which never happened).

In response, the coalition convened a National Latino Summit on the

Media in January 1995, bringing together delegates from thirty organizations in order to define a national strategy. They settled upon a boycott of
ABC. The boycott—which started with protests outside the network's owned
and operated stations but also included contacting advertisers for support—
functioned primarily as a public relations offensive, providing the coalition
with a platform for presenting its case to the public and generating "bad
press" for the network (Braxton, 1995a; 1995b; Snow, 1995; Braxton, 1995).[23]
For its part, ABC denied it had made a promise to the coalition, but shortly
thereafter initiated a Latino Freelance Writers Project (Snow, 1995). When
Walt Disney Co. announced its plans to purchase Capital Cities/ABC that
July, Nogales met with Michael Eisner but came away with no guarantees,
whereupon the coalition filed a petition to deny transfer (Snow, 1995). The
following fall, ABC launched a short-lived Latino sitcom, which Nogales
claimed as a partial victory (Braxton, 1996). But in the absence of lasting and
structural changes, the coalition extended its boycott to include both Disney
and ABC in April 1997, gaining support from Los Angeles County supervisor
Gloria Molina and, indirectly, from the newly formed U.S. Congressional Hispanic Task Force on Arts and Entertainment, which subsequently met with
Disney executives in Washington, D.C. (Snow, 1997; Leovy, 1997; Braxton,
1997; Snow, 1997a, 1997b). The coalition also filed petitions to deny license
renewal of Disney's three radio stations in the Los Angeles area.

One consequence of such sustained pressure from a group that can be
neither bought nor sold is that it increases the attractiveness of more moderate groups. Thus, in December 1997, ABC entered into an agreement with
the National Council of La Raza to air its two-hour awards ceremony during
prime time the following summer, while Disney gave money to the League
of United Latin American Citizens (LULAC).[24]

By 1999, several factors brought an end to the effectiveness of the industry's
divide and conquer strategy, leading to the first widespread Latino national
advocacy and policy efforts since the early 1970s. Most important, minority
representation hit an all-time low, one that was exemplified by the spring
announcements of the fall prime-time season, wherein the twenty-six new
series had all-white casts. Concurrently, the National Council of La Raza,
the Tomás Rivera Policy Institute, and the National Hispanic Foundation
for the Arts released important studies of representation and employment
within the industry. Then, in June, three hundred Latino producers came
together for the first time at a national conference in San Francisco. The
event offered a new model for media advocacy. First, the planning committee consisted of six organizations and ad hoc groups that had been fighting
for control of public television monies for Latino-themed programming. But

it also included crucial support from the National Council of La Raza and Nosotros. These groups agreed to work together on the understanding that the Latino community was now too large to be served by one organization, and that without some degree of unity their efforts would be easily undermined. Second, the planning committee expanded the focus beyond public television to include the entire "universe" for independent producers: cable, network, and Spanish-language television, but also foundations, international financing, and Hollywood itself (primarily through the guilds). Third, the conference participants endorsed the establishment of a membership-based organization, the National Association of Latino Independent Producers (NALIP), which would provide professional services and advocacy for independent producers working on both nonprofit and commercial projects. Since then, NALIP has staged nine annual conferences, as well as various regional workshops.

Inspired by the first NALIP conference and, in particular, its success in aligning competing groups to address larger structural issues regarding access, the National Hispanic Media Coalition joined numerous Latino civil rights groups to stage a "Brown Out" of the networks in fall 1999. By the end of 2000, the coalition had established working relations with African American, Asian American, and Native American groups, thereby forming a "Grand Coalition" in which three of the four cochairs were former U.S. congressmen. This group then negotiated comprehensive, legally binding memorandums of understanding with most of the major television networks. These agreements included reporting requirements that provided the Grand Coalition with both employment data and information on diversity efforts and the production pipeline. The agreements placed an emphasis on diversifying the executive ranks, calling for new "vice presidents of diversity" at each network. These new positions reported to the president/CEO and provided oversight of diversity efforts across the network.

Following on the heels of these efforts, new Latino series found a home on several cable networks: *Resurrection Blvd.* (Showtime), *The Garcia Brothers* (Nickelodeon), *Dora the Explorer* (Nickelodeon), and *Taina* (Nickelodeon). Though these gains were offset by cancellations on broadcast networks that reduced the number of Latino actors on prime time, they nonetheless signaled an increase in creative control, with *Resurrection Blvd.* becoming the first television series produced, written, and directed by Latinos (Adams, 2000). Since then, the networks have developed several Latino-themed programs, most notably the *George Lopez Show*, the first such network series since *Chico and the Man* in the 1970s. Other series included *Greetings from Tucson* and *Luis* (both cancelled), and unaired pilots for *The Ortegas* and

American Family. In an unusual arrangement, the latter series was allowed to move to PBS, where it completed three seasons. The coalition efforts provide a backdrop for the emergence of these new series; but in several instances the coalition also intervened directly in the programming process, leading a campaign to secure a second season for the *George Lopez Show* and facilitating the new life for *American Family* on public television.

If the coalition has helped redefine post–civil rights Latino advocacy, it has done so because its cultural politics are fundamentally different from the radical and reformist models of the 1960s and 1970s. Whereas earlier groups worked within an environment nominally open to social change, and thus developed a strategy predicated on being outside the system and defined by circulating knowledge about and against that system, the coalition worked within an environment defined by long-term deregulation and global technological and economic transformations. As such, their strategy depended not upon confronting the remnants of the state's regulatory system per se, but upon creating an appearance of power by tapping into the inherent instabilities within a deregulated and globalizing market.

To some extent, the coalition succeeded by inserting itself into the loop of an increasingly corporatist system wherein social claims find expression through economic representation. But rather than sell an "untapped market" on the promise of residual benefits, the coalition demanded equitable employment at all levels, trading its demand against the cost of slowing down mergers and acquisitions. In an undefined global media environment, speed became the basis upon which conglomerates "competed" for stability and advantage; and so for the coalition, time became power.

The Telecommunications Act of 1996 seriously undermined this strategy, followed two years later by a U.S. Court of Appeals ruling that rescinded the FCC affirmative action program.[25] The requirement that the electronic media reflect their public-*cum*-market no longer served a compelling public interest. For media reform groups, the only viable strategies included economic arguments, "bad press," and political pressure. Indeed, media advocates found they could now tap into a growing network of Latino political and business elites. Herein lay the new potential for the coalition and other reform groups. It is not that government will save the day, but, rather, that community groups can always attach the "and" of political contingency to their encounters with the corporate media. Political paradigms shift when they can no longer bear the weight of the supplement. For Nogales, then, the strategy was a simple one: "How do we get in their way? We're doing it through economics *and* politics *and* existing law."[26]

Current Policy Issues

The National Hispanic Media Coalition continues to be active on a number of fronts. The most pressing and defining issue for the coalition involves the Nielsen rating system for television, because the ratings data provide the basis for advertising rates as well as for program development and renewal. Under pressure from Latino media advocates in 1999, Nielsen Media Research agreed to implement a new protocol for measuring the Latino audience. Despite the implementation of the new protocol, Nielsen's methodology remains a trade secret that is closed to independent evaluation. In 2004, when Nielsen announced its plans to roll out a new "People Meter," media advocates argued that it would undercount black and Latino viewers. An independent market analysis of four cities suggested that Nielsen already undercounts English-language Latino viewers, thereby undermining efforts to increase Latino-themed programming.[27] Given the stakes—the ability to make market-based arguments for English-language Latino programming— the coalition has made Nielsen a priority for its current efforts.

Concurrent with these efforts, however, the coalition has grappled with its own lack of research data to counter those of Nielsen or the industry itself. In the 1970s and early 1980s, the regulatory system provided a viable outlet for social movement protests. Even in the late 1980s through the late 1990s, the regulatory system could be used, not as an end in itself but as leverage for more substantive negotiations with the industry. But since the Telecommunications Act of 1996, the coalition and other media reform groups have had to find another "and" of political contingency. Increasingly, these groups have shifted to the threat of bad public relations, combined with demographic- and market-based arguments. These arguments benefited from the networks' continued loss of viewers to cable, which itself intensified a more niche market approach to network programming, opening the door to recent efforts at Latino-themed programming. But, given their ad hoc funding, media advocacy groups are hard pressed to engage in such research, nor can they wait for scholars, who generally work on a longer time frame than that of the policy arena.

Throughout 2004, dialogues between media advocacy groups and communications scholars addressed this impasse and the possible areas of collaboration. Though such dialogue marks an important step in media advocacy at large, there remains a troubling gulf between the big issue advocacy groups in Washington, D.C., that address media as a vital part of our democratic process and the minority media advocacy groups in California and elsewhere, which place more emphasis on minority employment opportunities and creative control within the media industry. These are concerns that the former group has jettisoned as politically and judicially unviable inside the Beltway. After all, affirmative action has been legally undermined as a potential remedy. Even so, the problem of Latinos' limited access and representation within the media remains firmly in place, even if a once-viable regulatory tool has been removed. What appears likely, then, is that the coalition and other media reform groups will shift from traditional demands—for executive positions, trainee and internship programs, and development or pilot projects—to new ones aimed at industry support for research that can define the precise ways in which access and ratings/box office can mutually reinforce each other.

Notes

1. For an insightful overview of this act, the first overhaul of broadcast regulation since 1934, see Aufderheide (1999).

2. For more on Chicano and Latino media reform since the 1960s, see my book (2000).

3. See Santa Ana's (2002) excellent study of the *Los Angeles Times* coverage for Proposition 227 and other statewide initiatives.

4. In pointed contrast, former MALDEF director Mario Obledo reemerged in the same period, threatening to burn down a billboard calling California the "Illegal Immigration State" and to launch a boycott against Taco Bell for its Chihuahua-fronted television ads. The billboard message was removed. Sometimes atavism is the best alternative to an entrenched paradigm. See Reyes (1998).

5. Ibid.

6. Nicholas and Salladay (2005:B1, B10).

7. Morrison (2005:B15).

8. Personal interview with Alex Nogales, Los Angeles, September 18, 1995.

9. Ibid.; personal interview with Esther Rentería, Los Angeles, August 22, 1995; and personal interview with Armando Durón, Los Angeles, September 18, 1995.

10. Personal interview with Rentería.

11. Coalition members have included: Comisión Femenil, Congreso Para Pueblos Unidos, Hermandad Mexicana Nacional, Hispanic Urban Planners Association, L.A. County Chicano Employees Association, Latin Business Association, Latin Business and Professional Association, League of United Latin American Citizens, Mexican American Bar Association, Mexican American Correctional Association, Mexican American Grocers' Association, Mexican American Political Association, Mexican American Legal Defense and Education Fund, National Hispanic Leadership Conference, National G.I. Forum, Personnel Management Association of Aztlán, and the United Latino Artists of Los Angeles. Media-related groups have included: Alliance of Hispanic Media Professionals, Hispanic Academy of Media Arts and Sciences, Hispanic Public Relations Association, and Nosotros.

12. The phrase "incredible strength" is from Nogales. This point is reiterated by Durón and Rentería. Alinsky (1989:[1971] 127, emphasis in the original).

13. Personal interview with Rentería.

14. Thomas K. Van Amburg, vice president and general manager, KCBS-TV, letter to John E. Huerta, National Hispanic Media Coalition, March 31, 1987.

15. Unfortunately, the coalition expends a significant amount of time in "educating" incoming stations managers and news directors, who often have little understanding of the Los Angeles area. As Rentería explained, "I call them all migrant workers because they go from station to station, city to city, and they are never there too long." Personal interview with Rentería.

16. These include the National Puerto Rican Forum in New York and the Spanish American League Against Discrimination (SALAD) in Miami.

17. The National Puerto Rican Forum, G.I. Forum, and Telemundo also filed petitions, arguing that the transfer would reduce U.S. production and Latino employment. My account derives from my interviews with Durón, Rentería, and Nogales, as well as from coalition documents related to the Telemundo agreement.

18. For Spanish-language press coverage of these events, see Olivares (1989); Potes, (1989a; 1989b); Villalpando (1989); Navarro (1989). For English-language press coverage of these events, see Valle (1989a; 1989b; and 1989c).

19. See editor Sergio Muñoz's three-part series: (1989a, 1989b, and 1989c).

20. For a recent discussion of Miami as a nexus for Latin American and U.S. Latino entertainment, see Baxter (1998).

21. O'Steen (1993a, 1993b, 1993c, 1993d); Benson (1993); Robb (1993a, 1993b); Pristin (1993); Cerone (1993); Braxton (1993a, 1993b, 1994, 1996). See also reports on an ill-fated training program by one network: Braxton (1994); Chinea-Varela (1994); Snow (1995).

22. Lichter and Amundson (1994); Puig (1994); Du Brow (1994); Rivera (1994); Braxton (1996); Zamora (1996); Rivera (1996).

23. Braxton (1995); Braxton (1995); Braxton (1995); Braxton and Breslauer (1996). During this period, the coalition also became involved in protests against radio talk-show host Howard Stern after his disparaging remarks about the late Selena, convincing about fifteen sponsors to drop the program. Stern eventually issued a public apology in Spanish. Personal interview with Nogales and Crowe (1995).

24. The National Council of La Raza paid more than $500,000 for the time slot, but retained the advertising revenue, which came from Ford Motor Co., Coca-Cola Co., and General Motors, among others. Braxton (1997).

25. The FCC responded with a plan to increase recruitment of minorities and women applicants, but could no longer require goals in terms of actual hiring (*Los Angeles Times*, 1998).

26. Personal interview with Nogales.

27. Rincón and Associates (2004).

9. The Politics of Passion

Poetics and Performance of
La Canción Ranchera

OLGA NÁJERA-RAMÍREZ

Introduction

The Mexican *ranchera* is an expressive musical form intimately associated with Mexican cultural identity.[1] As an anthropologist concerned with the ways in which Mexican culture is constructed and perceived, I am intrigued by the *ranchera* as a critical site for exploring issues of *mexicanidad* (Mexican identity). Despite the widespread popularity of the *ranchera* on both sides of the United States–Mexico border, the scholarship on the *ranchera*, particularly that available in the English language, is limited in scope and depth.[2] Of particular concern in this scholarship is the stereotyped gender representation of Mexicans. On the one hand, the serious lack of attention to women as performers, composers, and consumers of *ranchera* music has rendered them silent. On the other hand, men have been stereotyped as overly passionate, irrational, macho, and fatalistic. This stereotype of Mexicans, most evident in the "culture of poverty" scholarship, became widely accepted by other scholars of that period, as noted in the following example: "The underlying sense of desperation of the lower-class Mexican male, the fatalism, and the view that *la vida no vale nada* (life is worth nothing) and of course large quantities of alcohol, give rise to the total rejection of reason and the indulgence of passion" (Foguelquist, 1975:60).[3]

In this paper, I contribute to the scholarship of the *ranchera* in two ways. First, drawing on recent scholarship on melodrama and performance studies, I argue that the *ranchera* embodies a poetics that resists facile and essential-ist interpretations. Specifically, I show how the *ranchera* may be considered a form of melodrama—a discursive space characterized by the intensity of emotion in which issues of profound social concern may be addressed. Second, I briefly explore several ways in which women *and men* have deployed the *ranchera* as a site through which they may challenge and even subvert traditional gender roles. In particular, I analyze a performance by Juan Gabriel, one of Mexico's leading singers and composers, to highlight the performance strategies he utilizes to decenter stereotypic images of Mexican masculinity.[4] But first, I will provide a brief history of the *ranchera* song genre.

La Ranchera

The term *canción ranchera* (literally, country song) first emerged in the early twentieth century during the postrevolutionary period, when Mexico experienced a surge in urban migration. Evoking a rural sensibility, the *ranchera* expressed nostalgia for a provincial lifestyle and projected a romanticized, idyllic vision of the past.[5] Considered an ideal expression of *lo mexicano* (Mexicanness) by romantic nationalists of the 1930s, the *ranchera* attained widespread popularity through radio and film, especially the *comedia ranchera* (western comedy).[6] According to ethnomusicologist Manuel Peña, "People respond, instinctively, to a ranchero sound, whether it be interpreted for them by a *conjunto,* an *orquesta* or a *mariachi*. And inevitably, by virtue of its symbolic association, it gives rise to vaguely articulated feelings of *mexicanismo*—momentary re-creations of a simpler and romanticized folk heritage, tempered nonetheless by the realization that it is an ineffable existence, lost forever like the elusive lover of most ranchera song lyrics" (1985:11). Particularly important in Peña's commentary is his suggestion that the nostalgic longing for another time or place becomes expressed metaphorically as the longing for an elusive lover. His insight anticipates my own argument that the *ranchera* has to be understood in poetic, rather than literal, terms. Peña's observation that the *canción ranchera* evokes a sentimental response among its (Mexican) audiences on both sides of the border is also noteworthy. Further, despite the explosion of newer forms of Latin music during the past two decades, the *canción ranchera* remains one of the most popular Latin genres in the United States.[7]

Punctuated with *gritos,* or soulful cries of emotion, the *ranchera* song is characterized by the intense expression of emotions, and in this respect may be favorably compared to the blues and country and western music.[8] Curiously, the passionate sentimentalism of the *ranchera* song has been interpreted by some scholars as a distinctive cultural attribute of the Mexican people rather than as a stylistic attribute of the song form. That is, scholars have tended to assume that because the *ranchera* gives voice to deep feelings,

that Mexicans must be exceptionally sentimental, thus conflating characteristics of the form of expression with the assumed characteristics of a cultural
community. Further, even those scholars who do not embrace the "culture
of poverty" stereotype quoted in the introduction nonetheless tend to assume that both the *ranchera* and the people to whom it speaks are simple,
unsophisticated, and therefore transparent in meaning. However, as Dr.
Américo Paredes skillfully demonstrated years ago, the failure to recognize
the artistic dimension of Greater Mexican[9] expressive culture has resulted in
gross interpretative inaccuracies by scholars who "proceed as if language had
only one level of meaning or as if informants were incapable of any kind of
language use but that of minimum communication" (1977:8).[10] Paredes's work
on proverbs is particularly instructive, for he clearly illustrates that brevity
and apparent simplicity of an expressive form are not accurate indicators of
the level of sophistication of the speaker or meaning of the message. Paredes's
insights help us appreciate emotional excess as a deliberate aesthetic quality
of the *ranchera,* rather than as an essential quality of Mexicans.[11]

The emphasis on the "emotional excess" of the *ranchera* points to its af-
finity with melodramatic forms and thus moves us farther away from essen-
tialist notions that Mexicans are uniquely and fundamentally sentimental.
Indeed, melodramatic forms are by definition a roller coaster of emotions.
As film theorist Marcia Landy observes, "Seduction, betrayal, abandonment,
extortion, murder, suicide, revenge, jealousy, incurable illness, obsession, and
compulsion—these are part of the familiar terrain of melodrama" (1991:14).
Appreciating melodrama as an aesthetic practice with its own strategies of
communication, cultural critics affirm that melodrama offers far more important insights into culture than had been previously considered (Brooks,
1976; Landy, 1991; Williams, 1991; Gledhill, 1987). Informed by this scholarship, I show that the *ranchera* is a melodramatic form that offers an important
lens through which we can learn much more about Mexican culture. But we
can only do so if we understand the strategies of communication at work in
the *ranchera.*

Melodrama calls for a performance style intended to induce emotional
responses from the audience (Landy, 1991:15). The emotions exhibited and
induced in the *ranchera* include sadness, despair, contempt, love, and pride.
Typically, the *ranchera* performance style includes not only a vocal display
of emotions but gestures (facial, hand, and body motions) and even tears.
During a concert in September 1999, singer/composer Juan Gabriel told
the audience, "*Fíjense en las manos, las manos dicen más que las palabras!*"
("Watch the hands, the hands say more than words.") Punctuating his performance with various gestures (such as "*¿y qué?*" and "*huevón*"[12]) Gabriel

delighted his audience by communicating an unspoken but richly nuanced subtext embedded in his songs.

In contrast to the claims that *rancheras* transparently express what the singers live, many *ranchera* singers claim they *live* what they sing *as* they perform, thus emphasizing the fact that it is a performance. For instance, in an interview I conducted with Lydia Mendoza, she explained to me, "*yo vivo lo que canto. Cuando estoy cantando siento como si estuviera viviendo aquellos sentimientos.*"[13] ("I live what I sing. When I am singing, I feel as if I was living those sentiments"). According to Mendoza, and judging by the audience's reactions to her live performances, her ability to sing as if she is experiencing the narrative is precisely what makes her music move others.

How well a *ranchera* singer executes a performance is a subject of great attention. The singer's ability to engage the audience depends on her/his ability to invoke a broad range of emotions even in a single song. Therefore, singers who merely sob through an entire song prompt such criticism as *es muy llorona* (he's/she's just a weeper) and lose the emotional tension that a skilled *ranchera* performer manages. For example, sadness can be expressed sweetly and tenderly or it can be expressed as a booming rage. A skilled *ranchera* singer will thus express the complexity and depth of his/her affective state not only by displaying different emotions but also by enacting different registers of those emotions.

In addition to an emphasis on sensibility and emotion, other characteristics of melodrama include the "dichotomizing of the world, its Manicheanism, and its inflation of personal conflicts and its internalization of external social conflicts" (Landy, 1991:16). This latter point has been especially evident in the recent research on Mexican melodramatic films by scholars such as Carlos Monsivais, Ana Lopez, and Laura Podalsky. They cogently assert that melodramatic films serve as fictional spaces in which issues of Mexican identity and social change are explored and represented (Monsivais, 1992; Lopez, 1991; Podalsky, 1993). As film critic Lopez concludes, "to dismiss melodrama as a simple 'tool of domination' is to ignore the complex intersections of strategies of representation and particular social relations of difference" (1991:47). These insights on Mexican film are particularly noteworthy because, as I noted earlier, the Mexican movie industry served as a critical site for the dissemination and popularization of the *ranchera* song.[14]

Understanding the *ranchera* as melodramatic form allows us to appreciate *rancheras* as a discursive space in which topics of emotional weight may be addressed in culturally appropriate ways. That is, *rancheras* may be considered culturally sanctioned sites in which the ideas, values, and concerns of a community are not merely displayed but, more important, produced, transmitted, and contested. Far from being transparent expressions of a simple people, *rancheras* are complex forms rife with contradictions. Moreover, *rancheras,* like other melodramatic forms, are "inextricable from social conflict, revealing, obliquely or directly, class, gender, and generational conflicts" (Landey, 1991:18). Because the *ranchera* relies heavily on the use of metaphor and performance style, the meanings are much more open-ended and situationally sensitive than scholars have heretofore suggested. Songs about abandonment, loss, and desire, for example, take on new meanings when examined within the context of the increased globalization that has intensified domestic as well as transnational migrations within Greater Mexico. Such displacements often rupture families (at least temporarily, sometimes permanently), threaten partnerships, and complicate preexisting notions of national identity. The nostalgia, longing, and despair that *mexicanos* experience in all aspects of their lives, not just their love lives, may be expressed through the *ranchera*.

Below, I provide excerpts from one *ranchera* to illustrate how the text allows listeners to bring to bear their own experiences to interpret the song:

"CRUZ DE OLVIDO"	"THE BURDEN OF FORGETTING"
Con el atardecer	At sunset
me iré de ti	I will leave you
me iré sin ti	I will leave without you
me alejaré	I will distance myself
de ti	from you
con un dolor dentro de mí	With a pain deep within me
Te juro corazón	I swear to you, sweetheart
que no es falta de amor	It's not for lack of love
pero es mejor así	But it's better this way
un día comprenderás	One day you'll understand
que lo hice por	That I did it for your own
tu bien	good
que todo fue por ti	That everything was for you

Clearly, the song speaks about the emotional turmoil experienced by a person who must leave a loved one. Although composer Juan Zaizar most likely wrote this song about an adult love relationship, the text is sufficiently fluid to apply to various situations. Engaged listeners can read the song according to their own experiences, filling in the specific details regarding exactly why the departure has to occur, and what the nature of the relationship is between the subject and the object. Considering the long history of labor migration within Greater Mexico, which has caused the fragmentation of families, I argue that for many listeners such songs may apply as much to parent-child separations as they do to separations experienced by two lovers.[15]

Moreover, the multiple meanings of the *canción ranchera* surely contribute to its enduring popularity. As Juan Gabriel candidly noted in an interview:

> My words are not educated but they are directed to the mind as well as to the heart, and they are a part of life's experiences. It's thanks to these songs—these safety valves—that I can let all of these feeling out and put it to music and give a good flavor to the music . . .
>
> Although songs are escape valves, they are being used to speak about hate. Hate is a word that can be *played with using phrases, a state of mind that talks about a disappointing love relationship,* but it does not get to the point of talking about protest. (Lannert, 1999, emphasis my own)

The notion of multiple, and even contested, meanings within melodrama also lays the groundwork for exploring issues of gender and sexual orientation. Gledhill observes, "in twentieth-century melodrama the *dual* role of woman as symbol for a whole culture and as representative of a historical, gendered point of view produces a struggle between male and female voices: the symbol cannot be owned but is contested" (Gledhill, 1987:37). Similarly, as Ana Lopez has argued, Mexican melodrama "always addresses questions of individual (gendered) identity within patriarchal culture" (1991:33). Extending their insights into my analysis of the *ranchera,* I argue that by participating actively in what was predominantly a male genre,[16] women have been able to employ the *ranchera* for their own purposes. In some cases, women highlight their subordination, and in other instances they talk back to that subordination, but they always call attention to their concerns, desires, experiences, and needs. In a longer version of this paper, I show that through the manipulation of text, costume, and performance style, women may use the *ranchera* to challenge, transgress, and even ameliorate gender constraints prevalent in Mexican society.[17] In what follows, I note a few examples.

Singers may manipulate the meaning of texts in subtle yet powerful ways. For example, without changing a single word, a woman singer can completely alter the meaning of a *ranchera* because the subjective "I" becomes a female and the "you" may become a male or, even more transgressive, remain a female. For example, a sexist double standard is blatantly revealed when a woman sings a "male song" such as, *"Ni en defensa propia"* ("Not Even in My Own Defense"), a song in which the male protagonist decides to leave his girlfriend when he discovers that she is not a virgin. The changes produced by transposing the gender roles in this case are monumental because they powerfully expose male privilege. Similarly, if the "I" and "you" roles are performed by women for women, or for that matter, by men for men, the *rancheras* can provide a safe space for articulating same-sex relationships that in other contexts remain clandestine, if not silenced.[18] This example thus illustrates how singers may *recontextualize* a text even when they do not change a single word. As Bauman and Briggs have argued, "to decontextualize and recontextualize a text is an act of control" (Bauman and Briggs, 1990:76). Hence, each performance presents singers with the opportunity to take control of the text to convey her/his own subversive message.

In recent years women have pushed to expand the scope of the *ranchera* by composing and performing songs that speak more openly about premarital sex, that "talk back" to the sexist tenets, and that project women as taking a more reflective and active stance in selecting and shaping a relationship. For instance, the songs entitled *"Es demasiado tarde"* ("It's Too Late") and *"Tu lo decidiste"* ("You Made the Decision"), composed and sung by Ana Gabriel, both feature a protagonist who refuses to take back her lover after their breakup. To illustrate, I provide the full text and translation of *"Es demasiado tarde"* below:

Tú quisiste estar allá	You wanted to be there
dijiste que quizá	You said that perhaps
ese era tu destino	that was your destiny
después que todo te falló	After everything failed you
hoy quieres regresar	Now you want to return
y ser felíz conmigo	and be happy with me
Pero tu no piensas	But you don't think
que mi amor	that my love
por siempre te olvido	has forgotten you forever
y exiges mi cariño	and you demand my affection
de veras lo siento no	I am truly sorry that I can't
podré volverme a enamorar	fall in love with you again
de ti ya no es lo mismo	it's just not the same anymore
(coro)	(chorus)
solo espero que entiendas	I just hope that you
que un amor	understand that love
se debe de cuidar	should be cared for
y no jugar con nadie	and never played with
porque yo te daba	because I gave you
mi querer	my love and
y aun si merecer	though I didn't deserve it
no te dolió dejarme	it didn't hurt you to leave me
ahora vuelves	Now you return,
buscando mi calor	looking for my warmth
diciendo que jamás	telling me you never
lograste olvidarme	managed to forget me
pero yo te aclaro	but I want to be perfectly clear

de una vez	once and for all
lo debes entender	you should understand
es demasiado tarde	that it's too late
yo no te guardo rencor	I don't resent you
pero tampoco amor	but I don't love you either
de ti ya nada queda	there's nothing left of you
	(for me)
no niego fue mucho	I don't deny that
mi dolor	it was very painful
pero eso ya pasó	but that's over now
mejor ya nunca vuelvas	it's best that you never return
(se repite el coro)	(repeat chorus)
porque tu quisiste	because you wanted
estar allá	to be there

Such songs are powerful because they do not assume a heterosexual relationship and because they portray women with agency staunchly refusing to become passive victims.

Entertaining Possibilities

I have argued that close attention to the poetics and performance of the *ranchera* is critical in order to conduct a more nuanced analysis of the *ranchera*. The best way to illustrate my point is by providing a brief analysis of a *ranchera* song performance by Juan Gabriel, one of Mexico's most prominent contemporary singers and composers. The performance I analyze was held in May 1990 at the *Palacio de Bellas Artes* in Mexico City, arguably the finest theater in the Mexican republic.[19] Below, I provide the lyrics he presented in this particular live performance, which differs from the original text.[20] As noted earlier, in most of his compositions, the text does not reveal the gender of the lover addressed by the singer. This ambiguity makes the song applicable to heterosexual or same-sex couples and thus appreciated by a broader audience.

"INOCENTE AMIGO"	"INNOCENT (NAIVE) FRIEND"
Te pareces tanto a mí	You are so much like me
Que no puedes	That you can't
Que no puedes engañarme	That you can't deceive me
¿Cuánto ganas?	How much do you earn?
¿Quién te paga por mentir?	Who pays you for lying?
Mejor dime la verdad	It's best you tell me the truth
al fin ya sé que	because I know that you're

vas a abandonarme	going to abandon me
Y sé muy bien	And I know very well
por quien lo hace	for whom you leave me
Crees, crees que	You think, you think that
yo no me doy cuenta	I'm not aware
Lo que pasa	The thing is that
es que no quiero	I don't want
Más problemas	anymore problems
con tu amor	with your love
Que te vas a ir con él	That you are leaving with him,
Está bien	that's fine
Te deseo que seas feliz	I hope that you are happy
Pero te voy a advertirte	But I want to warn you
Que si vuelves otra vez	That if you return again
Tu crees que yo no me	You think that I
daba cuenta	didn't know
Lo que pasa es que no quise	But it's just that I don't want
Más problemas con tu amor	any more problems with your love
Sé de un _____ tonto	I know a _____ fool
que te quiere	that loves you
Y sé que _____	And I know he's _____
Y sé bien que	I know that you both
los dos se entienden	understand each other
Que los dos se rien de me	That you both laugh at me
Tu crees que no	You think that
me he dado cuenta	I haven't been aware of it
Pues ya ves	Now you see that
que no es así	it's not that way
Hace tiempo que lo sé	I've known for a long time
Y yo jamás te dije nada	But I never told you anything
Y a pesar de tu traición	And in spite of your betrayal
Te di la oportunidad	I gave you an opportunity
De que recapacitaras	to come to your senses
Tu crees que yo	You think that
no me daba cuenta	I didn't know
Lo que pasa es	The truth is that
que no quiero más	I don't want
Problemas con tu	any more trouble with
requete mugroso amor	your filthy, stinking, dirty,
	rotten love

Y ese tonto	And that fool that
que te _____	fell in love with you
Y que se _____	And I know _____
No sabe lo que le espera	He doesn't know what he's in for
Piensa que va a ser felíz	He thinks he's going to be happy
Inocente pobre amigo	Innocent poor friend
No sabe que	He doesn't know that
va a sufrir	he's going to suffer
Sobre aviso no hay engaño	To be foretold is to be forewarned
Y se muy bien	And I know very well
que ya te vas	that you are leaving
Pues dile a ese	Well tell that one
que hoy te ama	who loves you today
Que para amarte nada mas	Just to love you
Que para eso a él	To love you
Le falta lo que yo	He needs (is lacking)

(At this point, Gabriel rubs hands on pants near his groin and mockingly tells the audience, "oh I sweat so much")

Lo que yo tengo de más	What I have an excess of
Te pareces tanto a mi	You are so like me
Que no puedes	That you can not
Que no pudiste	That you could not
Ni puedes	You cannot
Ni podrás	Will not
Engañarme	Deceive me

Backed by Mariachi "Arriba Juarez," Juan Gabriel makes a grand entrance on stage, wearing tight black pants and a matador-style black jacket heavily adorned with black and gold sequins. Despite the high-class status of the venue, Gabriel does not constrain his flamboyant behavior. From the opening lines—*te pareces tanto a mí* (you are so much like me) Juan Gabriel runs his hand through his hair to suggest that the person to whom he speaks resembles him with respect to looks, not just in personality. That line alone opens up the *possibility* that the other person is a man. In Bauman's (1977) terms, this action "keys" the performance of this particular song, alerting the crowd that they are in for a riveting show!

In the following stanza, he sings, *que te vas a ir con el?* (so you are leaving with him?). And instead of singing the original words, he sings *está bien* (that's fine); however, he makes the sign of the cross, a common gesture meaning, "have a safe trip." But then he extends his left foot as if to kick but quickly disguises the movement by rubbing his shoe against the back leg as if to polish it. This disrupted kicking action implies that although Gabriel has given his lover his blessing (to leave him), he is really thinking, "good riddance," thus causing the audience to laugh raucously. Later in the song, he sings, *pero te voy a advertir, que si vuelves otra vez* (I'm going to warn you, if you try to return). He completes his sentence by making various punching movements with his hands, suggesting that the ex-lover will receive a severe beating if s/he tries to return. Again, the audience laughs joyously at Gabriel's actions.

Feigning to have forgotten the next words, Gabriel invites the audience to "fill in the blanks." For example when he sings, *sé de un* (long pause) *tonto* (I know of a fool), the crowd offers him various profane terms to substitute for the word fool, causing lots of excitement and laughter. At other times, Gabriel extends the microphone to the audience to invite them to sing the song. Extending his hand over his heart to express his gratitude for the audience's compassion, Gabriel claps for them and then throws them a big kiss. The audience responds with roaring applause and *gritos*.

Toward the end of the song, Gabriel sings *dile a ese que hoy te ama . . . que para amarte . . . a él le falta* (tell the one who loves you today . . . that to love you he needs). Here Gabriel pauses quite decidedly and carefully rubs his hands near his groin area. Immediately, the audience bursts into laughter, at which Gabriel says quite innocently, "*ah sudo mucho, verdad?*" ("Oh, I sweat so much, right?") and he finishes the verse by saying *lo que yo tengo de más* (that of which I have an excess). He concludes the song by singing *no pudiste, no puedes, ni podrás* (you couldn't, you can't and you never will be able to deceive me). By using various verb tenses, Gabriel underscores the impossibility of ever being deceived by his lover.

This analysis, however brief, shows Juan Gabriel as a savvy performer who invokes various responses from the audience by employing a range of communicative strategies. Through his voice and his body, Gabriel expresses a range of emotions: indignation, pity, scorn, sadness, sarcasm, pride, and naughtiness. Clearly, he is intimately familiar with popular vernacular gestures that allow him to spice up his performances. Gabriel's flamboyant costume and stage persona provide a strong counterpoint to the stereotype of the "macho" *ranchera* singer, thus revealing the limits of that stereotype. More important, even though Juan Gabriel often assumes a flamboyant and effeminate persona, he appeals to heterosexual as well as nonheterosexual people because his performances are playful, suggestive, entertaining, and full of innuendoes. He introduces numerous possibilities with respect to the meanings of his performances, but he ultimately allows the audience to reach their own interpretation, thus making his music accessible and compelling to very different demographics. In sum, this example allows us to see that one reason the *ranchera* continues to be so popular among Mexicanos of all ages is because it is sufficiently fluid to allow for various readings, and thus engages an extremely diverse audience.

Conclusion

Clearly, the *ranchera* is a sophisticated art form that requires equally sophisticated analytical tools to avoid essentializing explications. The emotional excess in the *ranchera* is evidence that the *ranchera* is a melodramatic form rather than, as some have claimed, an essential, and in some cases negative, attribute of Mexican culture and identity. Further, as a melodramatic form, the *ranchera* provides a discursive space for contemplating personal, national, and global crises or anxieties in culturally appropriate ways. Perhaps this is why, despite the emergence of new Latino song forms, the *ranchera* song form, whether played by mariachi, *banda,* or *norteño* ensembles, remains so popular among *mexicanos* from different regions of Greater Mexico and across various generations. An examination of the poetics of the *ranchera,* along with the situated use of the *ranchera*— that is, the performance context—enables more specificity regarding issues of class, gender, ethnicity, and nationality. The point is that only in and through situated renderings can we see displayed, and therefore understand, certain cultural preoccupations expressed in the *rancheras.*

Notes

1. My understanding of the *ranchera* has been significantly enriched by the numerous conversations I had with close friends and family members over the years, in particular, Mrs. E. Nájera; Alicia, Elena, and John Nájera; Becky Silva; Rosita Ruíz; Josie Méndez Negrete; Laura Sobrino; and Russell Rodriguez. I also wish to thank members of the CLRC Transnational Popular Culture Research Cluster—Pat Zavella, Steve Nava, Elisa Huerta, Russell Rodriguez, Sarita Gaytán, and Deb Vargas—for their thoughtful critiques and suggestions on earlier drafts of this paper.

2. The majority of the studies focus on the historical roots of the *ranchera,* offering various definitions and trajectories (Grial, 1973; Geijerstam, 1976; Mayer-Serra, 1941; Reuter, 1983; and Saldivar, 1934). Among the most complete studies are those offered by Mendoza (1988 [1961]); Garrido (1974); and Moreno Rivas (1989). Interpretative studies of the *ranchera* are provided by Fogelquist (1975), Gradante (1982, 1983), Lamas (1978), and Monsivais (1977). Peña also offers important insights on the *ranchera* in his important work on *conjunto* music (1985).

3. This stereotyped construction of the Mexican male was particularly evident in the "culture of poverty" approach popularized by Oscar Lewis in the late 1960s. Equally problematic was the construction of Mexican women as submissive and fatalistic.

4. For more discussion on Juan Gabriel, see Geriola (1993); Lannert (1999); Monisivais (1988); and Sowards (2000).

5. For a good discussion of the concept of *lo ranchero* in English, see Peña (1985:10–12).

6. Mexican musicologist Garrido explains that the term *canción ranchera* did not emerge until the twentieth century, when this type of music became associated with Mexican sound film (1974:70).

7. According to journalist Gustavo Arellano, "Mexican regional music styles are the most popular Latin genres throughout the land. That's not salsa or the songs of blond-haired singers, but music some might think downright corny: mariachi-backed 'ranchera,' accordion-driven 'conjunto norteño' and brass-heavy 'banda.'" (Pacific News Service, September 12, 2002). As noted earlier in this paper, these three regional ensembles play a variety of music genres, including the ubiquitous *canción ranchera*.

8. Indeed, claiming that "country music, if you listen, is filled with the sounds of Mexico," Lewis notes the influence of the *ranchera* song on country music (1993, 94).

9. Following Américo Paredes, I use the term Greater Mexico to refer to "the areas inhabited by people of Mexico—not only within the present limits of the Republic of Mexico but in the United States as well in a cultural rather than a political sense" (1976:xiv).

10. In her insightful work on the blues and feminism, Angela Davis makes a similar claim, stating, "The realism of the blues does not confine us to literal interpretations. On the contrary, blues contain many layers of meanings and are often astounding in their complexity and profundity" (1998:24).

11. For a similar argument regarding country music, see Kathleen Stewart (1993).

12. Rooted in the word *huevo,* or egg, the term *huevo* is also a vernacular term used to refer to a man's testicles. A *huevón,* therefore, refers to someone who has big testicles, which may be interpreted as someone who is *muy hombre* (very manly) or someone who is "lazy or sluggish." The *huevón* gesture is made by an open hand facing upward to suggest the testicles are so big/heavy.

13. Interview conducted by author in Houston, Texas, July 30, 1984.

14. For discussions of the Mexican movie industry, see Reyes (1988) and Mora (1982). For a gender analysis of the *charro* in Mexican films, see Nájera-Ramírez (1994).

15. Many laborers migrate without their children and/or spouses to reduce the expense of relocation and to reduce the risk to the family. The idea is that typically, the laborer will send remittances to the family until they have accumulated sufficient resources to reunite as a family. Studies indicate, however, that instead of permanent reunification, families are increasingly constructing binational kin relations (see, for example, Zavella, 1997 and Rouse, 1992).

16. Although women have actively participated as singers of *ranchera,* the composers, musicians, and producers of this song form have been predominantly male.

17. See "Unruly Passions: Poetics, Performance, and Gender in the Ranchera Song," in *Chicana Feminisims: A Critical Reader,* (2003).

18. Juan Gabriel's songs commonly avoid the use of gendered pronouns, making them subject to a range of uses and interpretations; that is, he does not privilege a heterosexual male point of view. Yarbo-Bejarano makes a similar point in her discussion of Chabela Vargas (1997).

19. This performance is available on the videotape entitled *Juan Gabriel en el Palacio de Bellas Artes, Volumen 1* (1991).

20. The published lyrics are available in Verti (1997:524).

PART IV

Culture and Violence

10. Conflict Resolution and Intimate Partner Violence among Mexicans on Both Sides of the Border

YVETTE G. FLORES AND
ENRIQUETA VALDEZ CURIEL

Desde el primer momento en que un hombre te falta el respeto, eso es abuso

From the first moment a man disrespects you, that is abuse
—Maria, Woodland, California

By most accounts, intimate partner violence (IPV) has reached epidemic proportions in both the United States and Mexico (Ramos Lira et al., 2003, ENVIM, 2003, INEGI, 2004; Flores-Ortiz et al., 2003; Herrerias et al., 2003; Gobierno de México, 1999; Ramirez Rodriguez and Patiño Guerra, 1997). Moreover, most experts agree that IPV is a complex problem caused by a combination of factors, including individual psychological characteristics, family of origin legacies, relational problems and dysfunctions in couples, as well as ecological influences, particularly poverty, underemployment, and discrimination, which may cause alienation, despair, and rage among marginalized groups (Almeida et al., 1994; Flores-Ortiz, 2004). Clinical psychologists propose that experiences of migration may increase the risk for IPV among Latinos (Falicov, 1998), yet few studies have examined the role that migration may play in exacerbating preexisting intimate partner violence or propitiating such violence among immigrant couples.

This chapter reports the quantitative findings of a binational study of 390 heterosexual married couples in Tenamaztlán, Jalisco (77.9 percent) and northern California (22.1 percent). Utilizing the Conflict Tactics Scale (CTS) (Straus, 1990) we assessed the prevalence of various forms of violence and the impact of violence on how men and women perceive their relationship. The study also assessed qualitatively the challenges and benefits the immigrant couples experienced as a result of migrating from rural Mexico to northern California.

Intimate Partner Violence on Both Sides of the Border

In a recent study, Sorensen (2003) found that 45.5 percent of adult Californians had a friend, relative, or coworker who was a victim of domestic violence. Of these Californians, 40 percent knew a female victim and 5 percent knew a male victim. Furthermore, 35.7 percent knew the victim while the abuse was occurring. More than 86 percent of those who knew a victim reported that she had suffered physical injuries as a result of IPV, yet only 18.3 percent reported the maltreated woman had sought medical attention. Sorensen's sample included 666 "Hispanics"; reportedly there were no ethnic differences in her study sample in terms of knowing a victim. This study, as others conducted in Mexico (Herrerias et al., 2003, INEGI, 2004, Saltijeral et al., 2003), points to the widespread problem of IPV, the high rates of injuries suffered by women in abusive relationships, and the low rate of reporting and detection of IPV in medical settings. These authors note the importance of detection, treatment, and prevention of this significant public health problem.

A recent national survey of family dynamics in Mexico conducted by the Instituto Nacional de Geografía e Informática (INEGI) and the United Nations Population Fund for Women (2003) found that 47 percent of women surveyed reported some form of violence in their intimate relationships. The primary violence suffered was emotional, followed by economic, physical, and sexual abuse. Furthermore, 46.6 percent of the women reporting such violence were employed outside the home, 45.2 percent were housewives, and 39.7 percent were students. The groups at highest risk of suffering violence were women who worked outside the home and those who had attained higher levels of education (at least completed high school). The study findings suggest that as women become more economically independent, or have the potential to do so, their male partners may become threatened and potentially abusive. The INEGI study also found Jalisco to be one of the most violent states in the nation.

There are a number of problems with existing studies of IPV among Latinos on both sides of border. Many U.S.-based investigations do not identify the national origin or generational level of their subjects. For instance, in their major study of violence in U.S. families, Straus et al. (1990) found that about three hundred "Hispanic" individuals in their sample reported extremely high rates of spousal and child abuse. In particular, the respondents utilized more lethal means when they became violent (used guns and knives, kicked the spouse or partner in the stomach or genital area, choked their partner, and so forth). However, it is unknown how many of the participants in this study were immigrants or U.S.-born Latinos, or whether differences existed in the prevalence and incidence of specific acts of violence among Latinos of differing nationalities or generational levels. Furthermore, this study did not interview couples, thus it is not possible to determine whether men and women in these relationships reported similar levels and types of abuse or what, if any, relational factors may have contributed to the specific types of violence documented.

More recent studies (Abbott et al., 1996; Arbuckle et al., 1995; Diaz-Olavatierra and Sotelo, 1996; Flores-Ortiz, 2003; Herrerias et al., 2003) report prevalence estimates of partner abuse against adult women ranging from 11 percent to 65 percent in the United States, and from 33 percent to 61 percent in Mexico. However, as Peek-Asa et al. (2002) note, most of the IPV studies are not comparable, given different sampling practices, sample size, and the use of different instruments to measure IPV.

The problem of intimate partner violence has become the subject of study in Mexico only very recently (Ramos, 1999). The Instituto Estatal de las Mujeres (2003) examined the prevalence of domestic violence among 26,042 women who utilized public health-care services. They found a national prevalence rate of 60 percent for lifetime abuse (both in childhood and in adult intimate relationships.) Among the survey participants, 21.5 percent experienced violence with their current partner and 34.5 percent reported violence in previous relationships. Of those who reported violence in their current relationship, 19.6 percent indicated suffering psychological abuse, 9.8 percent reported physical abuse; 7 percent indicated they had suffered sexual violence, and 5.1 percent reported economic abuse. Saltijero et al. (2003) noted the limited information regarding rates of IPV across states in Mexico and the specific barriers that impede reporting for women in abusive relationships. A key barrier, these and other authors note, is the lack of screening for domestic violence generally done at medical centers or clinics. Moreover, the INEGI study is a significant step toward documenting violence in Mexico, given its methodology (57,000 households were sampled in eleven states). Its findings are all the more alarming given the representativeness of the sample.

There has been a general assumption in the literature that women, despite ethnic or racial differences, perceive IPV in the same manner. However, this assumption has been investigated empirically only recently. Peek-Asa et al. (2002) examined the differences in perception of the severity of domestic violence indicators in a sample of women from the United States and Mexico and found that women from both countries agreed on which indicators were most severe, but Mexican women rated fewer items as more severe. Their sample included 120 women from five groups in each country (twenty professional-level researchers, twenty clerical workers, twenty graduate students, twenty undergraduate students, and forty women drawn from health clinics participating in a study of domestic violence in Mexican American women). Utilizing a rating index drawn from Straus' Conflict Tactics Scale, the women were instructed to rate the severity of twenty-six specific events. For each group sampled, physical violence was ranked as most severe, followed by sexual and then emotional violence. U.S. women in each group rated each type of violence as more severe than the Mexican women. In fact, the U.S. women rated the overall severity of all events on the index to be twice as severe as women in Mexico. This study suggests that Mexican women may consider certain behaviors less abusive than women in the United States; this situation could affect patterns of reporting and seeking treatment. For instance, Wilt and Olson (1996) found that failure to provide adequate shelter and food (a measure of emotional abuse) was perceived as abusive by most Anglo women, but not by Mexican women in their study. When women do not recognize particular behaviors as abusive, or do not consider the behaviors to be severe, they may not view them as serious enough to report.

Flores-Ortiz et al. (2003), using the Conflict Tactics Scale (Straus et al., 1990), found that men and women in Mexico City and rural Jalisco did not classify intimate partner violence in terms of type, but rather focused on severity. For example, the sample of more than one thousand respondents defined *severe violence* as losing consciousness after being struck; needing to seek medical attention after a fight; partner destroying one's property; being struck by partner with an object that *could* cause harm; receiving insults that attack self esteem; sexual coercion utilizing physical force; partner using weapon (gun, knife) against one; being pushed or shoved against a wall. *Moderate violence* was described as beatings; threats; partner insisted on sexual relations but not using force; spouse left the house in anger during a fight; needing medical attention after a fight but not seeking it. *Minor physical aggression* included: suffering bruises during a fight; partner twisted a limb or pulled hair; being forced by partner to have unprotected sex; being pushed by partner; partner throwing something at her/him that could have caused damage. These findings mirror Peek-Asa et al.'s (2002) in that many behaviors clearly considered serious abuse in the United States (throwing objects that could cause harm, twisting limbs, forced unprotected sex, and so forth) were considered minor forms of violence by both female and male Mexican respondents.

Flores-Ortiz (1993, 1994, 1997, 1998, 1999a, 1999b, with Bauer et al., 2000, with Rodriguez et al., 1998) examined patterns of violence among Latinos in the United States and proposed a theoretical model to understand and intervene in the cycle of violence. Central to the model is the assertion that specific modes of interaction within couples (relational dynamics) influence the ways in which couples negotiate and resolve differences. Furthermore, in a dialectic fashion, intimate violence affects the way in which couples perceive their relationship, specifically the desire for and feelings of closeness toward their partner and the extent to which spouses are willing to hear the other's position and negotiate nonviolent resolutions to their disagreements.

Moreover, few studies have examined family and couple dynamics with Mexican samples (Diaz-Loving and Andrade Palos, 1996). These authors developed a scale to assess theoretically derived dimensions of couple interaction. Through a factor analysis of data from 497 individuals (272 men and 224 women, including 289 single and 208 married persons) the authors obtained four dimensions of couple interaction. The first, "desire for interaction," includes items that measure the desire for, pleasure with, or interest in sharing activities with the partner or spouse; the second, "fear-distancing," measures the degree of fear or apprehension evoked by the partner's behavior and treatment toward the respondent; the third, "displeasure-frustration," measures feelings of frustration and anger as a result of interactions with the spouse; and the fourth, "desire to get to know," measures a respondent's interest in knowing the partner better and knowing more about him or her. The study found a negative relationship between fear-distancing and displeasure-frustration and desire to know the partner for women, but not for men. For men, desire to know the partner decreases with greater displeasure-frustration. The authors suggest that women have a more global evaluation of the relationship; that is, when women perceive negative consequences in any aspect of the relationship, they evaluate it negatively, with a corresponding decrease in their desire to interact or get to know the spouse better. However, when men experience fear-distancing, their desire to interact with the partner decreases. The authors suggest that experiencing fear in an intimate relationship produces an aversive reaction in Mexican men. Diaz-Loving and Andrade Palos also found that the more children a couple had, the less fear the women experienced; concomitantly, the more children they had, the more men expressed a desire to interact with the partner. According to these authors, among Mexican couples, fulfillment of sociocultural mandates of getting married and having a large family increases their satisfaction with the relationship. To what extent this sociocultural mandate of *familismo* deters women from reporting violence has not been investigated.

In earlier studies, Flores-Ortiz, Valdez Curiel, and Andrade Palos (2003) examined the relationship between physical, sexual, and psychological violence and men's and women's desire for closeness and interaction with their partner. We found that both men and women who have been violent toward their partner experience more fear of their partner and less desire to know and interact with him or her. Furthermore, we found that not only the spouse who experiences violence suffers fear and distance from the partner, but the perpetrator experiences such fear as well. In addition, our study examined the influence of traditional gender role ideals on perceived couple interactions and use of violent tactics for conflict resolution. Though there were no *significant* differences between men's and women's beliefs on the superiority of males, these beliefs were more prevalent in women who have used violence against their partners. The data suggest that women who used verbal aggression and occasional minor physical violence toward their spouses (slapping, throwing things that could cause harm) hold more traditional views of male superiority than women who do not aggress in this fashion. Qualitative findings obtained in this study may shed some light on these data. A number of women in rural Mexico who use violence toward their spouses explained it as a way to *not* tolerate the male's machismo. By putting themselves at the level of the man (*ponerse al par, de tu a tu*), the women attempted to put an end to the abuse they experienced. They saw it as a way to challenge the man's superiority. These findings point to the interactive nature of intimate partner violence. Women disclosed using violence to resolve conflicts, to be heard, and to be respected, and their use of violence was related to greater fear of their spouse and a decreased desire for intimacy with them. Women victimized by spousal violence also feared their spouses and expressed a decreased desire for interaction. However, none of the women considered leaving the spouse as an option, primarily owing to economic need, the desire to keep the family together, and because they loved the spouse.

Straus (1996) proposes that couples resort to violence when all other efforts to problem solve or negotiate have failed. Indeed this form of violence has been labeled *relational violence* by Johnson and Leone (2005) and must be distinguished from what they term intimate terrorism, which is the violence perpetrated by men against women within a context of power and control. Straus developed the Conflict Tactics Scale (CTS) to determine the frequency with which individuals utilize particular strategies to negotiate or resolve conflict. This scale is used widely to measure IPV. Though our earlier studies have not measured directly what Johnson terms intimate terrorism, utilizing the CTS scales we have found primarily a pattern of relational violence among Mexican couples. Mexican women are more likely to aggress verbally and psychologically, or to utilize minor physical aggression, whereas males are more likely to utilize verbal and moderate to severe physical aggression against their partners.

IPV studies point to the complexity of couple violence and the need to investigate more precisely how the cycle of violence is initiated among Mexican couples from urban and rural settings. Likewise, it is necessary to assess the role migration-related stress may play in the incidence of intimate partner violence. In the study reported here, we examined the prevalence of relational violence among Mexicans from rural settings on both sides of the border. To obtain a deeper understanding of the experience of migration and the ways in which couples' immigrant status might influence their relational conflict, a qualitative component was added to the study. Thus, the couples in California were interviewed regarding the challenges and opportunities posed by their immigration to the United States.

Situating Our Study

The study aimed first to determine the prevalence of IPV among couples from rural Jalisco (Tenamaxtlán) and couples from Jalisco and Michoacán who had migrated to northern California, and second, to identify the challenges and benefits experienced by the immigrant couples as a result of their migration.

For the Mexican couples a quantitative methodology was used; because none of the couples interviewed in Mexico had migrated to the United States, only a survey measuring the prevalence of IPV was conducted. For the California sample, a combined methodology was used in order to determine both the prevalence of IPV as well as to examine, through open-ended questions and subsequent interviews, their experiences of migration and the possible impact of a transnational migration on their couple relationship.

The couples recruited for this study were Mexican nationals who resided in the municipality of Tenamaxtlán, Jalisco, including the communities of Atengo, Soyatlán, and Miraplanes. In Tenamaxtlán, a community health worker and medical students under the direction of Dr. Valdez Curiel canvassed randomly selected households and interviewed both spouses utilizing the Conflict Tactics Scale, IRIP (couple interaction scale), and the Machismo Scales. These data were collected from fall of 2002 to fall of 2003.

Initially, we had sought to recruit individuals who had married brothers or sisters residing in Woodland, Davis, Vacaville, or Sacramento, California. We planned to identify couples whose relatives had resided in the United States for at least two years and who were currently in California. The Mexican couples

were to be asked to provide the research team with the information necessary to contact their relatives in California. Once the Mexican couples had
been contacted, their relatives in California would be contacted and invited
to participate in the study. However, we ran into significant obstacles with
this methodology. First, prospective participants were unwilling to disclose
if they had relatives in the United States, in fear that such knowledge would
lead to their kidnapping or that of their relative abroad. In a few instances,
parents were willing to provide information regarding their children in the
United States but did not want the California research team to disclose who
had provided their name and contact information. Second, Mexican prospective participants feared that the California team would contact immigration
officials and cause the deportation of their relatives in California. As a result,
the principal investigators modified the recruitment protocol. Thus, the participants were not related. We sought California residents who originated
from Jalisco and Jalisco residents who had relatives in the United States.

In California, undergraduate students under the direction of Dr. Yvette
Flores obtained a sample of married couples in Woodland and San Jose and
interviewed them utilizing the same scales. In addition, open-ended questions were asked regarding the challenges and benefits of migration. Data
collection took place from fall of 2002 to summer of 2003.

Instruments

Four instruments were utilized, including a demographic questionnaire con-
sisting of sixteen questions addressing primarily sociodemographic information and family composition, and four open-ended questions regarding
problems the couple had faced and the challenges and benefits of migrating
to the United States.

The Conflict Tactics Scale (CTS) was used to measure the frequency of
violent and nonviolent strategies couples utilize to resolve their conflicts.
Half of the items refer to tactics the subject has experienced from his or her
partner. The other half refers to tactics the subject has utilized toward his
or her partner. This is a seventy-eight–item scale developed by Strauss et al.
(1996) and modified for use with a Spanish population by Medina and Barbaret (1996). The Spanish version of the CTS was revised and modified for
an earlier study with Mexican couples by Flores-Ortiz et al. (2000) and was
validated for use with Mexico City and Tenamaxtlán residents (Flores-Ortiz
et al., 2003). Though the CTS examines both the perpetration and experience
of violence, the scales do not help determine who initiates and who responds
to violence with violence. Moreover, this is the most widely used scale to
measure the prevalence of violence among couples and individuals.

The Inventario de Reacciones ante la Interacción de Pareja (IRIP) (Inventory of Reactions toward a Partner or Spouse) was used to measure perceptions and reactions toward the couple relationship. This scale consists of forty items and was developed and validated with a Mexican population (Díaz-Loving et al., 1998). This scale was also validated for use with urban and rural Mexican subjects (Flores-Ortiz et al., 2003).

Finally, the Machismo Scale was developed by Andrade-Palos and Valdez Curiel (2001) to measure traditional beliefs and values generally held by Mexican families. The scale utilizes as a foundation the items comprising the machismo dimension of the Historical and Sociocultural Foundations of the Mexican Family Scale (Díaz-Guerrero, 1979). The scale was factor-analyzed and validated in previous studies utilizing items measuring attitudes regarding women's and men's roles.[1] The items include: Do you think men are more intelligent than women? Do you think men should be more aggressive? Do you think it is better to be a man than a woman? Do you think that life is harder for a man than for a woman? Do you think men are superior to women? Do you think women live happier lives than men?

Participants

In Tenamaxtlán, Jalisco, 165 women and 139 men (constituting 139 couples and twenty-six women whose husbands refused to participate) were randomly selected from households in the city. In northern California forty-four women and forty-two men participated in the study. The majority of the participants (68 percent) were obtained through snowball technique and from solicitation at local Catholic churches and Mexican supermarkets. Thus, recruitment in California required a more personal approach than the door-to-door canvassing that was effective in Jalisco.

Table 10.1 presents key demographic characteristics of the subjects in each city. Although the samples were derived differently, they have a similar sociodemographic profile. Couples from both regions ranged in age from twenty to sixty-one years of age; the Jalisco sample included older persons. The majority of the Tenamaxtlán residents worked in agriculture, while in Woodland the majority of women were unemployed. The majority of men in northern California held service-related jobs. Consistent with their age, the majority of Jalicienes had lived longer with their spouses and had more children than the northern California sample.

The northern California sample had lived in the United States for at least two years. However, 40.9 percent had lived in the United States between five and ten years. A smaller percentage (6.8) had lived in the United States between eleven and fifteen years and 11.4 percent had lived there more than twenty years. Both the male and female immigrants had a higher degree of high school completion than their counterparts in rural Jalisco. Quantitative data were obtained from forty-two couples in northern California. Couples with incomplete data were excluded from the quantitative analysis.

Table 10.1. Demographic data

Characteristics	Jalisco		Woodland	
	Women (N = 165)	Men (N = 139)	Women (N = 44)	Men (N = 42)
Age				
Less than 20 years	0.6	0	2.3	0
From 21 to 30 years	20.0	12.2	27.3	31.0
From 31 to 40 years	32.1	28.8	40.9	31.0
From 41 to 50 years	19.4	23.0	22.7	23.8
From 51 to 60 years	15.2	15.8	2.3	9.5
More than 61 years	12.1	20.1	4.5	2.4
Didn't answer	0.6	0	0	2.4
Education				
Finished primary	27.3	27.3	25.0	35.7
4-5 of primary	6.1	10.1	4.5	4.8
1-3 of primary	15.2	22.3	4.5	4.8
Finished junior high	21.8	12.9	11.4	26.2
Didn't finish junior high	1.8	0	9.1	4.8
Finished high school	4.8	5.8	25.0	9.5
Didn't finish high school	3.6	2.9	6.8	4.8
Technical/Academic career	7.3	0	0	0
Professional career	9.1	12.9	11.4	7.1
No education, but literate	0	2.2	0	0
Illiterate	3.0	2.9	0	2.4
Didn't answer	0	0.7	2.3	0
Occupation				
Farmworker - Agriculture - Laborer	77.0	41.0	20.5	23.8
Mason	11.5	7.2	0	4.8
Business (butcher)	4.8	9.4	0	0
Employed (taxi driver, chauffeur)	4.2	9.4	27.3	19.0
Professional (professor, teacher, orthodontist)	2.4	7.9	4.5	2.4
Service provider (carpenter, musician, gardener, electrician)	0	11.5	11.4	40.5
Unemployed	0	4.3	31.8	2.4
Other (fisher)	0	0.7	0	2.4
Sales	0	7.9	4.5	4.8
Didn't answer	0	0.7	0	0

Table 10.1. Con't.

Characteristics	Jalisco		Woodland	
	Women (N = 165)	Men (N = 139)	Women (N = 44)	Men (N = 42)
Marital Status				
Married	94.5	94.2	0	2.4
Single	5.5	5.8	86.4	83.3
Separated	0	0	2.3	2.4
Divorced	0	0	4.5	2.4
Living together	0	0	6.8	9.5
Didn't answer	0	0	0	0
Time Living with Partner				
Less than 5 years	1.8	24.5	25.0	23.8
From 6 to 10 years	20.0	7.2	29.5	23.8
From 11 to 15 years	17.0	13.7	6.8	16.7
From 16 to 20 years	13.9	14.4	11.4	7.1
From 21 to 30 years	23.6	18.7	15.9	16.7
More than 30 years	22.4	20.1	4.5	7.1
Didn't answer	1.2	1.4	6.8	4.8
Number of Marriages				
Median	1.06	1.12	1.05	1.00
Children				
None	8.5	2.2	9.1	9.5
1 to 3 kids	41.8	47.5	70.5	71.4
4 to 5 kids	26.7	30.2	13.6	14.3
More than 5 kids	22.4	19.4	4.5	4.8
Didn't answer	0.6	0.7	2.3	0

Findings

Our study obtained several important findings, which are discussed in detail below. First, couples reported suffering and perpetrating primarily psychological or verbal violence; very few reported use of physical aggression severe enough to cause injury. Second, couples in Jalisco reported more violence than those in California. Third, couples who suffered or perpetrated physical or sexual violence experienced decreased satisfaction with their relationship and tended to hold more *machista* views.

Types and Frequency of Aggression Utilized and Received by the Couples

A principal components analysis of the CTS was conducted, resulting in nine factors or subscales, which account for 60.2 percent of the variance. Six of these were utilized for subsequent analysis given their conceptual clarity and reliability. These factors are named physical and psychological violence (alpha .89), sexual violence (alpha .69), negotiation (alpha .73), moderate physical violence (alpha .73), verbal violence (alpha .67), and severe violence (alpha .73).[2] A factor analysis of the Couple Interaction Scale (IRIP) yielded five factors, which account for 53 percent of the variance.[3] Four of these factors were utilized in subsequent analysis: apprehension or mild fear (alpha .76), desire to interact (alpha .67), desire to know the other (alpha .71), and being afraid of the other (alpha .57).

In comparing the percentages of the different strategies for conflict resolution the subjects utilized one or more times, it is evident that subjects in Jalisco (both men and women) utilized both psychological and physical aggression more frequently than the subjects in northern California. Women in Guadalajara reported suffering mostly threats and insults as well as being shoved and pushed. They reported threatening to leave their husbands and insults as their primary forms of aggression. The couples reported using and receiving similar levels of and types of aggression.

Women in northern California reported being shoved and pushed and threatened with being left by their spouses. The women related slapping their spouses. Their husbands reported threatening to leave their spouses, insulting, and destroying their wife's possessions. Moreover, the men reported that their wives insult them and threaten to leave them. Thus, there was less agreement between spousal reports of specific types of aggression.

The northern California sample also disclosed causing more injuries to their partners than did the participants from Jalisco. Both groups reported a low prevalence of sexual coercion, although it is higher among the immigrant sample. Women in both countries did report experiencing pressure from their spouses to have sex, without the use of force. Men in both countries acknowledged such pressure.

Both groups reported a high use of negotiation strategies for problem solving. The participants reported mostly utilizing respect for the feelings of the other and suggesting ways of reaching agreements as tactics of negotiation. However, it is important to note that nearly one-third of the participants expressed that their partners had never made them feel loved in a moment of disagreement, nor that they have been willing to attempt the solution offered by their spouse. Thus, while the majority of the couples in both countries reported using negotiation strategies to problem solve, these do not completely prevent the use of physical aggression, threats, and verbal abuse in their relationship. It is not clear from the quantitative data whether couples are just as likely to negotiate as to use violence, or whether violence follows failed attempts at negotiating differences.

Moderate or severe violence had a low incidence, particularly among northern California residents, with only 2.3 percent of the women and 9.5 percent of the men reporting using such violence. It is notable, however, that all respondents denied attempting to strangle or shove their partner against a wall, even though several women and men reported having suffered this type of abuse. Finally, nearly half of the sample of men and women in both cities disclosed yelling and insulting their partner and as well as receiving such treatment from the partner (Table 10.2).

Conflict Resolution by Country and Gender

In Table 10.3 we present the different forms of violence respondents reported using on his/her partner as well as receiving from their partner. Verbal violence is the most frequent form used by both men and women in both countries. Psychological and physical violence was the next set of tactics used and received most often by men and women in the United States and women in Mexico. Men in Mexico reported less use of physical and psychological violence (42.4 percent) than their partners reported receiving (46.7 percent), whereas women in Woodland reported receiving less of this type of violence (47.7 percent) than their spouses reported committing (52.4 percent). This finding suggests that women in Woodland and men in Mexico underreported or minimized the severity of certain types of aggression. This finding is similar to Peek et al. (2002) and may be indicative of different levels of awareness among women in both countries of what constitutes violence. Men in Guadalajara reported lower levels of physical and psychological abuse (both used and received) than men in California and women in both countries. This may reflect reluctance among these men to report being physically or psychologically victimized by their partner because of concerns about their masculinity (55.2 percent of the women reported using these tactics, while only 38.1 percent of the men related receiving these tactics). The underreporting of such violence is also evident in men who reside in California (61.4 percent of the women reported using such tactics and only 52.4 percent of the men admitted receiving such tactics). Moreover, the incongruence between reported and received patterns of violence among couples in both countries may also indicate different perceptions between men and women, and between Mexicans on both sides of the border, of what constitutes intimate partner violence. It is important to note that the majority of the respondents indicated having used negotiation; nevertheless, this does not imply the absence of violence in the relationship.

Table 10.2. Prevalence (%) of tactics and answers received

Tactics	Frequencies	Jalisco				Woodland			
		Women		Men		Women		Men	
		Use	Receive	Use	Receive	Use	Receive	Use	Receive
Physiological and physical violence:									
8. My partner threw something at me.	1. It never occurred.	86.7	83.0	86.2	89.1	84.1	93.2	88.1	88.1
	2. Never occurred in the last 12 mo.	8.5	9.7	5.8	4.3	11.4	2.3	9.5	11.9
	3. One or more times in the last 12 mo.	4.8	7.3	8.0	6.5	4.5	4.5	2.4	0
11. I had a sprain, bruise, or small cut because of a fight with my partner.	1. It never occurred.	90.8	84.2	91.2	94.9	83.7	84.1	90.5	97.6
	2. Never occurred in the last 12 mo.	4.9	10.3	4.4	2.2	9.3	11.4	7.1	2.4
	3. One or more times in the last 12 mo.	4.3	5.5	4.4	2.9	7.0	4.5	2.4	0
18. My partner pushed or shoved me.	1. It never occurred.	87.3	82.4	83.2	88.3	77.3	77.3	81.0	83.3
	2. Never occurred in the last 12 mo.	6.1	11.5	7.3	4.4	18.2	18.2	14.3	16.7
	3. One or more times in the last 12 mo.	6.7	6.1	9.5	7.3	4.5	4.5	4.8	0
22. My partner used a gun or a knife on me.	1. It never occurred.	98.2	97.6	99.3	97.1	100	97.7	97.6	100
	2. Never occurred in the last 12 mo.	1.8	1.8	0	1.5	0	2.3	2.4	0
	3. One or more times in the last 12 mo.	0	0.6	0.7	1.5	0	0	0	0
26. My partner insulted me saying, for example, I'm useless and I'm not worth anything.	1. It never occurred.	82.4	81.8	82.5	85.4	81.4	90.9	83.3	78.6
	2. Never occurred in the last 12 mo.	6.1	8.5	8.8	5.1	11.4	2.3	14.3	14.3
	3. One or more times in the last 12 mo.	11.5	9.7	8.8	9.5	6.8	6.8	2.4	7.1
28. My partner punched/hit me with something that could hurt.	1. It never occurred.	95.8	92.7	93.4	94.9	88.6	100	95.2	97.6
	2. Never occurred in the last 12 mo.	2.4	6.1	4.4	2.2	9.1	0	4.8	2.4
	3. One or more times in the last 12 mo.	1.8	1.2	2.2	2.9	2.3	0	0	0
30. My partner destroyed something belonging to me.	1. It never occurred.	90.3	89.1	91.3	88.4	97.7	90.9	83.3	88.1
	2. Never occurred in the last 12 mo.	5.5	7.9	5.1	8.7	2.3	9.1	9.5	11.9
	3. One or more times in the last 12 mo.	4.2	3.0	3.6	2.9	0	0	7.1	0

| | | Jalisco | | | | Woodland | | | |
| | | Women | | Men | | Women | | Men | |
Tactics	Frequencies	Use	Receive	Use	Receive	Use	Receive	Use	Receive
46. My partner threatened me.	1. It never occurred.	90.9	86.7	92.1	91.4	90.9	93.2	83.3	90.5
	2. Never occurred in the last 12 mo.	3.0	5.5	2.2	2.9	9.1	4.5	16.7	9.5
	3. One or more times in the last 12 mo.	6.1	7.9	5.8	5.8	0	2.3	0	0
52. My partner smacked me.	1. It never occurred.	93.9	84.2	94.2	92.8	77.3	95.3	92.9	90.5
	2. Never occurred in the last 12 mo.	2.4	9.7	3.6	3.6	13.6	2.3	7.1	9.5
	3. One or more times in the last 12 mo.	3.6	6.1	2.2	3.6	9.1	2.3	0	0
66. My partner threatened to hit or throw something at me.	1. It never occurred.	95.1	90.9	89.9	89.9	90.9	90.9	83.3	92.9
	2. Never occurred in the last 12 mo.	1.2	3.0	6.5	5.0	6.8	6.8	14.3	4.8
	3. One or more times in the last 12 mo.	3.7	6.1	3.6	5.0	2.3	2.3	2.4	2.4
67. I had physical pain the day after fighting with my partner.	1. It never occurred.	92.1	82.3	93.5	93.5	93.2	81.8	92.9	95.2
	2. Never occurred in the last 12 mo.	1.8	6.7	2.9	2.2	2.3	9.1	7.1	4.8
	3. One or more times in the last 12 mo.	6.1	11.0	3.6	4.3	4.5	9.1	0	0
72. My partner threatened to leave me.	1. It never occurred.	57.6	73.3	76.3	78.3	54.5	72.7	69.0	69.0
	2. Never occurred in the last 12 mo.	21.8	12.1	10.8	8.7	25.0	11.4	19.0	21.4
	3. One or more times in the last 12 mo.	20.6	14.5	12.9	13.0	20.5	15.9	11.9	9.5
Sexual violence:									
16. My partner forced me to have a sexual relationship.	1. It never occurred.	95.8	92.1	90.6	95.7	90.9	88.6	95.2	97.6
	2. Never occurred in the last 12 mo.	1.2	3.0	2.9	2.2	2.3	6.8	2.4	0
	3. One or more times in the last 12 mo.	3.0	4.8	6.5	2.2	6.8	4.5	2.4	2.4
20. My partner used force to make me have oral or anal sex.	1. It never occurred.	98.8	93.3	97.8	97.8	100	97.7	100	100
	2. Never occurred in the last 12 mo.	1.2	3.6	1.5	1.5	0	2.3	0	0
	3. One or more times in the last 12 mo.	0	3.0	0.7	0.7	0	0	0	0
23. I passed out from being hit on the head by my partner in a fight.	1. It never occurred.	100	96.4	99.3	98.5	100	100	97.6	100
	2. Never occurred in the last 12 mo.	0	2.4	0.7	0	0	0	2.4	0
	3. One or more times in the last 12 mo.	0	1.2	0	1.5	0	0	0	0
50. My partner insisted on having sex when I did not want to (but did not use physical force).	1. It never occurred.	95.8	84.1	89.2	94.2	93.2	86.4	85.7	92.9
	2. Never occurred in the last 12 mo.	1.2	3.0	2.9	2.9	6.8	11.4	4.8	2.4
	3. One or more times in the last 12 mo.	3.0	12.8	7.9	2.9	0	2.3	9.5	4.8

continues

| | | Jalisco | | | | Woodland | | | |
| | | Women | | Men | | Women | | Men | |
Tactics	Frequencies	Use	Receive	Use	Receive	Use	Receive	Use	Receive
62. My partner accused me of being a lousy lover.	1. It never occurred.	95.2	93.3	95.0	95.7	95.5	93.2	95.2	92.9
	2. Never occurred in the last 12 mo.	1.2	1.2	2.9	2.9	2.3	0	4.8	4.8
	3. One or more times in the last 12 mo.	3.6	5.5	2.2	1.4	2.3	6.8	0	2.4
Negotiation:									
2. My partner showed care for me even though we disagreed.	1. It never occurred.	28.5	22.4	19.6	31.7	27.3	31.8	21.4	28.6
	2. Never occurred in the last 12 mo.	9.7	11.5	6.5	9.4	9.1	11.4	9.5	9.5
	3. One or more times in the last 12 mo.	61.8	66.1	73.9	59.0	63.6	56.8	69.0	61.9
4. My partner explained their side of a disagreement to me.	1. It never occurred.	18.8	26.7	19.4	20.1	16.3	27.9	14.3	23.8
	2. Never occurred in the last 12 mo.	9.1	7.9	15.8	12.9	9.3	9.3	9.5	2.4
	3. One or more times in the last 12 mo.	72.1	65.5	64.7	66.9	74.4	62.8	76.2	73.8
14. My partner showed respect for my feelings about an issue.	1. It never occurred.	4.8	9.7	6.5	7.2	6.8	11.4	0	11.9
	2. Never occurred in the last 12 mo.	5.5	7.3	5.1	6.5	9.1	9.1	11.9	7.1
	3. One or more times in the last 12 mo.	89.7	83.0	88.4	86.2	84.1	79.5	88.1	81.0
40. My partner was sure we could work out a problem.	1. It never occurred.	14.0	19.5	15.1	17.3	25.0	25.6	23.8	28.6
	2. Never occurred in the last 12 mo.	7.3	7.3	13.7	15.1	11.4	11.6	14.3	14.3
	3. One or more times in the last 12 mo.	78.7	73.2	71.2	67.6	63.6	62.8	61.9	57.1
58. My partner suggests compromises to agree with me.	1. It never occurred.	9.1	15.8	15.8	16.5	13.6	18.6	11.9	16.7
	2. Never occurred in the last 12 mo.	4.2	4.8	2.9	5.8	4.5	2.3	9.5	7.1
	3. One or more times in the last 12 mo.	86.7	79.4	81.3	77.7	81.8	79.1	78.6	76.2
74. My partner agreed to try a solution I suggested.	1. It never occurred.	26.7	25.6	26.6	23.7	11.4	11.6	16.7	16.7
	2. Never occurred in the last 12 mo.	4.8	6.1	12.9	10.1	11.4	9.3	11.9	14.3
	3. One or more times in the last 12 mo.	68.5	68.3	60.4	66.2	77.3	79.1	71.4	69.0
Moderate physical violence:									
31. I went to the doctor because of a fight with my partner.	1. It never occurred.	98.8	92.7	97.8	97.1	97.7	93.2	92.9	100
	2. Never occurred in the last 12 mo.	1.2	4.3	0.7	1.5	2.3	6.8	7.1	0
	3. One or more times in the last 12 mo.	0	3.0	1.4	1.5	0	0	0	0

| | | Jalisco | | | | Woodland | | | |
| | | Women | | Men | | Women | | Men | |
Tactics	Frequencies	Use	Receive	Use	Receive	Use	Receive	Use	Receive
44. My partner gave me a beating.	1. It never occurred.	100	93.9	95.7	97.1	97.7	97.7	92.9	95.2
	2. Never occurred in the last 12 mo.	0	4.8	3.6	2.2	2.3	2.3	7.1	4.8
	3. One or more times in the last 12 mo.	0	1.2	0.7	0.7	0	0	0	0
70. My partner kicked me.	1. It never occurred.	96.4	92.1	94.2	96.4	95.5	95.5	97.6	92.9
	2. Never occurred in the last 12 mo.	1.2	5.5	4.3	1.4	0	4.5	2.4	7.1
	3. One or more times in the last 12 mo.	2.4	2.4	1.4	2.2	4.5	0	0	0
Verbal violence:									
6. My partner insulted me.	1. It never occurred.	50.3	46.1	55.1	61.6	46.5	52.3	54.8	57.1
	2. Never occurred in the last 12 mo.	12.7	16.4	13.8	10.1	18.6	20.5	21.4	21.4
	3. One or more times in the last 12 mo.	37.0	37.6	31.2	28.3	34.9	27.3	23.8	21.4
36. My partner yelled at me.	1. It never occurred.	49.1	49.1	46.8	58.3	45.5	51.2	47.6	52.4
	2. Never occurred in the last 12 mo.	11.5	13.9	16.5	10.8	9.1	14.0	23.8	23.8
	3. One or more times in the last 12 mo.	39.4	37.0	36.7	30.9	45.5	34.9	28.6	23.8
47. I left my house furious after a fight with my partner.	1. It never occurred.	62.2	72.1	83.3	64.0	70.5	70.5	78.6	57.1
	2. Never occurred in the last 12 mo.	16.5	14.5	9.4	12.9	15.9	15.9	7.1	21.4
	3. One or more times in the last 12 mo.	21.3	13.3	7.2	23.0	13.6	13.6	14.3	21.4
Severe violence:									
34. My partner tried to strangle me.	1. It never occurred.	99.4	95.2	94.2	95.7	100	95.5	100	97.6
	2. Never occurred in the last 12 mo.	0.6	2.4	3.6	2.2	0	2.3	0	0
	3. One or more times in the last 12 mo.	0	2.4	2.2	2.2	0	2.3	0	2.4
38. My partner threw me up against a wall.	1. It never occurred.	94.5	87.8	94.2	95.6	97.7	84.1	90.5	95.2
	2. Never occurred in the last 12 mo.	2.4	6.1	2.2	2.2	2.3	6.8	9.5	2.4
	3. One or more times in the last 12 mo.	3.0	6.1	3.6	2.2	0	9.1	0	2.4
56. My partner threatened me so that I would have oral or anal sex.	1. It never occurred.	99.4	97.6	98.6	97.8	100	93.0	100	92.9
	2. Never occurred in the last 12 mo.	0	0.6	0.7	0.7	0	0	0	2.4
	3. One or more times in the last 12 mo.	0.6	1.8	0.7	1.4	0	7.0	0	4.8

Table 10.3. Frequencies of CTS by city and gender

| | Jalisco | | | | Woodland | | | |
| | Men | | Women | | Men | | Women | |
Type of violence	P	A	P	A	P	A	P	A
Psychological and physical violence								
Used	42.4	57.6	55.2	44.8	52.4	47.6	61.4	38.6
Received	38.1	61.9	46.7	53.3	52.4	47.6	47.7	52.3
Sexual violence								
Used	15.8	84.2	10.9	89.1	19.0	81.0	13.6	86.4
Received	9.4	90.6	26.1	73.9	16.7	83.3	18.2	81.8
Negotiation								
Used	97.8	2.2	98.2	1.8	97.6	2.4	100	0
Received	98.6	1.4	98.8	1.2	97.6	2.4	100	0
Moderate physical violence								
Used	7.2	92.8	6.1	93.9	14.3	85.7	11.4	88.6
Received	5.0	95.0	12.7	87.3	11.9	88.1	13.6	86.4
Verbal violence								
Used	64.7	35.3	68.5	31.5	64.3	35.7	61.4	38.6
Received	61.2	38.8	69.1	30.9	64.3	35.7	59.1	40.9
Severe violence								
Used	7.9	92.1	6.1	93.9	9.5	90.5	2.3	97.7
Received	5.8	94.2	13.9	86.1	11.9	88.1	18.2	81.8

Key: P = present; A = absent.

Violence, Couple Interaction, and Machista Attitudes

We examined whether there was a relationship between particular forms of violence and respondents' perception of the couple relationship. In the next three tables, we report the relationship between verbal aggression and the four dimensions of couple interaction as measured by the IRIP, as well as the relationship between *machista* attitudes and whether violence was present or absent.

Verbal Abuse

An examination of the relationship between verbal abuse perpetrated, couple interaction, and machismo in both countries found that both men and women who are verbally abusive experience more fear of their partners, hold more *machista* views, and report less desire to get to know their partners better than those who have not perpetrated such violence. Similarly, those who have experienced verbal abuse reported fear of their spouse and held *machista* views (Table 10.4).

Table 10.4. Means of IRP and verbal abuse committed and received

	Verbal Abuse															
	Committed								Received							
	Jalisco				Woodland				Jalisco				Woodland			
	Women		Men		Women		Men		Women		Men		Women		Men	
	P	A	P	A	P	A	P	A	P	A	P	A	P	A	P	A
Fear	1.47	1.38	1.44	1.41	1.44	1.41	1.40	1.34	1.47	1.39	1.44	1.41	1.46	1.39	1.39	1.37
Desire to get to know each other	1.93	1.97	1.91	1.98	1.89	1.96	1.85	1.92	1.93	1.98	1.92	1.95	1.89	1.95	1.86	1.91
Desire to interact	1.92	1.91	1.95	1.99	1.91	1.98	1.92	1.92	1.90	1.96	1.96	1.99	1.92	1.96	1.92	1.92
Scared	1.09	1.02	1.05	1.05	1.11	1.02	1.09	1.04	1.09	1.03	1.05	1.05	1.11	1.02	1.08	1.04
Machismo	1.17	1.01	1.17	.966	1.15	1.00	1.14	1.00	1.17	1.01	1.16	1.00	1.16	1.00	1.14	1.00

Key: P = present; A = absent.

Physical and Psychological Violence

Examining the relationship of physical and psychological violence utilized against a partner, we found that men and women in both countries who have utilized such means expressed greater fear of their partners, as well as more *machista* attitudes and less desire to know their partner (see Table 10.5).[4] The same pattern is evident with regard to physical and psychological violence experienced or received from the partner (See Tables 10.5). There were no significant differences between men and women or between participants in each country.

Sexual Violence

In the dimension of sexual violence, both men and women in both countries who have used these types of violence expressed being scared of their partner and hold stronger *machista* views (see Table 10.6). For instance, women in Jalisco who have suffered sexual violence (mean of 1.22) are more scared of their husbands than women who did not suffer such violence (mean of 1.08).[5] Likewise, across all groups, perpetrators and recipients of sexual violence hold more *machista* views than those who did not engage in or receive such tactics. Both men and women receiving sexual violence expressed greater fear and less desire to know their partner and held stronger *machista* views (see Table 10.6), irrespective of country of residence.

Moderate Violence

Individuals utilizing moderate physical violence (seeing a doctor as a result of a fight, being beaten, kicking partner) expressed greater fear of their partner and more *machista* views. For example, women in Jalisco who suffered such violence had a mean of 1.42 in terms of machismo, compared to women in the same state who did not suffer such violence (mean of 1.07). Men in Jalisco who committed such violence had a mean of 1.73 versus 1.05 for men who did not commit such violence. Furthermore, there was a significant interaction by country, with men and women in northern California expressing more fear of their partners and those in Jalisco expressing more *machista* views (Table 10.7).

Those who have received this type of abuse also expressed more fear of their spouses, less desire to know them, and more *machista* views. There was a significant interaction by country, with women in northern California expressing less fear of their spouses and both men and women in Jalisco showing more *machista* views (see Table 10.7).

Table 10.5. Means of IRIP dimensions of physical and psychological violence committed and received

Physical and Psychological Violence

	Committed								Received							
	Jalisco				Woodland				Jalisco				Woodland			
	Women		Men		Women		Men		Women		Men		Women		Men	
	P	A	P	A	P	A	P	A	P	A	P	A	P	A	P	A
Fear	1.49	1.39	1.47	1.40	1.45	1.39	1.43	1.32	1.49	1.40	1.48	1.40	1.45	1.41	1.40	1.36
Desire to get to know each other	1.92	1.98	1.90	1.96	1.89	1.95	1.84	1.92	1.92	1.96	1.89	1.96	1.90	1.93	1.84	1.91
Desire to interact	1.90	1.94	1.95	1.98	1.94	1.93	1.93	1.90	1.92	1.92	1.95	1.98	1.95	1.92	1.91	1.92
Scared	1.10	1.02	1.06	1.04	1.12	1.00	1.12	1.02	1.12	1.03	1.07	1.03	1.16	1.00	1.12	1.01
Machismo	1.21	1.00	1.26	.979	1.15	1.00	1.17	1.00	1.23	1.02	1.26	.994	1.18	1.01	1.17	1.00

Key: P = present; A = absent.

Table 10.6. Means of IRIP dimensions of sexual violence committed and received

Sexual Violence

	Committed								Received							
	Jalisco				Woodland				Jalisco				Woodland			
	Women		Men		Women		Men		Women		Men		Women		Men	
	P	A	P	A	P	A	P	A	P	A	P	A	P	A	P	A
Fear	1.47	1.44	1.49	1.42	1.59	1.40	1.45	1.36	1.48	1.43	1.46	1.42	1.43	1.43	1.45	1.37
Desire to get to know each other	1.92	1.95	1.89	1.94	1.97	1.91	1.80	1.89	1.89	1.96	1.83	1.94	1.87	1.93	1.86	1.88
Desire to interact	1.90	1.92	1.95	1.97	2.00	1.93	1.91	1.92	1.83	1.95	1.96	1.97	1.97	1.93	2.00	1.90
Scared	1.09	1.07	1.12	1.04	1.28	1.04	1.17	1.05	1.15	1.04	1.18	1.04	1.12	1.06	1.14	1.06
Machismo	1.28	1.10	1.29	1.06	1.30	1.06	1.27	1.05	1.22	1.08	1.40	1.06	1.33	1.04	1.33	1.04

Key: P = present; A = absent.

Table 10.7. Means of IRIP dimensions of moderate physical violence committed or received

	Moderate Physical Violence															
	Committed								Received							
	Jalisco				Woodland				Jalisco				Woodland			
	Women		Men		Women		Men		Women		Men		Women		Men	
	P	A	P	A	P	A	P	A	P	A	P	A	P	A	P	A
Fear	1.51	1.44	1.51	1.42	1.54	1.41	1.64	1.34	1.56	1.43	1.47	1.47	1.12	1.47	1.43	1.37
Desire to get to know each other	1.88	1.95	1.82	1.94	1.92	1.92	1.83	1.88	1.86	1.96	1.86	1.94	1.87	1.93	1.84	1.88
Desire to interact	1.80	1.92	1.95	1.97	2.00	1.93	2.00	1.91	1.88	1.82	2.00	1.97	1.96	1.93	1.95	1.91
Scared	1.27	1.06	1.27	1.03	1.27	1.05	1.33	1.03	1.25	1.04	1.24	1.04	1.11	1.07	1.27	1.04
Machismo	1.57	1.09	1.73	1.05	1.10	1.09	1.28	1.06	1.42	1.07	1.59	1.07	1.28	1.06	1.30	1.06

Key: P = present; A = absent.

Severe Violence

Severe violence refers to being strangled, being thrown against a wall, or being threatened to engage in oral sex. The prevalence of this violence was very low in both countries. However, when present, such violence was associated with more fear of their partner and more *machista* views. Examination of the interaction of violence committed, by country, finds that women in Jalisco who commit severe violence hold more *machista* views as do men in northern California. Likewise, fear is greater among those in Guadalajara who perpetrate or suffer severe violence (see Table 10.8). Women in Guadalajara and men in Woodland who reported using severe violence hold more *machista* views than their partners. Men and women in Guadalajara and women in Woodland who suffer such violence also reported stronger *machista* views than those who did not. There was no difference in terms of machismo between men in Woodland who receive and do not receive such violence (Table 10.8).

It is important to note that the men and women who experienced moderate and severe physical abuse requiring medical attention did not seek it. The women in Mexico had very limited access to health care and did not obtain medical attention as a result both of economic reasons and the shame and stigma associated with intimate partner violence. Men in Mexico did not disclose the reasons for not seeking medical attention; it is likely that limited access served as a barrier. It is also possible that men did not want to disclose being physically abused by their spouse.

Summary of Findings

The quantitative findings of this study indicate that both men and women in Tenamaxtlán, Jalisco, and northern California utilize primarily verbal abuse to resolve conflicts. Those who perpetrate or experience severe or moderate physical violence reported experiencing fear of their spouse, a reduced desire to know them better, and hold more *machista* views than their conationals who do not utilize such tactics. The findings lend support to the systemic hypothesis that violence in intimate relationships creates fear and a reduced desire to interact with the partner. This in turn may propitiate further violence as the couple's intimacy needs are not met in the relationship.

Machismo can be viewed as a set of culturally influenced behaviors and attitudes that privilege men over women. Individuals in our sample who held traditional views of male superiority and female subordination (items in the Machismo Scale) reported using and receiving more verbal, physical, and psychological abuse than those who did not hold such views. The

Table 10.8. Means of IRIP dimensions of severe physical violence committed and received

	Severe Physical Violence															
	Committed								Received							
	Jalisco				Woodland				Jalisco				Woodland			
	Women		Men		Women		Men		Women		Men		Women		Men	
	P	A	P	A	P	A	P	A	P	A	P	A	P	A	P	A
Fear	1.41	1.45	1.44	1.43	1.28	1.43	1.61	1.36	1.50	1.44	1.45	1.43	1.50	1.41	1.28	1.39
Desire to get to know each other	1.88	1.95	1.80	1.94	2.00	1.92	2.00	1.86	1.89	1.95	1.82	1.94	1.95	1.91	1.80	1.89
Desire to interact	1.87	1.92	1.91	1.97	2.00	1.93	2.00	1.91	1.89	1.92	1.94	1.97	1.94	1.94	1.90	1.92
Scared	1.20	1.06	1.21	1.04	1.33	1.07	1.42	1.03	1.22	1.05	1.21	1.04	1.12	1.06	.933	1.09
Machismo	1.45	1.10	1.02	1.05	1.00	1.10	1.29	1.07	1.38	1.07	1.67	1.06	1.23	1.06	1.00	1.10

Key: P = present; A = absent.

quantitative data do not shed light on whether the *machista* views develop as a result of the intimate partner violence or were precursors to the abuse. However, our qualitative data suggest that women who hold more *machista* views are more likely to view the abuse they suffer as part and parcel of their married life. Many of these women expressed hopelessness about their situation. A few, however, transcend their fear and retaliate. Women who physically aggressed against their husbands felt satisfied with their behavior and asserted that while the aggression between them continued, it was now more egalitarian. Furthermore, several asserted that they were capable of arguing, yelling, and verbally offending their husbands, even more than the men. One of the participants stated: "*En un pleito, le metí un golpe con todas mis ganas y le tumbé un diente. Ahora si te voy a matar," me dijo. Le dije: "pues hazme lo que quieras, pero no me voy a dejar." Desde entonces ya nunca me ha levantado la mano. Se le quito la maña de golpearme; pero después siguió con las maltratadas pero al menos los golpes se acabaron.*" ("In a fight I hit him with all my force and knocked out a tooth. He told me, 'Now I am going to kill you.' I said 'well, do whatever you want, but I am not going to take it any more.' Since then he hasn't lifted a hand, but he continued with the verbal abuse, but at least the hitting stopped.")

In Their Own Voice: Northern California Couples

Through open-ended questions and semistructured interviews, couples in Woodland were asked about their migration and the challenges it posed to their relationship. We aimed to shed light on the context in which northern California couples negotiated their intimate relationships and identify potential stressors that might increase the risk of IPV.

Relational Challenges and Problems

In order to understand the relational context of immigrant couples, we asked them to name the most pressing problems they experienced in their marriage. The majority of the women named lack of communication with their spouse and financial difficulties as consistent challenges. Several women reported spousal alcohol abuse and infidelity as major challenges to their relationship. The majority of the men indicated that financial problems, uncertainty about their immigration status, and fear of deportation were key problems. A few of the men indicated their wives' lack of understanding of their "need" to drink as a major challenge to their relationship. Both men and women mentioned concerns about their children and disagreements about child rearing as key problems in their marriage.

Though few of the immigrant couples reported physical or sexual abuse, they reported episodes of pushing, yelling, and storming out of the house when angry. These incidents were not considered severe or moderate abuse, but rather ways of venting or "letting off steam" when problems became overwhelming. None of the couples that had experienced intimate partner violence in the past had sought assistance or reported the incidents to authorities. Several of the women who had suffered violence earlier in the marriage attributed the abuse to the man's drinking, which once reduced in frequency or ceased altogether had resulted in less violence. The two women who had suffered the most serious violence indicated their abuse had occurred prior to migration. Though many of the couples engaged in psychological abuse, they did not consider it severe enough to seek help.

Men tended to minimize the severity of the abuse they had imparted on their partners or received from them. One man jokingly stated: "*Yo solo tengo dos vicios, el alcohol y las mujeres*" ("I only have two vices, alcohol and women") and blamed his wife's lack of understanding of his vices as the reason for their problems. In this man's case, his wife would fight with him when he came home inebriated. He did not see his drinking as a problem, rather her lack of tolerance as the cause of their conflict.

Benefits of Being Married

Couples also were asked what they liked about being married. The majority of respondents mentioned companionship, having someone to share their life with, and having a family. Two of the women and three of the men, including two of the couples who disclosed IPV, could not think of anything good about being married. Nevertheless, some of the respondents who had experienced violence in the past stated that it was important to be patient and withstand problems such as violence because it was important to keep the family together. One woman stated that eventually men mellow out and stop the violence. She felt women should be patient and give men time to change, as long as her life was not threatened. The majority of women expressed great empathy for the difficulties their husbands faced in their work life. They viewed their spouses as overburdened (*sobrecargados*) and saw their verbal outbursts, drinking, and occasional physical violence as a way to relieve their distress. All of the women who had been abused felt they had needed to be understanding and forgiving. However, all of them stated they would never forget the abuse. This finding sheds light on the reported decreased desire to know and interact with their partner (as measured by the IRIP) evident in women who suffer or perpetrate abuse.

Women who had abusive spouses explained the violence in terms of situational issues: too much work, being overburdened, problems with documentation status, being under the influence. Men, however, attributed their wives' violence to characterological or personality traits: being *corajuda* (ill tempered), hard headed, or intolerant, and expressed less empathy for their wives' aggression than did the women.

Challenges of Migration

A content analysis of the interviews generated three main themes relative to the challenges posed by migration, which we have named "acculturative stressors," "longing and loss," and "socioeconomic stressors."

Acculturative Stressors

Most couples mentioned the difficulties they have encountered and may continue to face in getting accustomed to the new country and its traditions and practices, their lack of English skills, and lack of contacts and support networks. For men, the primary stressors were looking for and finding work, which invariably is poorly paid and does not provide insurance. A man stated, "*el no encontrar trabajo, el no saber inglés*" (not finding work, not speaking English). For those who were undocumented, the major challenges had to do with crossing the border without documents, fear of deportation, and the limited work opportunities they face as a result of their status.

Several respondents described the challenges of crossing the border itself: the fear of detection and the dangers they encountered. One woman told of the harrowing rape experience she suffered as she tried to come into the United States to join her husband.

Longing and Loss

Both men and women recounted the sadness of leaving their loved ones, sometimes parents, often spouses and children, and the continued longing for Mexico and the familiar. One man stated: "*dejar el país que quiere y con la esperanza de volver*" (to leave a country one loves and hopes to return to). Most women mentioned the pain of leaving their parents, family, and children behind as the most difficult aspect of their migration.

Socioeconomic Pressures

Most respondents discussed the hardships they experienced upon arrival to the United States as they tried to find work, housing, and a means of bringing their relatives. For the men who came ahead of their families with hopes of reuniting with them in the United States, the main task was finding work and stability. For several of the men, many years passed before they could bring their wives and children. A few of the women had migrated alone, at a young age and before marriage, and struggled, as did the men, to find work to help support their families back in Mexico. Most men and women continued to face economic hardship. When asked if such economic hardship had affected their marriage, several respondents indicated that financial problems did stress the marriage and may have contributed to their "loss of control."

Benefits of Migration

Two main themes emerged in the interviews: the first centered on greater economic opportunities in the United States, which allowed immigrants to help their relatives in Mexico; the second focused on the increased educational opportunities available for their children here.

Most respondents noted that the best thing about their migration was that here their children could go to school and not have to work in childhood, as many had to do in Mexico: "*mis hijos están aprendiendo inglés*" ("my children are learning English"), which parents saw as essential for a better life, in particular given their own struggles with finding employment because of their limited English proficiency.

The majority of respondents had no more than an elementary education from Mexico and associated their limited employment options to their lack of skills. They foresaw a brighter future for their children and for themselves though education: Having the ability to study and prosper, fulfilling the "American Dream."

A number of female respondents also mentioned that coming to the United States gave them the opportunity to meet and marry their husbands and start a family. A few women also mentioned being reunited with their spouses as a benefit of migration.

In sum, men tended to focus on economics—their ability to work and help their family on both sides of the border—as both the challenges and opportunities accompanying their migration to the United States. Although we did not ask whether their migration was documented, several men volunteered that they were undocumented. They expressed fear of deportation and the stress of trying to live their lives "below the radar." Two men stated that they were still awaiting the benefits of migration: "*los beneficios todavía no los descubro*" ("the benefits I yet have to discover"). Women tended to focus primarily on relational aspects or the welfare of their children as benefits of migration, and longing for Mexico and the familiar culture and the loss of relationships as the major detriments.

Though the couples did not directly connect their migration narratives or experiences to the violence that had occurred or was currently occurring in their marriages, both men and women acknowledged the difficulties managing stress and the cultural changes and discontinuities brought forth by migration. Moreover, most women prioritized their children and their welfare and considered their improved economic situation worth the difficulties of adjusting to a new country. Those who had experienced violence in the past viewed IPV as something intrinsic to their married life, as another obstacle that was overcome. The couples who were experiencing violence in the present did not express such optimism. Indeed, their suffering was not attenuated by the benefits of migration.

Awareness of Resources

None of the couples who had experienced violence had sought services or reported the abuse. Few of the women who were undocumented or whose spouses were undocumented were aware of the legal protection afforded to victims of intimate partner violence. Moreover, those who knew their legal rights did not trust the authorities enough to report. Furthermore, all of the women felt compelled to protect their husbands from the authorities. Several named family loyalty *¿el que dirán?* (what will people say?) and shame over their situation as constraints against reporting. For those who faced economic hardship, the absence of the husband through incarceration or deportation would have meant severe economic problems, thus they were reluctant to report abuse. None of the couples were aware of the community services in Woodland that could provide counseling to deal with their relational conflicts in nonviolent ways. Few were interested in pursuing these services once we apprised them of the available resources. As in other studies, economic and cultural factors emerge as significant barriers to reporting IPV and seeking help. For the undocumented couples in the study, fear of deportation of the male was a major deterrent. One woman stated: *"¿que haria yo si se lo llevan, quien me ayudaría a mantener los niños?"* (who would help me if he were deported, who would help me support my kids?).

Discussion

Prevalence of Violence

Although couples in Jalisco and northern California reported a low prevalence of physical violence, sexual coercion, and violence resulting in injuries, the rates were greater among couples in Jalisco. Women in northern California reported suffering more physical violence, more injuries, but less sexual coercion than women in Tenamaxtlán. Both immigrant men and women reported suffering from and perpetrating high rates of verbal aggression. The low prevalence of physical violence may be attributable in part to the age of the sample and the length of marriage. Several women noted that early in the marriage they had suffered a great deal of abuse; however, as the men aged they became "mellower" and less violent. Most men and women reported few instances of physical aggression in the preceding twelve months. However, the high rate of psychological aggression and the minimization of its importance are important to note. Many couples viewed verbal aggression and other forms of disrespect as hurtful but not serious enough to warrant attention or change.

It is notable that immigrant couples exhibited more fear and less desire to know and interact with their partner than did their Mexican counterparts. The extent to which the financial difficulties and migration-related challenges immigrant couples faced account for these findings cannot be determined. But the qualitative data suggest these immigrant couples face major stressors and have few sources of support to negotiate the stress. The psychological aggression reported may be a manifestation of that stress. Clearly, for undocumented couples, living in fear of detection and deportation creates a chronic state of uncertainty and duress.

The study found that both men and women who perpetrated or suffered violence held *machista* views. This finding indicates a link between problematic cultural views and IPV. It is unknown, however, whether these views propitiate abusive relationships or are the result of suffering and perpetrating injustice. It is likely, however, that attitudes that privilege men over women serve to normalize gender injustice. Women who are aggressors hold these traditional views as well; the qualitative data suggest that perhaps, for them, using violence is a reaction to the injustice they experience.

As indicated, none of the women in northern California who had suffered physical abuse had sought medical, legal, or social assistance. As Saltijeral et al. (2003) found, few Mexican women who have suffered abuse and injuries seek medical assistance in Mexico, where they speak the language and health services are more accessible and available. In California, health services for immigrants are more limited; for undocumented women the resources are even more limited. Despite the fact that legal protection exists for women in abusive relationships, lack of information regarding their rights, fear, and family loyalty deters immigrant Mexican women from seeking social service help, including use of shelters. Furthermore, few of the shelters on either side of the border have sufficient space to accommodate the numbers of women in need. In northern California, limited bilingual services compounds the problem (Bauer et al., 2000). For immigrant women in this study, social and linguistic isolation created a significant barrier to seeking and receiving help.

Limitations of the Study

Recruiting couples in northern California after new immigration laws had been passed in the United States proved very difficult. Initially, couples were reluctant to speak to researchers for fear that their legal status might be reported to the authorities. Most participants were willing to engage in in-depth conversation about sensitive topics once the research team gained their trust. The majority of couples were recruited through a church or at a neighborhood grocery store after the research team had been present for several months. Because this was a community sample, which volunteered for participation, it is likely that individuals involved in more severe types of violence were less willing to participate. Thus, the recruitment methods used and small sample size preclude generalizations of the data obtained with immigrant couples. Nevertheless, the findings of this study point to important areas for future research with regard to the patterns of couple interaction that may propitiate IPV.

Policy Implications

Though our study found low rates of physical aggression and sexual coercion among Mexicans on both sides of the border, the high rates of psychological aggression, particularly among the immigrant couples, merit attention. Community education campaigns need to target this type of abuse by providing educational materials and increasing awareness of the deleterious effects of such aggression on victims, perpetrators, and the children who witness such abuse.

This study, as well as others, found a lack of reporting IPV. A major disincentive to report among undocumented immigrant couples was fear of detection and deportation. Clearly, educational campaigns need to inform potential victims that there is protection under the law for victims of domestic violence, irrespective of immigration status. Likewise, the minimization of the severity of various forms of abuse calls for educational campaigns to teach both men and women about the various forms of violence and their deleterious effect on family and individual well-being. Likewise, there is a need for community-based programs to teach immigrant and nonimmigrant couples alternatives to violence. If these programs are viewed as familistic and nonpunitive, Latinos are more likely to use them (Flores-Ortiz, 1993).

Finally, the qualitative data highlight the stresses Mexican immigrants face as well as their dreams and aspirations. Many of these couples would have benefited from networks of support, outreach from social services, and access to adult education. In terms of preventing IPV among immigrant populations, it is necessary to increase awareness about the severity of any act of physical aggression and the detrimental effects of psychological abuse. As we have noted elsewhere (Flores-Ortiz, 1998), few Latinos ever separate as a result of IPV; thus, strategies for promoting justice in relationships and efforts to promote the resiliency evident among immigrants will go a long way to reduce intimate partner violence.

Notes

This material is based upon work supported by a grant from the University of California Institute for Mexico and the United States (UC MEXUS) and the Consejo Nacional de Ciencia y Tecnología (CONACYT), Yvette Flores-Ortiz and Enriqueta Valdez Curiel, coinvestigators. The authors acknowledge the special contributions of Magdalena Arceo (project manager, U.C. Davis, 2001–2003), Elizabet Covarrubias (project manager, U.C. Davis, 2003–2004), and Patricia Andrade Palos, Ph.D., UNAM, for her statistical consultation.

1. Six items comprising a scale with an alpha value of .65 were used in this study (Flores-Ortiz et al., 2003). The alpha value reflects the strength of a significant difference. Typically an alpha value of .60 or greater is considered a strong validation of the relationship being analyzed.

2. The alpha value here indicates a strong association among the items of the subscale, so that they logically correspond to the same construct or idea; the higher the score, the greater the association of the items. The original CTS scale includes three additional subscales: verbal abuse, injuries, and psychological abuse. In our previous study, as in the one reported here, Mexican respondents did not differentiate in terms of type of abuse. Instead, the items clustered in terms of severity.

3. The variance is a measure of how spread out a distribution is. That is how far the scores cluster around a mean. Furthermore, an unexplained variance is typically that which is not accounted for by such factors as education, age, occupation, etc.

4. A higher mean reflects greater fear, for instance a mean of 1.49 among women in Jalisco who commit physical or psychological aggression indicates greater fear than those

who do not commit such violence, a mean of 1.40. Likewise, women in Guadalajara who receive such violence (mean of 1.49) expressed greater fear than women who do not receive such violence (mean of 1.39).

5. This difference is statistically significant at .05, which suggests that there is a five in one hundred chance that the difference is not real, but in fact a statistical error.

Bibliography

Abott, J., R. Johnson, J. Koziol-McLain, and S. R. Lowenstein, 1995. "Domestic Violence Against Women. Incidence and Prevalence in an Emergency Department Population." *JAMA* 26322: 1763–67.

Acuña, R., 1972. *Occupied America: The Chicano's Struggle Toward Liberation*. San Francisco: Canfield Press.

Adams, T., 2000. "The Networks Barely Hear the Latin Boom Outside." *New York Times*, October 29, 35, 38.

Aguirre, A., and R. Martinez, 1993. "Chicanos in Higher Education: Issues and Dilemmas for the 21st Century." *ASHE-ERIC Higher Education Report No. 3*. Washington, D.C.: The George Washington University, School of Education and Human Development.

Alexander, K. L., D. R. Entwisle, and S. L. Dauber, 1993. "First-Grade Classroom Behavior: Its Short- and Long-Term Consequences for School Performance." *Child Development* 64: 801–14.

Alinsky, S. D., 1989 [1971]. *Rules for Radicals: A Pragmatic Primer for Realistic Radicals*. New York: Vintage Books.

Almaguer, T., 1971. "Toward the Study of Chicano Colonialism." *Aztlán* 2: 7–21.

Almaguer, T., 1974. "Historical Notes on Chicano Oppression: The Dialectics of Race and Class Domination in North America." *Aztlán* 5: 27–56.

Almaguer, T., 1975. "Class, Race, and Chicano Oppression." *Socialist Revolution* 25: 71–99.

Almaguer, T., 1989. "Ideological Distortions in Recent Chicano Historiography." *Aztlán* 18: 7–27.

Almaguer, T., 1994. *Racial Fault Lines: The Historical Origins of White Supremacy in California*. Berkeley: University of California Press.

Almeida, R., R. Woods, T. Messineo, R. J. Font, and C. Heer, 1994. "Violence in the Lives of Racially and Sexually Different: A Public and Private Dilemma." In *Expansions of Feminist Family Theory through Diversity*. Ed. R. Almeida. New York: Harrington Park/Haworth, 99–126.

Alvirez, D., and F. D. Bean, 1976. "The Mexican American Family." In *Ethnic Families in America: Patterns and Variations.* Eds. C. H. Mindel and R. W. Habenstein. New York: Elsevier, 271–92.

Anderson, B., 1983. *Imagined Communities.* London: Verso.

Anzaldúa, G., 1987. *Borderlands—La Frontera: The New Mestiza.* San Francisco: Spinsters/ Aunt Lute.

Aparicio, F. R., 2004. "U.S. Latino Expressive Cultures." In *The Columbia History of Latinos in the United States since 1960.* Ed. D. G. Gutiérrez. New York: Columbia University Press, 355–90.

Arbuckle, J., L. Olson, M. Howard, J. Brillman, C. Anctil, and D. Skylar, 1996. "Safe at Home? Domestic Violence and Other Homicides Among Women in New Mexico." *Annals of Emergency Medicine* 272: 210–15.

Arellano, G., 2003. "Fear of a Brown Planet." *OC Weekly*: 16–21.

Armor, D., 2003. *Maximizing Intelligence.* Somerset, U.K.: Transaction Publishers.

Ashton, P. T., and R. B. Webb, 1986. "Making a Difference: Teacher's Sense of Efficacy and Student Achievement." *The Future of Children* 5: 25–50.

Astin, A., 1982. *Minorities in Higher Education.* San Francisco: Jossey-Bass.

Aubry, E. J., 1993. "Day Laborers Rankle Residents." *Los Angeles Times,* April 11.

Aufderheide, P., 1999. *Communications Policy and the Public Interest: The Telecommunication Act of 1996.* New York: The Guilford Press.

August, D., and T. Shanahan, 2006. *Developing Literacy in Second Language Learners: Report of the National Literacy Panel on Language Minority Children and Youth.* New York: Lawrence Erlbaum Associates.

Bada, X., J. Fox, and A. D. Selee, 2006. "Invisible No More: Mexican Migrant Civic Participation in the United States." Washington, D.C.: Woodrow Wilson International Center for Scholars.

Bakke v. Regents of the University of California, 1978. 438 U.S. 265.

Barnett, W. S., 1995. "Long-Term Effects of Early Childhood Programs on Cognitive and School Outcomes." *The Future of Children* 5: 25–50.

Barrera, M., 1979. *Race and Class in the Southwest: A Theory of Racial Inequality.* Notre Dame, Ind.: Notre Dame University Press.

Barrera, M., C. Muñoz, and C. Ornelas, 1972. "The Barrio as an Internal Colony." *Urban Affairs Annual Reviews* 6: 465–98.

Bauer, H., M. Rodriguez, S. S. Quiroga, and Y. G. Flores-Ortiz, 2000. "Barriers to Health Care for Abused Latina and Asian Immigrant Women." *Journal of Health Care for the Poor and Underserved* 111: 33–44.

Bauman, R., 1977. *Verbal Art as Performance.* Prospect Heights, Ill.: Waveland Press.

Bauman, R., and C. Briggs, 1990. "Poetics and Performance as Critical Perspectives on Language and Social Life." *Annual Review of Anthropology* 19: 59–88.

Baumeister, R. F., 1998. "The Self." In *The Handbook of Social Psychology, Vol. One.* Eds. D. T. Gilbert, S. T. Fiske, and G. Lindzey. New York and Oxford: Oxford University Press, 680–740.

Baxter, K., 1998. "Latin America Looks to Miami, Not Hollywood, for Music, Film." *Los Angeles Times,* August 26, D1, D5.

Bean, F. D., C. G. Swicegood, and R. Berg, 2000. "Mexican-Origin Fertility: New Patterns and Interpretations." *Social Science Quarterly* 81: 404–20.

Beard, K. M., and J. R. Edwards, 1995. "Employees at Risk: Contingent Work and the Psychological Experience of Contingent Workers." In *Trends in Organizational Behavior.* Eds. C. L. Cooper and D. M. Rousseau. Chichester, U.K.: Wiley, 2: 109–26.

Belous, R. S., 1989. *The Contingent Economy: The Growth of the Temporary, Part Time and Subcontracted Workforce.* Washington, D.C.: National Planning Association.

Benner, C., L. Leete, and M. Pastor, 2007. *Staircases or Treadmills: Labor Market Intermediaries and Economic Opportunity in a Changing Economy.* New York: Russell Sage Press.

Bennet, K. K., D. J. Wiege, and S. S. Martin, 2002. "Children's Acquisition of Early Literacy Skills: Examining Family Contributions." *Early Childhood Research Quarterly* 17: 295–317.

Benson, J., 1993. "NHMC Fights B'Casters: Claims Hispanics Underemployed at TV Stations." *Variety*: 5, 43.

Bernstein, J., E. McNichol, and K. Lyons, 2006. "Pulling Apart: A State-by-State Analysis of Income Trends." Washington, D.C.: Economic Policy Institute/Center on Budget and Policy Priorities.

Betts, J. R., K. S. Rueben, and A. Danenberg, 2000. *Equal Resources, Equal Outcomes? The Distribution of School Resources and Student Achievement in California.* San Francisco: Public Policy Institute of California.

Betts, J. R., A. C. Zau, and L. Rice, 2003. *Determinants of Student Achievement: New Evidence from San Diego.* San Francisco: Public Policy Institute of California.

Blauner, R., 1969. "Internal Colonialism and Ghetto Revolt." *Social Problems* 16: 393–408.

Blauner, R., 1972. *Racial Oppression in America.* New York: Harper & Row.

Blauner, R., 2001. *Still the Big News: Racial Oppression in America.* Philadelphia: Temple University Press.

Bowen, W. G., and D. Bok, 1998. *The Shape of the River. Long-Term Consequences of Considering Race in College and University Admissions.* Princeton, N.J.: Princeton University Press.

Braxton, G., 1993. "Networks, Studios Won't Discuss Minority Reports." *Los Angeles Times,* June 17, B1, B4.

Braxton, G., 1994. "KCBS to Establish Minority Employee Panel." *Los Angeles Times,* March 19, F11.

Braxton, G., 1995a. "Latinos to Press for Boycott of ABC-TV." *Los Angeles Times,* January 13, B1, B4.

Braxton, G., 1995b. "Latinos Protest at ABC Stations." *Los Angeles Times,* April 27, F1, F8.

Braxton, G., 1995c. "Cancellations Upset Minority Groups." *Los Angeles Times,* May 17, F4.

Braxton, G., 1996a. "U.S. to Examine Hiring of Minorities in Entertainment." *Los Angeles Times,* February 22, F2, F3.

Braxton, G., 1996b. "Latinos on TV: Mixed Findings, Progress." *Los Angeles Times,* April 16, F1, F6.

Braxton, G., 1997a. "Latinos Split over Disney's Motivations." *Los Angeles Times,* December 13, F1, F22.

Braxton, G., 1997b. "Molina Joins in Protest over Alleged Disney Discrimination." *Los Angeles Times,* June 27, F2, F17.

Brimelow, P., 1995. *Alien Nation: Common Sense about America's Immigration Disaster.* New York: Random House.

Brooks, P., 1997. *The Melodramatic Imagination: Balzac, Henry James, Melodrama, and the Mode of Excess.* New Haven, Conn.: Yale University Press.

Brooks-Gunn, J., and L. B. Markman, 2005. "The Contribution of Parenting to Ethnic and Racial Gaps in School Readiness." *The Future of Children* 15: 139–68.

Brown, E., 1992. *A Taste of Power: A Black Woman's Story.* New York: Pantheon Books.

Brown, I., and M. Joya, 2003. "The Intersection of Gender and Race in the Labor Market." *Annual Review of Sociology* 29: 487–513.

Brown, M., M. Carnoy, E. Currie, T. Duster, D. B. Oppenheimer, M. M. Shutz, and D. Wellman, eds., 2003. *White-Washing Race, The Myth of a Color-Blind Society.* Berkeley: University of California Press.

Brown, M. N. V., and A. Domenzain, 2002. "Voices from the Margins: Immigrant Workers' Perceptions of Health and Safety at the Workplace." Los Angeles: UCLA-Labor Occupational Safety and Health Program Report.

Broyles-Gonzalez, Y., 2002. "Ranchera Music and the Legendary Lydia Mendoza: Performing Social Location and Relations." In *Chicana Traditions: Continuity and Change.* Eds. N. Cantu and O. Nájera-Ramírez. Champaign: University of Illinois Press.

Buchanan, P. J., 1994. "What Will America Be in 2050?" *Los Angeles Times,* October 28.

Buchanan, P. J., 2002. *The Death of the West: How Dying Populations and Immigrant Invasions Imperil Our Country and Civilization.* New York: St. Martins Press.

Burchinal, M. R., E. Peisner-Feinberg, R. Pianta, and C. Howes, 2002. "Development of Academic Skills from Preschool through Second Grade: Family and Classroom Predictors of Developmental Trajectories." *Journal of School Psychology* 40: 415–36.

Burciaga V. R., 2003. "Access to Illness Care and Health Insurance." In *Latinos and Public Policy in California: an Agenda for Opportunity.* Eds. D. López and A. E. Jiménez. Berkeley, Calif.: Berkeley Public Policy Press, 189–239.

Burr, R., 1996. "Women Helping Drive Thriving Mexican Market." *Billboard* 10833, August 17.

Calderon, J. S., S. Foster, and S. Rodriguez, 2002. "Organizing Immigrant Workers: Action Research and Strategies in the Pomona Day Labor Center." In *Communities and Political Activism.* Eds. E. C. Ochoa and G. L. Ochoa. Philadelphia: Temple University Press.

California Department of Education, 2000–2001. Educational Demographics Office.

California Department of Education, 2004. Standardized Testing and Reporting STAR Results. http://www.dof.ca.gov/html/Demograp/K12ethtb.htm.

California Department of Finance, 2000. Demographics Unit.

California Department of Finance, 2003. California Public K-12 Enrollment Projections by Ethnicity: 2002 Series. http://www.dof.ca.gov/html/Demograp/K12ethtb.htm.

Camarillo, A., 1979. *Chicanos in a Changing Society: From Mexican Pueblos to American Barrios in Santa Barbara and Southern California, 1848–1930.* Cambridge, Mass.: Harvard University Press.

Carmichael, S. and C. V. Hamilton, 1967. *Black Power: The Politics of Liberation in America.* New York: Vintage Books.

Carvajal, M. P., 2000. "Day Labor Work: Bottom of the Barrel or Viable Alternative." M.A. thesis, University of California, Los Angeles.

Castaneda et al. v. T. R. o. t. U. o. C. e. a., 1999. Case N. C99-0525SI, United States District Court, Northern District of California.

Castells, M., and A. Portes, 1989. "World Underneath: The Origins, Dynamics, and Effects of the Informal Economy." In *The Informal Economy: Studies in Advanced and Less Developed Countries.* Eds. A. Portes, M. Castells, and L. A. Benton. Baltimore: John Hopkins University Press.

Castillo, A., 1995. *Massacre of the Dreamers: Essays on Xicanisma.* Albuquerque: University of New Mexico Press.

Catanzarite, L., 2000. "Brown Collar Jobs: Occupational Segregation and Earnings of Recent-Immigrant Latinos." *Sociological Perspectives* 431: 45–75.

Cerone, D., 1993. "TV Not Representative of Society, Study Finds." *Los Angeles Times,* June 16, F9.

Chang, E. T., and R. C. Leong, eds., 1993. *Los Angeles—Struggles toward Multiethnic Community: Asian American, African American & Latino Perspectives.* Seattle: University of Washington Press.

Chapa, J., and R. Valencia, 1993. "Latino Population Growth, Demographic Characteristics, and Educational Stagnation: An Examination of Recent Trends." *Hispanic Journal of Behavioral Sciences* 15: 165–87.

Chapin, J., 1998. "Closing America's 'Back Door.'" *GLQ: A Journal of Lesbian and Gay Studies* 4(3): 403–22.

Chaturvedi, V., ed., 2000. *Mapping Subaltern Studies and the Postcolonial.* London: Verso.

Chavez, L., E. Flores, and M. Lopez-Garza, 1990. "Here Today, Gone Tomorrow? Undocumented Settlers and Immigration Reform." *Human Organization* 493 (Fall): 193–205.

Chavez, L. R., 1991. "Outside the Imagined Community: Undocumented Settlers and Experiences of Incorporation." *American Ethnologist* 18: 257–78.

Chavez, L. R., 1997. "Immigration Reform and Nativism: The Nationalist Response to the Transnationalist Challenge." In *Immigrants Out! The New Nativism and the Anti-Immigrant Impulse in the United States.* Ed. J. Perea. New York: New York University Press.

Chavez, L. R., 2001. *Covering Immigration: Popular Images and the Politics of the Nation.* Berkeley: University of California Press.

Chavez, L. R., 2004. "A Glass Half Empty: Latina Reproduction and Public Discourse." *Human Organization* 63: 173–88.

Chavez, L. R., 2007. "The Spectacle in the Desert: The Minuteman Project on the U.S.–Mexico Border." In *Global Vigilantes.* Eds. D. Pratten and A. Sen. London: Hurst & Company Publishers.

Chavez, L. R., 2008. *The Latino Threat: Constructing Immigrants, Citizens, and the Nation.* Stanford, Calif.: Stanford University Press.

Chinea-Varela, M., 1994. "Second-Class Writers." *Los Angeles Times,* October 20, B7.

Clark, K., 1965. *Dark Ghetto.* New York: Harper & Row.

Cleeland, N., 2000. "AFL-CIO Calls for Amnesty for Illegal U.S. Workers." *Los Angeles Times,* February 17.

Cohen, J., 1988. *Statistical Power Analysis for the Behavioral Sciences.* Hillsdale, N.J.: Erlbaum.

Cole, B., and M. Oettinger, 1978. "Petition to Deny: Heavy Artillery." In *Reluctant Regulators: The FCC and the Broadcast Audience.* Reading, Mass.: Addison-Wesley: 204–25.

Coleman, J. S., 1990. *Equality and Achievement in Education.* San Francisco: Westview Press.

Coleman, J. S., E. Q. Campbell, C. J. Hobson, J. McPartland, A. M. Mood, F. D. Weinfeld, and R. L. York, 1966. *Equality of Educational Opportunity.* Washington, D.C.: U.S. Government Printing Office.

Collins, P. H., 2002. *Black Feminist Thought.* New York: Routledge.

Commission on the Future of Advanced Placement Program, 2001. *Access to Excellence.* New York: College Entrance Examination Board.

Cooper, H., K. Charlton, J. C. Valentine, and L. Muhlenbruck, 2000. "Making the Most of Summer School: A Meta-analytic and Narrative Review." *Monographs of the Society for Research in Child Development* 65: 1–118.

Cornelius, W. A., 1998. "The Structural Embeddedness of Demand for Mexican Immigrant Labor: New Evidence from California." In *Crossings: Mexican Immigration in Interdisciplinary Perspectives.* Ed. M. M. Suarez-Orozco. Cambridge, Mass.: Harvard University Press.

Cosden, M., J. Zimmer, C. Reyes, and M. del Rosario Gutierrez, 1995. "Kindergarten Practices and First-Grade Achievement for Latino Spanish-Speaking, Latino English-Speaking, and Anglo Students." *Journal of School Psychology* 33: 123–41.

Cotler, J., 1970. "The Mechanics of Internal Domination and Social Change in Peru." In *Masses in Latin America.* Ed. I. L. Horowitz. New York: Oxford University Press, 407–44.

Crowe, J., 1995. "Latinos to Stern: Apology Is Not Accepted." *Los Angeles Times,* April 11, F2, F6.

Cruse, H., 1968. "Revolutionary Nationalism and the Afro-American." In *Rebellion or Revolution?* New York: William Morrow & Co.

Currie, J., and T. Duncan, 1999. "Does Head Start Help Hispanic Children?" *Journal of Public Economics* 74: 235–62.

Currie, J., and D. Thomas, 1995. "Does Head Start Make a Difference?" *American Economic Review* 85: 341–64.

Curtius, M., 2005. "House Moving to Tighten Immigration." *Los Angeles Times,* December 16, A22.

Daniel et al. v. The State of California, 1999. Superior Court of the State of California, Los Angeles Superior Court, Case No. BC 214156.

Darder, A., and R. D. Torres, 1998. *The Latino Studies Reader: Culture, Economy & Society.* Malden, Mass.: Blackwell Publishers.

Darling-Hammond, L., B. Berry, and A. Thoreson, 2001. "Does Teacher Certification Matter? Evaluating the Evidence." *Educational Evaluation and Policy Analysis* 23: 57–77.

Davis, A. Y., 1998. *Blues Legacies and Black Feminism: Gertrude "Ma" Rainey, Bessie Smith, and Billie Holiday.* New York: Pantheon Books.

Delgado, R., and J. Stefancic, eds., 1998. *The Latino Condition: A Critical Reader.* New York: New York University Press.

del Olmo, F., 1989a. "El Mito de la Unidad Hispana." *La Opinión,* May 29, 5.

del Olmo, F., 1989b. "La Diversidad Latina y el Mito de la Unidad." *La Opinión,* June 11.

del Olmo, F., 1989c. "TV Dispute Sheds Light on the 'Hispanic' Myth." *Los Angeles Times,* May 29, 5.

Diaz Olavatierra, C., and J. Sotelo, 1996. "Letter from Mexico City: Domestic Violence in Mexico." *JAMA* 27524: 1937–41.

Diaz-Loving, R., and P. A. Palos, 1996. "Inventario de Reacciones ante la Intervención de Pareja IRIP." *Revista de Psicología Contemporánea* 31: 90–96.

Domina, T., 2005. "Leveling the Home Advantage: Assessing the Effectiveness of Parental Involvement in Elementary School." *Sociology of Education* 78: 233–49.

Donato, R., M. Menchaca, and R. R. Valencia, 1991. "Segregation, Desegregation, and Integration of Chicano Students: Problems and Prospects." In *Chicano School Failure and Success: Research and Policy Agenda for the 1990s.* Ed. R. Valencia. New York: The Falmer Press, 27–63.

Dornbusch, S. M., P. L. Ritter, P. H. Leiderman, D. F. Roberts, and M. J. Fraleigh, 1987. "The Relation of Parenting Style to Adolescent School Performance." *Child Development* 58: 1244–57.

Doss, Y. C., 1996. "Network TV: Latinos Need Not Apply." *Frontera* 2: 20–21, 43.

Du Brow, R., 1994a. "Portrayals of Latinos on TV Regressing." *Los Angeles Times,* September 7, A5.

Du Brow, R., 1994b. "Latino Roles Still Mired in Stereotypes." *Los Angeles Times,* October 1, F1, F17.

Dube, A., and M. Reich, 2005. "Wage and Employment Impacts of a Citywide Minimum Wage, Labor and Employment Relations Association." Proceedings of the 57th Annual Meeting.

Duncan, G. J., and K. A. Magnuson, 2005. "Can Family Socioeconomic Resources Account for Racial and Ethnic Test Score Gaps?" *The Future of Children,* 1535–54.

Economic Policy Institute, 2002. "Pulling Apart: A State-by-State Analysis of Income Trends." Washington, D.C.: Economic Policy Institute.

Entwisle, D., K. L. Alexander, and L. S. Olson, 1997. *Children, Schools, and Inequality.* Boulder, Colo.: Westview Press.

Entwisle, D. R., and K. L. Alexander, 1995. "A Parent's Economic Shadow: Family Structure versus Family Resources as Influences on Early School Achievement." *Journal of Marriage and the Family* 57: 399–409.

Esbenshade, J., 2000. "The 'Crisis' Over Day Labor: The Politics of Visibility and Public Space." *Working U.S.A.* 36: 27–70.

Estadísticas Gobierno de Mexico, 1999. *Víctimas de Violencia Sexual y Familiar Atendidas en el CAVI, Enero-Septiembre 1997.* Mexico City: Prontuario Estadístico de la Mujer.

Falcón, L., 1995. "Social Networks and Employment for Latinos, Blacks, and Whites." *New England Journal of Public Policy* 111: 17–28.

Falcone, M., 2002. "Former Chancellor Kerr Remembers UC History." *UCLA Daily Bruin,* May 16.

Falicov, C. J., 1998. *Latino Familias in Therapy: A Guide to Multicultural Practice.* New York: Guilford Press.

"FCC Urges New Rules for Broadcaster Hiring." 1998. *Los Angeles Times,* November 20, C5.

Feige, E. L., 1990. "Defining and Estimating Underground and Informal Economics." *World Development* 187: 989–1002.

Fenstermaker, S., and C. West, eds., 2002. *Doing Gender, Doing Difference. Inequality, Power, and Institutional Change.* New York: Routledge.

Fernandez-Kelly, M. P., and A. M. Garcia, 1989. "Informalisation at the Core: Hispanic Women, Homework, and the Advanced Capitalist State." *Environment and Planning* D8: 459–83.

Fine, M., L. Wies, L. C. Powell, and L. M. Wong, eds., 1996. *Off White: Readings on Society, Race and Culture.* New York: Routledge.

Finn, J. D., and C. M. Achilles, 1999. "Tennessee's Class Size Study: Findings, Implications, Misconceptions." *Educational Evaluation and Policy Analysis* 21: 97–110.

Finn, J. D., G. M. Pannozzo, and K. E. Voelkl, 1995. "Disruptive and Inattentive-Withdrawn Behavior and Achievement among Fourth Graders." *Elementary School Journal* 95: 421–34.

Flores-Ortiz, Y., 1993. "La Mujer y La Violencia: A Culturally Based Model for Understanding the Treatment of Domestic Violence in Chicana/Latina Communities." In *Chicana Critical Issues.* Eds. N. Alarcon, M. Melville, T. D. Rebolledo, C. Sierra, and D. Gonzales. Berkeley, Calif.: Third Woman Press, 169–82.

Flores-Ortiz, Y., 1997. "The Broken Covenant: Incest in Latino Families." *Voces: A Journal of Chicana/Latina Studies* 11: 48–70.

Flores-Ortiz, Y., 1998. "Fostering Accountability: A Reconstructive Dialogue with a Couple with a History of Violence." In *101 More Interventions in Family Therapy.* Eds. T. Nelson and T. Trepper. New York: Haworth Press, 389–96.

Flores-Ortiz, Y., 1999a. "Migración, Identidad y Violencia/Migration, Identity and Violence." In *Breaking Barriers: Diversity in Clinical Practice.* Eds. M. Mock, L. Hill, and D. Tucker. Sacramento, California: California State Psychological Association.

Flores-Ortiz, Y., 1999b. "Injustice in the Family." In *Family Therapy with Hispanics.* Eds. M. Flores and G. Carey. Boston: Allyn & Bacon.

Flores-Ortiz, Y., E. V. Curiel, and P. A. Palos, 2001. "Conflict Resolution and Couple Relationship among Mexican Couples from Mexico City and Tenamaxtlán, Jalisco." UC MEXUS-CONACYT, University of California, Riverside.

Flores-Ortiz, Y., E. V. Curiel, and P. A. Palos, 2002. "Intimate Partner Violence and Couple Interaction among Mexican Workers from Mexico City and Jalisco." *Journal of Border Health* 71: 21–32.

Flores-Ortiz, Y., M. Esteban, and R. Carrillo, 1994. "La Violencia en la Familia: Un Modelo, Contextual de Terapia Intergeneracional." *Revista Interamericana de Psicología* 282: 235–50.

Fogelquist, M., 1975. "Rhythm and Form in the Contemporary Son Jalisciense." M.A. thesis, University of California, Los Angeles.

Foucault, M., 1980. *Power/Knowledge.* Brighton, U.K.: Harvester.

Fowler, E., 1996. *San'ya Blues: Laboring Life in Contemporary Tokyo.* Ithaca, N.Y.: Cornell University Press.

Fox, J., and G. Rivera-Salgado, eds., 2004. *Indigenous Mexican Migrants in the United States.* La Jolla, University of California, San Diego: Center for U.S.-Mexican Studies and Center for Comparative Immigration Studies.

Frank, A. G., 1966. "The Development of Underdevelopment." *Monthly Review* 18: 17–31.

Frank, A. G., 1969. *Latin America: Underdevelopment or Revolution.* New York: Monthly Review Press.

Frank, A. G., 1972. "Economic Dependence, Class Structure, and Underdevelopment Policy." In *Dependence and Underdevelopment: Latin America's Political Economy.* Eds. A. G. Frank and D. L. Johnson. Garden City, N.Y.: Anchor Books, 19–45.

Franklin, J. H., and A. A. Moss Jr., 1988. *From Slavery to Freedom: A History of Negro Americans.* New York: McGraw-Hill.

Fregoso, R.-L., 2003. *meXicana Encounters. The Making of Social Identities on the Borderlands.* Berkeley: University of California Press.

Fuhrman, S. H., and R. F. Elmore, 2004. *Redesigning Accountability Systems for Education.* New York: Teachers College Press.

Gallimore, R., and C. Goldenberg, 2001. "Analyzing Cultural Models and Settings to Connect Achievement and School Improvement Research." *Educational Psychologist* 36: 45–56.

Gandara, P., R. W. Rumberger, J. Maxwell-Jolly, and R. Callahan, 2003. "English Learners in California Schools: Unequal Resources, Unequal Outcomes." *Educational Policy Analysis Archives* 11: 36.

Gaouette, N., 2006. "Bush Signs Fence Bill, Pushes Back." *Los Angeles Times,* October 26, A26.

Garcia, A. M., 1997. *Chicana Feminist Thought: The Basic Historical Writings.* New York: Routledge.

Garcia, E., 2001. *Hispanic Education in the United States: Raices y Alas.* Oxford: Rowman & Littlefield.

García, I. M., 1989. *United We Win: The Rise and Fall of La Raza Unida Party.* Tucson: Mexican American Studies Research Center, University of Arizona.

Garrido, J. S., 1974. *Historia de la Música Popular de México.* Mexico City: Editorial Extemporaneos.

Geijerstam, C., 1976. *Popular Music in México.* Albuquerque: University of New México Press.

Gellene, D., 1998. "In Their Own Images: TV Ad Seeks to Broaden the Public's View of Latinos." *Los Angeles Times,* April 2, D4.

Geriola, G., 1996. "Juan Gabriel: Cultura Popular y Sexo de los Angeles." *Latin American Music Review* 142: 232–67.

Geyer, G. A., 1996. *Americans No More.* New York: Atlantic Monthly Press.

Giamo, B., 1994. "Order, Disorder and the Homeless in the United States and Japan." *American Studies International* 31: 1–19.

Gilchrist, J., and J. R. Corsi, 2006. *Minutemen: The Battle to Secure America's Borders.* Los Angeles: World Ahead Publishing.

Gill, T., 1994. "Sanya Streetlife under the Heisei Recession." *Japan Quarterly* 41 (3): 270–86.

Gill, T., 2001. *Men of Uncertainty: The Social Organization of Day Laborers in Contemporary Japan.* New York: State University of New York Press.

Gledhill, C., 1987. "Introduction." In *Home Is Where the Heart Is: Studies in Melodrama and the Woman's Film.* Ed. C. Gledhill. London: BFI.

Gonzales, R., 2001. *Message to Aztlán: Selected Writings.* Houston: Arte Público Press.

Gonzalez, J., 2000. *Harvest of Empire: A History of Latinos in the United States.* London: Penguin Books.

González Casanova, P., 1963. "Sociedad Plural, Colonialismo Interno y Desarrollo." *América Latina* 6: 15–32.

Gorey, K. M., 2001. "Early Childhood Education: A Meta-analytic Affirmation of the Short- and Long-Term Benefits of Educational Opportunity." *School Psychology Quarterly* 16: 9–30.

Gorman, A., and S. Enriquez, 2005. "Ad Putting L.A. in Mexico Called Slap in Face." *Los Angeles Times,* April 27, B3.

Government Accounting Office, U.S., 2000. Contingent Workers: Incomes and Benefits Lag Behind Those of Rest of Workforce. U.S. General Accounting Office, Washington, D.C. 20548-0001. Go/HEHS-00-76.

Gradante, W., 1982. "El Hijo del Pueblo: José Alfredo Jimenez and the Mexican Canción Ranchera." *Latin American Music Review* 31: 36–59.

Gradante, W., 1983. "Mexican Popular Music at Mid-Century: The Role of José Alfredo Jimenez and the Canción Ranchera." *Studies in Latin American Popular Culture* 2: 99–114.

Granados, C., 2001. "La Nueva Latina. Unbound by Traditional or Modern Expectations, We're Creating Our Own Models of Success." *Latina* 5: 100–104.

Gratz et al. v. Bollinger et al., 2003. No. 02-516, Slip Opinion of the U.S. Supreme Court.

Green, R. J., and P. Wemer, 1996. "Intrusiveness and Closeness–Caregiving; Rethinking the Concept of Family 'Enmeshment.'" *Family Process* 352: 115–36.

Grial, H. d., 1973. *Músicos Mexicanos.* Mexico City: Editorial Diana.

Grieco, E., 2003. "The Foreign Born from Mexico in the United States." *Migration Policy Institute* 1 (October): 1–4.

Griffith, D., E. Kissam, J. Camposeco, A. García, M. Pfeffer, D. Runsten, and M. Pizzini, eds., 1995. *Working Poor: Farmworkers in the United States.* Philadelphia: Temple University Press.

Griffith, J. 1998. "The Relation of School Structure and Social Environment to Parent Involvement in Elementary Schools." *Elementary School Journal* 9953–80.

Grissom, J. B., and L. A. Shepard, 1989. "Repeating and Dropping Out of School." In *Flunking Grades: Research and Policies on Retention.* Eds. L. A. Sheppard and M. L. Smith. New York: Falmer Press.

Griswold del Castillo, R., 1979. *The Los Angeles Barrio, 1850–1890: A Social History.* Berkeley: University of California Press.

Grutter et al. v. Bollinger et al., 2003. No. 02-241, Slip Opinion of the U.S. Supreme Court.

Guo, G., and K. M. Harris, 2000. "The Mechanisms Mediating the Effects of Poverty on Children's Intellectual Development." *Demography* 37: 431–47.

Gurin, P., A. Hurtado, and T. Peng, 1994. "Group Contacts and Ethnicity in the Social Identities of Mexicanos and Chicanos." *Personality and Social Psychology Bulletin* 205: 521–32.

Gurin, P., A. H. Miller, and G. Gurin, 1980. "Stratum Identification and Consciousness." *Social Psychology Quarterly* 43 (1): 30–47.

Gutiérrez, D. G., 2004. *The Columbia History of Latinos in the United States since 1960.* New York: Columbia University Press.

Gutiérrez, G. 1984. *Teología de la Liberación: Perspectivas.* Lima: Cep.

Gutiérrez, J. A., 1999. *The Making of a Chicano Militant: Lessons from Cristal.* Madison: University of Wisconsin Press.

Gutiérrez, R. A., 1976. "Mexican Migration to the United States, 1880–1930: The Chicano and Internal Colonialism." M.A. thesis, University of Wisconsin.

Gutiérrez, R. A., 1993. "Community, Patriarchy and Individualism: The Politics of Chicano History." *American Quarterly* 45: 44–72.

Gándara, P., 1995. *Over the Ivy Walls: The Educational Mobility of Low-Income Chicanos.* Albany: State University of New York Press.

Haney Lopez, I., 2005. "Race on the 2010 Census: Hispanics and the Shrinking White Majority." *Daedalus* (Winter): 42–52.

Haney Lopez, I. F., 2003. *Racism on Trial: The Chicano Fight for Justice.* Cambridge, Mass.: Harvard University Press.

Hanson, V. D., 2003. *Mexifornia: A State of Becoming.* San Francisco: Encounter Books.

Hanushek, E. A., 1997. "Assessing the Effects of School Resources on Student Performance: An Update." *Educational Evaluation and Policy Analysis* 19: 141–64.

Hanushek, E. A., 1999. "Some Findings from an Independent Investigation of the Tennessee STAR Experiment and from Other Investigations of Class Size Effects." *Educational Evaluation and Policy Analysis* 21: 143–63.

Hanushek, E. A., J. F. Kain, J. M. Markman, and S. G. Rivkin, 2003. "Does Peer Ability Affect Student Achievement?" *Journal of Applied Economics* 18 (5): 27–44.

Harlem Youth Opportunities Unlimited, 1964. *Youth in the Ghetto: A Study of the Consequences of Powerlessness and a Blueprint for Change.* New York: Harlem Youth Opportunities Unlimited.

Hayes, L. B., 1994. Letter to the Editor: "California's Prop. 187." *New York Times,* October 15.

Hayes-Bautista, D., P. Hsu, A. Perez, and M. I. Kahramanian, 2003. "The Latino Majority Has Emerged. Latinos comprise More than 50 Percent of All Births in California." Center for the Study of Latino Health and Culture, School of Medicine. University of California, Los Angeles.

Hayes-Bautista, D. E., 1993. "Mexicans in Southern California: Societal Enrichment or Wasted Opportunity?" In *The California-Mexico Connection.* Eds. A. F. Lowenthal and K. Burgess. Stanford, Calif.: Stanford University Press.

Hayes-Bautista, D. E., W. O. Schink, and J. Chapa, 1987. *The Burden of Support: Young Latinos in an Aging Society.* Stanford, Calif.: Stanford University Press.

Hedges, L. V., R. D. Laine, and R. Greenwald, 1994. "Does Money Matter? A Meta-analysis of Studies of the Effects of Differential School Inputs on Student Outcomes." *Educational Researcher* 23: 5–14.

Henson, K. D., 1996. *Just a Temp.* Philadelphia: Temple University Press.

Herrerias, C., A. G. Mata, and R. L. Ramos, 2003. "The Face of Violence against Women in Mexico and the United States." *Journal of Border Health* 71: 3–19.

"Hispanic Org Mulls Protest." 1995. *Variety,* August 3, 4.

Hondagneu-Sotelo, P., 1994. *Gendered Transitions: Mexican Experiences of Immigration.* Berkeley: University of California Press.

Hondagneu-Sotelo, P., 2001. *Doméstica: Immigrant Workers Cleaning and Caring in the Shadows of Affluence.* Berkeley: University of California Press.

Hondagneu-Sotelo, P., and E. Avila, 1997. " 'I'm Here, but I'm There': The Meanings of Latina Transnational Motherhood." *Gender and Society*: 11548–71.

Hondagneu-Sotelo, P., and C. Riegos, 1997. "Sin Organización, No Hay Solución: Latina Domestic Workers and Non-traditional Labor Organizing." *Latino Studies Journal* 8: 54–81.

Houseman, S., 1996. "Temporary, Part-Time, and Contract Employment in the United States: A Report on the W.E. Upjohn Institute's Employer Survey on Flexible Staffing Policies." Kalamazoo, Mich.: W.E. Upjohn Institute for Employment Research.

Huerta, J. A., 1982. *Chicano Theater: Themes and Forms.* Tempe, Ariz.: Bilingual Press.

Huntington, S. P., 2000. "The Special Case of Mexican Immigration: Why Mexico is a Problem." *The American Enterprise* (December): 20–22.

Huntington, S. P. 2004. "The Hispanic Challenge." *Foreign Policy* (March/April): 30–45.

Hurtado, A. 1996. "Strategic Suspensions: Feminists of Color Theorize the Production of Knowledge." In *Knowledge, Difference and Power: Essays Inspired by Women's Ways of Knowing.* Eds. N. Goldberger, J. Tarule, B. Clinchy, and M. Belenky. New York: Basic Books.

Hurtado, A., 1997. "Understanding Multiple Group Identities: Inserting Women into Cultural Transformations." *Journal of Social Issues* 532: 299–328.

Hurtado, A., 2003. *Voicing Chicana Feminisms: Young Women Speak Out on Sexuality and Identity.* New York: New York University Press.

Hurtado, A., and A. J. Stewart, 1997. "Through the Looking Glass: Implications of Studying Whiteness for Feminist Methods." In *Off White: Readings on Society, Race, and Culture.* Eds. M. Fine, L. C. Powell, L. Weis, and L. M. Wong. New York: Routledge.

Ibarra, M. d. l. L., 2000. "Mexican Immigrant Women and the New Domestic Labor." *Human Organization* 594: 452–64.

Ibarra, M. d. l. L., 2002. "Emotional Proletarians in a Global Economy: Mexican Immigrant Women and Elder Care Work." *Urban Anthropology* 31 (3–4): 317–51.

Ibarra, M. d. l. L., 2003. "The Tender Trap: Mexican Immigrant Women and the Ethics of Elder Care Work." *Aztlán* 28: 87–113.

Inda, J. X., 2000. "Foreign Bodies: Migrants, Parasites, and the Pathological Nation." *Discourse: Journal for Theoretical Studies in Media and Culture* 22: 46–62.

Inda, J. X., 2002. "Biopower, Reproduction, and the Migrant Woman's Body." In *Decolonial Voices: Chicana and Chicano Cultural Studies in the 21st Century.* Eds. A. J. Aldama and N. H. Quinones. Bloomington: Indiana University Press.

INEGI, 2004. "Resumen de los Resultados de un Estudio Nacional sobre la Violencia contra las Mujeres."

Instituto Nacional de Salud Pública, 2003. "Encuesta Nacional sobre Violencia contra las Mujeres." México City: Instituto Estatal de la Mujer, 73–75.

Jencks, C., and M. Phillips, 1998. *The Black-White Test Score Gap.* Washington, D.C.: Brookings Institute.

Jencks, C., M. Smith, H. Acland, M. J. Bane, D. Cohen, H. Gintis, B. Heyns, and S. Michelson, 1972. *Inequality: A Reassessment of the Effects of Family and Schooling in America.* New York: Basic Books.

Jepsen, C., and S. G. Rivkin, 2002. *Class Size Reduction, Teacher Quality, and Academic Achievement in California Public Elementary Schools.* San Francisco: Public Policy Institute of California.

Jimerson, S., G. Anderson, and A. D. Whipple, 2002. "Winning the Battle and Losing the

War: Examining the Relation between Grade Retention and Dropping Out of High School." *Psychology in the Schools* 39: 441–57.

Johnson, M. P., and J. M. Leone, 2005. "The Differential Effects of Intimate Terrorism and Situational Couple Violence." *Journal of Family Issues* 26: 322–49.

Johnson, T. A., 1966. "Harlem Likened to a New Nation." *New York Times,* December 11, 10.

Kalleberg, A. L., 2002. "Nonstandard Employment Relations: Part-Time, Temporary and Contract Work." *Annual Review of Sociology* 26: 31–45.

Kaplan, E. A., 1992. *Motherhood and Representation: The Mother in Popular Culture and Melodrama.* New York: Routledge.

King, M. L., Jr., 1968. *Where Do We Go from Here: Chaos or Community?* Boston: Beacon Press.

Kochhar, R., 2003. "Jobs Lost, Jobs Gained: The Latino Experience in the Recession and Recovery." In *Pew Hispanic Center Report.* Washington, D.C.: Pew Hispanic Center.

Kosambi, M., 1995. "An Uneasy Intersection: Gender, Ethnicity, and Crosscutting Identities in India." *Social Politics* 2: 181–94.

Kotkin, J., T. Tseng, and E. Ozuna, 2002. "Rewarding Ambition: Latinos, Housing, and the Future of California." Malibu, Calif.: Davenport Institute, School of Public Policy, Pepperdine University.

Krasnow, E. G., L. D. Longley, and H. A. Terry, 1982. *The Politics of Broadcast Regulation.* New York: St. Martin's Press.

Ladson-Billings, G., 1996. "Silences as Weapons: Challenges of a Black Professor Teaching White Students." *Theory into Practice* 35: 79–85.

Ladson-Billings, G., and W. Tate, 1995. "Toward a Critical Race Theory of Education." *Teachers College Record* 97: 47–68.

Lamas, M., 1978. "De Abandonada a Leona: La Imagen de la Mujer en la Canción Ranchera." *Fem* 26: 20–28.

Landy, M., 1991. "Introduction." In *Imitations of Life: A Reader on Film and Television Melodrama.* Ed. M. Landy. Detroit: Wayne State University Press.

Lannert, J., 1999. "Juan Gabriel: The Billboard Interview." *Billboard* 11140: 56.

Lawrence, C. R., III, and M. J. Matsuda, 1997. *We Won't Go Back. Making the Case for Affirmative Action.* Boston and New York: Houghton Mifflin.

Lee, J., 2002. "Racial and Ethnic Achievement Gap Trends: Reversing the Progress Toward Equity." *Educational Researcher* 31: 3–12.

Lee, V. E., and A. S. Bryk, 1989. "A Multilevel Model of the Social Distribution of High School Achievement." *Sociology of Education* 62: 172–92.

Leovy, J., 1997. "Latino Group to Launch Disney Boycott." *Los Angeles Times,* April 24, D2.

Lewin, K., 1948. *Resolving Social Conflicts, Selected Papers on Group Dynamics, 1935–1946.* New York: Harper & Brothers.

Lewis, G. H., 1993. "Mexican Musical Influences on Country Songs and Styles." In *All That Glitters: Country Music in America.* Ed. G. Lewis. Bowling Green, Ohio: Bowling Green University Popular Press.

Liang, X., B. Fuller, and J. D. Singer, 2000. "Ethnic Difference in Child Care Selection: The Influence of Family Structure, Parental Practices, and Home Language." *Early Child Research Quarterly* 15: 357–84.

Light, I., 1979. "Disadvantaged Minorities in Self-Employment." *International Journal of Comparative Sociology* 20: 31–45.

Light, I., and E. Roach, 1996. "Self-Employment: Mobility Ladder or Economic Lifeboat." In *Ethnic Los Angeles*. Eds. R. Waldinger and M. Bozorgmehr. New York: Russell Sage Foundation.

Lin, J., 1995. "Polarized Development and Urban Change in New York's Chinatown." *Urban Affairs Review* 303: 332–54.

Lopez, A., 1991. "Celluloid Tears: Melodrama in the 'Old' Mexican Cinema." *Iris* 13: 29–51.

López, E., and R. M. Moller, 2003. *The Distribution of Wealth in California, 2000.* Sacramento: California Research Bureau, California State Library.

López, E., E. Ramirez, and R. I. Rochin, 1999. *Latinos and Economic Development in California.* Sacramento: California Research Bureau.

López Tijerina, R., 2000. *They Called Me "King Tiger": My Struggle for the Land and Our Rights.* Houston: Arte Público Press.

Los Angeles Unified School District, 2001. Student Enrollment by School, Grade, and Ethnicity, Fall 2001.

Lozano, C., 1992. "Moorpark: Council Hears from Opponents of Day Laborer's Hiring Site." *Los Angeles Times*, January 9.

Magnuson, K. A., and J. Waldfogel, 2005. "Early Childhood Care and Education: Effects on Ethnic and Racial Gaps in School Readiness." *Future of Children* 15: 169–96.

Marcelli, E. A., and W. A. Cornelius, 2001. "The Changing Profile of Mexican Migrants to the United States: New Evidence from Southern California." *Latin American Research Review* 363: 105–31.

Marez, Curtis, 2004. *Drug Wars: The Political Economy of Narcotics.* Minneapolis: University of Minnesota Press.

Marr, M. D., 1997. "Maintaining Autonomy: The Plight of the American Skid Row and the Japanese Yoseba." *Journal of Social Distress and the Homeless* 63: 229–50.

Massey, D. S., J. Durand, and N. J. Malone, 2002. *Beyond Smoke and Mirrors: Mexican Immigration in an Era of Economic Integration.* New York: Russell Sage Foundation.

Matsuda, M., C. Lawrence, R. Delgado, and K. Crenshaw, eds., 1993. *Words That Wound: Critical Race Theory, Assaultive Speech, and the First Amendment.* Boulder, Colo.: Westview Press.

Mauricio Gastón Institute for Latino Community Development and Public, 1994. "Barriers to Employment and Work-Place Advancement of Latinos, Report to the Glass Ceiling Commission." U.S. Department of Labor.

McClelland, M. M., F. J. Morrison, and D. L. Holmes, 2000. "Children at Risk for Early Academic Problems: The Role of Learning-Related Social Skills." *Early Childhood Research Quarterly* 15: 307–29.

Medina, J. J., and R. Barbaret, 1999. "A Spanish Version of the CTS." In *Handbook for the Conflict Tactics Scales*. Ed. M. Straus. Durham: University of New Hampshire, Family Research Laboratory.

Mendoza, V. T., 1988 [1961]. *La Canción Mexicana.* Mexico City: Fondo de Cultura Económica.

Merickel, A., R. Linquanti, T. B. Parrish, M. Pérez, M. Eaton, and P. Esra. 2003. Effects of the Implementation of Proposition 227 on the Education of English Learners, K–12:

Year 3 Report. Palao Alto, Ca.: American Institutes for Research. Retrieved July 28, 2004 from http://www.air.org/publications/documents/Yr%203%20FinalRpt.pdf.

Milkman, R., and R. E. Dwyer, 2002. "Growing Apart: The 'New Economy' and Job Polarization of California, 1992–2000." In *The State of California Labor 2002.* Ed. R. Milkman. Berkeley: University of California Press.

Millard, A. V., and J. Chapa, 2004. *Apple Pie & Enchiladas: Latino Newcomers in the Rural Midwest.* Austin: University of Texas Press.

Min, P. G., 1988. "Ethnic Business Enterprise: Korean Small Business in Atlanta." New York, Center for Migration Studies.

Monsivais, C., 1988. *Escenas de Pudor y Livianad.* Mexico City: Editorial Grijalbo.

Monsivais, C., 1992. "Las Mitologias del Cine Mexicano." *Intermedios* 2 (June-July): 12–23.

Monsivais, C., 1993. "Se Sufre, pero Se Aprende: El Melodrama y las Reglas de la Falta de Limites." *El Melodrama Mexicano* 16: 5–19.

Monsivais, C., 1994. *Amor Perdido.* Mexico, City: Bibilioteca Era.

Moore, J., 1970. "Colonialism: The Case of Mexican Americans." *Social Problems* 17: 463–72.

Mora, C., 1982. *Mexican Cinema.* Berkeley: University of California Press.

Moraga, C., 1981. "La Güera." In *This Bridge Called My Back: Writings by Radical Women of Color.* Eds. C. Moraga and G. Anzaldúa. Watertown, Mass.: Persephone Press.

Moraga, C., 1983. *Loving in the War Years: Lo que Nunca Pasó por Sus Labios.* Boston: South End Press.

Moraga, C., and G. Anzaldúa, eds., 1981. *This Bridge Called My Back: Writings by Radical Women of Color.* Watertown, Mass.: Persephone Press.

Morales, R., and F. Bonilla, eds., 1993. *Latinos in a Changing U.S. Economy.* Newbury Park, Calif.: Sage Publications.

Moreno, J., ed., 1999. *The Elusive Quest for Equality: 150 Years of Chicano/Chicana Education.* Cambridge, Mass.: Harvard Educational Review.

Moreno Rivas, Y., 1989. *Historia de la Música Popular Mexicana.* Mexico City: Alianza Editorial Mexicana, Consejo Nacional para la Cultura y las Artes.

Morrison, P., 2005. "A Sign of Controversy over Immigration." *Los Angeles Times,* May 4, B15.

Mozingo, J., 1997. "Injured Worker Finds Little Aid." *Los Angeles Times,* November 25, B1.

Murphy, P. J., 2004. *Financing California's Community Colleges.* San Francisco: Public Policy Institute of California.

Muñoz, S., 1989a. "¿La TV en Español Sufre un Proceso de Cubanización?" *La Opinión,* May 10, 1, 11.

Muñoz, S., 1989b. "Miami y Los Angeles, Dos Ciudades Incomparables." *La Opinión,* May 11, 1, 10.

Muñoz, S., 1989c. "Crónica de un Despido Anunciado." *La Opinión,* June 9, 1, 7.

National Association of Color Women's Clubs, Inc. and Youth Affiliates. Retrieved December 11, 2006, from http://www.nacwc.org/intro.htm.

National Research Council and Institution of Medicine, 2000. *From Neurons to Neighborhoods: The Science of Early Childhood Development.* Washington, D.C., National Academic Press.

Navarro, A., 2000. *La Raza Unida Party: A Chicano Challenge to the U.S. Two-Party Dictatorship*. Philadelphia: Temple University Press.

Navarro, B., 1989. "Mi Experiencia en KVEA TV." *La Opinión,* June 16, 4.

Nesiah, V., 2000. "Toward a Feminist Internationality. A Critique of U.S. Feminist Legal Scholarship." In *Global Critical Race Feminism. An International Reader.* Ed. A. K. Wing. New York and London: New York University Press.

Neumark, D., 2002. *How Living Wage Laws Affect Low-Wage Workers and Low-Income Families.* San Francisco: Public Policy Institute of California.

Nicholas, P., and R. Salladay, 2005. "Gov. Praises 'Minuteman' Campaign." *Los Angeles Times,* April 29, B1, B10.

Noriega, C. A., 2002. "Ready for Prime Time: Minorities on Network Entertainment Television." In *Latino Policy & Issues Brief.* Los Angeles: UCLA Chicano Studies Research Center.

Noriega, C. A., 2003. "Out of Sync, Out of Focus: A Report on the Film and Television Industries." The National Association for the Advancement of Colored People.

Noriega, C. A., and A. Hoffman, 2004. "Looking for Latino Regulars on Prime-Time Television: The Fall 2004 Season." *CSRC Research Report:* 4.

Nájera-Ramírez, O., 1994. "Engendering Nationalism: Identity, Discourse, and the Mexican Charro." *Anthropological Quarterly* 671: 1–14.

Nájera-Ramírez, O., 2003. "Unruly Passions: Poetics and Performance in the Ranchera Song." In *Chicana Feminisms: A Critical Reader.* Eds. A. H. Gabriela Arredondo, Norma Klahn, Olga Nájera Ramirez, and Patricia Zavella. Durham, N.C.: Duke University Press.

O'Steen, K., 1993a. "White Male Pens Still Busiest: Study Finds H'wood Lags in Hiring Minority, Female Writers." *Variety:* June 15, 1, 42.

O'Steen, K., 1993b. "Face of Prime Time TV is Still White." *Variety,* June 21, 4.

O'Steen, K., 1993c. "Guild Study Finds TV Bias." *Variety,* June 28, 37.

O'Steen, K., 1993d. "TV Distorts Minorities, Study Finds." *Variety:* June 16, 1, 40.

Oakes, J., 1985. *Keeping Track: How Schools Structure Inequality.* New Haven, Conn.: Yale University Press.

Oakes, J., J. Rogers, R. J. McDonough, P. Solórzano, D. Mehan, and P. Noguera, 2000. "Remedying Unequal Opportunities for Successful Participation in Advanced Placement Courses in California High Schools: A Proposed Action Plan." An expert report submitted on behalf of the Defendants and the American Civil Liberties Union in the case of *Daniel v. the State of California.*

Obler, S., 1992. "The Politics of Labeling." *Latin American Perspectives* 4 (Fall): 18–36.

Ogbu, J. U., 1992. "Understanding cultural diversity and learning." *Educational Researcher* 21: 5–14.

Olivares, J., 1989. "Piden Aclaraciones a Telemundo: Coalición Nacional Hispana Desea Discutir Problemas Surgidos en KVEA." *La Opinión,* May 11, 1, 10.

Orfield, G., and F. Monfort, 1992. *Status of School Desegregation: The Next Generation.* Cambridge, Mass.: Metropolitan Opportunity Project, Harvard University.

Ornelas, A., and D. Solórzano, 2004. "The Transfer Condition of Latina/o Community College Students in California: Policy Recommendations and Solutions." *Community College Journal of Research and Practice* 28: 233–48.

Palerm, J. V., 1991. *Farm Labor Needs and Farm Workers in California, 1970–1989.* Sacramento: California Agricultural Studies, Employment Development Department.

Palerm, J. V., 1999. "The Expansion of California Agriculture and the Rise of Peasant-Worker Communities." In *Immigration: A Civil Rights Issue for the Americas*. Eds. S. Jonas and S. D. Thomas. Wilmington, Del.: Scholarly Resources.

Palerm, J. V., 2000. "Farmworkers Putting Down Roots in Central Valley Communities." *California Agriculture* 541: 33–34.

Paredes, A., 1977. "On Ethnographic Work among Minorities: A Folklorist's Perspective." *New Scholar* 6: 1–32.

Paredes, A., 1982. "Folklore, Lo Mexicano and Proverbs." *Aztlán* 13: 1–11.

Parker, R., 1994. *Flesh Peddlers and Warm Bodies: The Temporary Help Industry and Its Workers*. New Brunswick, N. J.: Rutgers University Press.

Passel, J., 2004. "Mexican Immigration to the US: The Latest Estimates." *Migration Policy Institute* (March): 1–3.

Passel, J. S., 2005. *Estimates of Size and Characteristics of the Undocumented Population*. Washington, D.C.: Pew Hispanic Center.

Pastor, M., 2003. "Rising Tides and Sinking Boats: The Economic Challenge for California's Latinos." In *Latinos and Public Policy in California: An Agenda for Opportunity*. Ed. D. Lopez and A. Jimenez. Berkeley, Calif.: Berkeley Public Policy Press.

Pastor, M., Jr., P. Dreier, J. E. Grigsby, and M. Lopez-Garza, 2000. *Regions that Work: How Cities and Suburbs Can Grow Together*. Minneapolis: University of Minnesota Press.

Pastor, M., and E. A. Marcelli, 2000. "Men N the Hood: Skill, Spatial, and Social Mismatch for Male Workers in Los Angeles County." *Urban Geography* 21: 474–96.

Pastor, M., and J. Scoggins, 2006. *Working Poverty in California: A Multi-Measure Comparison Using the 2000 and 1990 Public Use Microdata Samples*. Santa Cruz, Calif.: Center for Justice, Tolerance, and Community.

Pastor, M., and C. Zabin, 2002. "Recession and Reaction: The Impact of the Downturn on California Labor." In *The State of California Labor 2002*. Ed. R. Milkman. Berkeley: University of California Press.

Peck, J., and N. Theodore, 1998. "The Business of Contingent Work: Growth and Restructuring in Chicago's Temporary Employment Industry." *Work, Employment & Society* 124: 655–74.

Peck, J., and N. Theodore, 2001. "Contingent Chicago: Restructuring the Spaces of Temporary Labor." *International Journal of Urban and Regional Research* 253: 471–96.

Peek-Asa, C., L. Garcia, D. McArthur, and R. Castro, 2002. "Severity of Intimate Partner Abuse Indicators as Perceived by Women in Mexico and the United States." *Women and Health* 352–53: 165–80.

Peña, M., 1985. *The Texas-Mexican Conjunto: History of a Working-Class Music*. Austin: University of Texas Press.

Perea, J., ed., 1997. *Immigrants Out! The New Nativism and the Anti-Immigrant Impulse in the United States*. New York: New York University Press.

Perez, G. M., 2004. *The Near Northwest Side Story: Migration, Displacement, and Puerto Rican Families*. Berkeley: University of California Press.

Pesquera, B., and D. A. Segura, 1993. "There Is No Going Back: Chicanas and Feminism." In *Chicana Critical Issues*. Eds. N. Alarcón, R. Castro, E. Perez, B. Pesquera, A.S. Ridell, and P. Zavella. Berkeley, Calif.: Third Woman Press.

Pesquera, B., and D. A. Segura, 1996. "With Quill and Torch: A Chicana Perspective on the

American Women's Movement and Feminist Theories." In *Social, Economic, and Political Change.* Eds. D. R. Maciel and I. D. Ortiz. Tucson: University of Arizona Press.

Phinney, J. S., 1996. "When We Talk about American Ethnic Groups, What Do We Mean?" *American Psychologist* 519: 918–27.

Pianta, R. C., and M. W. Stuhlman, 2004. "Teacher–Child Relationships and Children's Success in the First Years of School." *School Psychology Review* 33: 444–58.

Podalsky, L., 1993. "Disjointed Frames: Melodrama, Nationalism and Representation in 1940s México." *Studies in Latin American Popular Culture* 12: 57–73.

Polivka, A. E., 1996. "Contingent and Alternative Work Arrangements, Defined." *Monthly Labor Review* (October): 3–9.

Polivka, A. E., and T. Nardone, 1989. "The Quality of Jobs: On the Definition of Contingent Work." *Monthly Labor Review* (December): 9–14.

Portes, A., 1994. "The Informal Economy and its Paradoxes." In *The Handbook of Economic Sociology.* Eds. N. J. Smelser and R. Swedberg. Princeton, N.J.: Princeton University Press.

Portes, A., and L. A. Benton, 1984. "Industrial Development and Labor Absorption: A Reinterpretation." *Population and Development Review* 10: 589–611.

Portes, A., M. Castells, and L. A. Benton, 1989. *Informal Economy: Studies in Advanced and Less Developed Countries.* Baltimore: Johns Hopkins University Press.

Portes, A., and S. Sassen, 1987. "Making It Underground: Comparative Material on the Urban Informal Sector in Western Market Economies." *American Journal of Sociology* 93: 30–61.

Portes, A., and A. Stepick, 1993. *City on the Edge: The Transformation of Miami.* Berkeley: University of California Press.

Potes, C. I., 1989a. "Levin da Su Versión sobre Cambios en el Equipo Noticioso de Canal 52." *La Opinión,* 3.

Potes, C. I., 1989b. "Grupos Mexicoamericanos Protestan Cambios en Equipo Noticioso de Canal 52." *La Opinión,* 3.

Prebisch, R., 1950. *The Economic Development of Latin America and Its Principal Problems.* New York: United Nations Department of Social and Economic Affairs.

Pristin, T., 1993. " 'Substantial Barriers' to Minority Writers, Survey Finds." *Los Angeles Times,* June 15, F2.

Puig, C., 1994. "Study No Surprise to Latinos." *Los Angeles Times,* September 8, F1, F9.

Quesada, J., 1999. "From Central American Warriors to San Francisco Latino Day Laborers: Suffering and Exhaustion in a Transnational Context." *Transforming Anthropology* 81–82: 162–85.

Ramos, L. L., G. Borges, C. Cherpitel, M. Medina-Mora, and L. Mondragon, 2003. "Domestic Violence: A Hidden Problem in the Healthcare System. The case of emergency services." *Journal of Border Health* 71: 43–54.

Ramírez Rodríguez, J. C., and M. C. Patiño Guerra, 1997. "Algunos Aspectos sobre la Magnitud y Trascendencia de la Violencia Doméstica contra la Mujer: un Estudio Piloto." *Salud Mental*: 202.

Raudenbush, S. W., and A. S. Bryk, 2002. *Hierarchical Linear Models: Applications and Data Analysis Methods.* Thousand Oaks, Calif.: Sage Publications.

Reardon, S. F., 2003. *Sources of Educational Inequality: The Growth of Racial/Ethnic and*

Socioeconomic Test Score Gaps in Kindergarten and First Grade. University Park: Population Research Institute, Pennsylvania State University.

Reese, L., and R. Gallimore, 2000. "Immigrant Latinos' Cultural Model of Literacy Development: An Evolving Perspective on Home-School Discontinuities." *American Journal of Education* 108: 103–34.

Reuter, J., 1983. *La Música Popular de México: Origen e Historia de la Música que Canta y Toca el Pueblo Mexicano.* Mexico City: Panorama Editorial.

Reyes, A. d. l., 1988. *Medio siglo de Cine Mexican 1896–1947.* Mexico City: Editorial Trillas.

Reyes, B. I., 2001. *A Portrait of Race and Ethnicity in California: An Assessment of Social and Economic Well-Being.* San Francisco: Public Policy Institute of California.

Reyes, D., 1991. "Victims of Economy." *Los Angeles Times,* August 8.

Reyes, D., 1998. "Seasoned Activist's Passions Burn Bright Again." *Los Angeles Times,* August 2, A3, A32, A33.

Rincón & Associates, 2004. Latino Television Study, National Hispanic Media Coalition.

Rivera, M., 1994. "When Will TV Reflect Latino Audience?" *Los Angeles Times,* December 12, F3.

Rivera, M., 1996. "Film and TV Perpetuate Invisibility." *Hispanic,* June: 12–13.

Rivkin, S. G., 2001. "Tiebout Sorting, Aggregation and the Estimation of Peer Group Effects." *Economics of Education Review* 20: 201–9.

Robb, D., 1993. "Kids TV Gets Worst Marks on Minority Images." *The Hollywood Reporter,* 1, 8, 33.

Robb, D., 1993. "WGAW: Minorities 'Typecast': Modest Gains Said Overshadowed by Little If Any Access. *The Hollywood Reporter,* 1, 12, 14.

Rodney, W., 1972. *How Europe Underdeveloped Africa.* Dar es Salaam: Tanzania Publishing House.

Rodriguez, G., 1996. *The Emerging Latino Middle Class.* Malibu, Calif.: Institute for Public Policy, Pepperdine University.

Rodriguez, M., H. M. Bauer, Y. Flores-Ortiz, and S. Szkupinski-Quiroga, 1998. "Factors Affecting Patient-Physician Communication for Abused Latina and Asian Immigrant Women." *Journal of Family Practice* 47: 309–11.

Rodriguez, R., 1982. *Hunger of Memory: The Education of Richard Rodriguez.* New York: Bantam Books.

Romero, M., 1992. *Maid in the U.S.A.* New York: Routledge.

Romero, M., P. Hondagneu-Sotelo, and V. Ortiz, eds., 1997. *Challenging Fronteras: Structuring Latina and Latino Lives in the U.S.: An Anthology of Readings.* New York: Routledge.

Rosales, F. A., 2000. *Testimonio: A Documentary History of the Mexican American Struggle for Civil Rights.* Houston: Arte Público Press.

Roscigno, V. J., 2000. "Family/School Inequality and African-American/Hispanic Achievement." *Social Problems* 47: 266–90.

Rosenblatt, R., 1997. "Another Day, Another 73 cents? Non-Standard Jobs Offer More or Less." *Los Angeles Times,* August 31.

Rosenthal, R., 1994. "Parametric Measures of Effect Size." In *The Handbook of Research Synthesis.* Eds. H. Cooper and L. V. Hedges. New York: Russell Sage Foundation.

Rostow, W. W., 1960. *The Stages of Economic Growth: A Non-Communist Manifesto.* London: Cambridge University Press.

Rothstein, R., 2004. *Class and Schools: Using Social, Economic, and Educational Reform to Close the Black-White Achievement Gap.* Washington, D.C.: Economic Policy Institute.

Rouse, C. E., and L. Barrow, 2006. "U.S. elementary and secondary schools: Equalizing opportunity or replicating the status quo?" *The Future of Children* 16: 99–123.

Rouse, R., 1992. "Making Sense of Settlement: Class Transformation, Cultural Struggle, and Transnationalism among Mexican Migrants in the United States." *Annals of the New York Academy of Sciences* 645: 25–82.

Rowan, B., S. Raudenbush, and S. J. Kang, 1991. "Organizing design in high schools: A multilevel analysis." *American Journal of Education* 99: 238–68.

Ruiz, V. L., 1987. "By the Day or the Week: Mexicana Domestic Workers in El Paso." In *Women on the U.S.-Mexico Border: Responses to Change.* Eds. V. L. Ruiz and S. Tiano. Boston: Allen & Unwin.

Rumberger, R., 1991. "Chicano Dropouts: A Review of Research and Policy Issues." In *Chicano School Failure and Success: Research and Policy Agenda for the 1990s.* Ed. R. Valencia. New York: The Falmer Press.

Rumberger, R. W., and B. A. Anguiano. 2004. *Investigating the Latino Achievement Gap in California During Early Elementary School: Technical Appendix.* Retrieved July 28, 2004 from http://education.ucsb.edu/rumberger/.

Rumberger, R. W., and K. A. Larson, 1998. "Toward Explaining Differences in Educational Achievement among Mexican-American Language Minority Students." *Sociology of Education* 71: 69–93.

Rumberger, R. W., and G. J. Palardy, 2005. "Does Segregation Still Matter? The Impact of Student Composition on Academic Achievement in High School." *Teachers College Record* 107: 1999–2045.

Rumberger, R. W., and L. Tran, 2006. *Preschool Participation and the Cognitive and Social Development of Language Minority Students.* Los Angeles: Center for the Study of Evaluation, Graduate School of Education and Information Studies, University of California.

Ryan, A. M., 2000. "Peer groups as a context for the socialization of adolescents' motivation, engagement, and achievement in school." *Educational Psychologist* 35: 101–11.

Said, E. W., 1978. *Orientalism.* New York: Random House.

Saldivar, G., 1934. *Historia de la Música en México.* Mexico City: Secretaría de Educación Pública.

Saldívar-Hull, S., 2000. *Feminism on the Border: Chicana Gender Politics and Literature.* Berkeley: University of California Press.

Saltijeral, M. T., L. R. Lira, and M. A. Cabellero, 1998. "Las Mujeres que han sido Victimas de Maltrato Conyugal: Tipos de Violencia Experimentada y Algunos Efectos en la Salud Mental." *Salud Mental* 212: 10–18.

Sanderson, A. R., B. Dugoni, T. Hoffer, and L. Selfa, 2000. "Doctorate Recipients from United States Universities: Summary Report, 1999." Chicago: National Opinion Research Center at the University of Chicago.

Sandoval, C., 2000. *Methodology of the Oppressed.* Minneapolis: University of Minnesota Press.

Santa Ana, O., 2002. *Brown Tide Rising: Metaphors of Latinos in Contemporary American Public Discourse.* Austin: University of Texas Press.

Sassen, S., 1989. "New York City's Informal Economy." In *The Informal Economy: Studies in Advanced and Less Developed Countries*. Eds. A. Portes and M. Castells. Baltimore: John Hopkins University Press.

Sassen-Koop, S., 1987. "Growth and Informalization at the Core: A Preliminary Report on New York City." In *The Capitalist City: Global Restructuring and Community Politics*. Eds. M. P. Smith and J. R. Feagin. Malden, Mass.: Blackwell Publishers.

Schacter, J., and Y. M. Thum, 2004. "Paying for High- and Low-Quality Teaching." *Economics of Education Review* 23: 411–30.

Scheer, R., 2000. "Surprise! Immigration Hasn't Ruined Us." *Los Angeles Times*, February 22.

Schlesinger, A. M., Jr., 1992. *The Disuniting of America*. New York: W.W. Norton.

Segura, D., 2003. "Navigating between Two Worlds. The Labyrinth of Chicana Intellectual Production in the Academy." *Journal of Black Studies* 341: 28–51.

Smith, D., 1997. "Food Stamp Extension Granted to Legal Immigrants; Counties Given Option of Continuing Aid until Aug. 22." *Fresno Bee*, March 21.

Smith, J. F., and E. Chen, 2001. "Bush to Weigh Residency for Illegal Mexican Immigrants." *Los Angeles Times*, September 7.

Smith, V., 1997. "New Forms of Work Organization." *Annual Review of Sociology* 23: 315–39.

Snow, C., W. S. Barnes, J. Chandler, I. F. Goodman, and L. Hemphill, 1991. *Unfulfilled Expectations: Home and School Influences on Literacy*. Cambridge, Mass.: Harvard University Press.

Snow, S., 1995a. "Morning Report: Latino Training Program Dropped." *Los Angeles Times*, May 2, F2.

Snow, S., 1995b. "Morning Report: ABC Versus Latinos." *Los Angeles Times*, May 9, F2.

Snow, S., 1996. "Morning Report: KCAL Protest." *Los Angeles Times*, August 3, F2.

Snow, S., 1997a. "Morning Report: Boycotting ABC, Disney." *Los Angeles Times*, April 25, F2.

Snow, S., 1997b. "Morning Report: Mickey's Defense." *Los Angeles Times*, June 28, F2.

Snow, S., 1997c. "Morning Report: Latinos and Disney." *Los Angeles Times*, July 26, F2.

Solórzano, D., 1994. "The Baccalaureate Origins of Chicana and Chicano Doctorates in the Physical, Life, and Engineering Sciences: 1980–1990." *Journal of Women and Minorities in Science and Engineering* 1: 253–72.

Solórzano, D., 1995. "The Baccalaureate Origins of Chicana and Chicano Doctorates in the Social Sciences." *Hispanic Journal of Behavioral Sciences* 17: 3–32.

Solórzano, D., 1997. "Images and Words That Wound: Critical Race Theory, Racial Stereotyping, and Teacher Education." *Teacher Education Quarterly* 24: 5–19.

Solórzano, D., 1998. "Critical Race Theory, Racial and Gender Microaggressions, and the Experiences of Chicana and Chicano Scholars." *International Journal of Qualitative Studies in Education* 11: 121–36.

Solórzano, D., and A. Ornelas, 2004a. "A Critical Race Analysis of Advance Placement Classes and Selective Admissions." *High School Journal* 87: 15–26.

Solórzano, D., and A. Ornelas, 2004b. "The Transfer Condition of Latina/o Community College Students in California: Policy Recommendations and Solutions." *Community College Journal of Research and Practice* 28: 233–48.

Solórzano, D., and R. Solórzano, 1995. "The Chicano Educational Experience: A Proposed Framework for Effective Schools in Chicano Communities." *Educational Policy* 9: 293–314.

Solórzano, D., and T. Yosso, 2000. "Toward a Critical Race Theory of Chicana and Chicano Education." In *Chartering New Terrains of Chicana(o)/Latina(o) Education*. Eds. C. Tejeda, C. Martinez, Z. Leonardo, and P. McLaren. Cresskill, N.J.: Hampton Press.

Solórzano, D. G., and D. Delgado Bernal, 2001. "Examining Transformational Resistance Through a Critical Race and LatCrit Theory Framework: Chicana and Chicano Students in an Urban Context." *Urban Education* 36: 308–42.

Solórzano, D. G., and A. Ornelas, 2002. "A Critical Race Analysis of Advanced Placement Classes: A Case of Educational Inequality." *Journal of Latinos in Education* 1: 215–29.

Sorensen, S. B., 2003. "Funding Public Health: The Public's Willingness to Pay for Domestic Violence Prevention Programming." *American Journal of Public Health* 9311: 1934–38.

Sorensen, S. B., and C. A. Taylor, 2003. "Personal Awareness of Domestic Violence: Implications for Health Care Providers." *Journal of the American Medical Women's Association* 581 (Winter): 4–9.

Sowards, S., 2000. "Juan Gabriel and Audience Interpretation: Cultural Impressions of Effeminacy and Sexuality in Mexico." *Journal of Homosexuality* 392: 133–58.

Stavenhagen, R., 1970. "Class, Colonialism, and Acculturation." In *Masses in Latin America*. Vol. I. Ed. L. Horowitz. New York: Oxford University Press.

Stecher, B. M., and G. W. Bohrnstedt, 2002. *Class Size Reduction in California: Findings from 1999–00 and 2000–01*. Sacramento: California Department of Education.

Steinberg, L., S. M. Bombusch, and B. B. Brown, 1992. "Ethnic Differences in Adolescent Achievement." *American Psychologist* 47: 723–29.

Steiner, S., 1970. *La Raza: The Mexican Americas*. New York: Harper Colophon Books.

Stepick, A., 1989. "Miami's Two Informal Sectors." In *The Informal Economy: Studies in Advanced and Less Developed Countries*. Eds. A. Portes, M. Castells, and L. A. Benton. Baltimore: John Hopkins University Press.

Stewart, A., and C. McDermott, 2004. "Gender in Psychology." *Annual Review of Psychology* 55: 519–44.

Stewart, K., 1993. "Engendering Narratives of Lament in Country Music." In *All That Glitters: Country Music in America*. Ed. G. Lewis. Bowling Green, Ohio: Bowling Green University Popular Press, 221–25.

Stipek, D., 2004. "Teaching Practices in Kindergarten and First Grade: Different Strokes for Different Folks." *Early Childhood Research Quarterly* 19: 548–68.

Stone, I. F., 1966. "Review of *People without a Country: The American Negro*." In *The New York Review of Books*. Eds. T. Parsons and K. B. Clark.

Straus, M. A., 1979. "Measuring Intrafamily Conflict and Violence: The Conflict Tactics CT Scales." *J. Mar. Fam.* 41: 75–88.

Straus, M. A., and R. J. Gelles, 1990. *Physical Violence in American Families: Risk Factors and Adaptations to Violence in 8,145 Families*. New Brunswick, N.J.: Transaction.

Suarez-Orozco, M. M., and M. M. Paez, eds., 2002. *Latinos: Remaking America*. Berkeley: University of California Press.

Tajfel, H., 1981. *Human Groups and Social Categories: Studies in Social Psychology*. London: Cambridge University Press.

Tancredo, T., 2006. *In Mortal Danger: The Battle for America's Border and Security.* Nashville: Cumberland House Publishing.

Tate, W., 1997. "Critical Race Theory and Education: History, Theory, and Implications." *Review of Research in Education* 22: 195–247.

Taylor, J. E., P. Martin, and M. Fix, eds., 1997. *Poverty Amid Prosperity: Immigration and the Changing Face of Rural California.* Washington, D.C.: The Urban Institute Press.

Thernstrom, S., and A. Thernstrom, 2003. *No Excuses: Closing the Racial Gap in Learning.* New York: Simon and Schuster.

Thomas, J. J., 1992. *Informal Economic Activity.* Harvester Wheatsheaf, U.K.: Hemel Hempstead.

Tierney, W., 1993. *Building Communities of Difference: Higher Education in the Twenty-First Century.* Westport, Conn: Bergin & Garvey.

Tijerina, R. L., 2000. *They Call Me "King Tiger": My Struggle for the Land and Our Rights.* Houston: Arte Público Press.

Tilly, C., 1994. *Half a Job: Bad and Good Part-Time Jobs in a Changing Labor Market.* Philadelphia: Temple University Press.

Toma, R. S., and J. Esbenshade, 2001. "Day Laborer Hiring Sites: Constructive Approaches to Community Conflict." Los Angeles County Human Relations Commission Report.

Torres, A., 1998. "La Gran Familia Puertorriqueña 'Ej Prieta de Beldá' The Great Puerto Rican Family Is Really Really Black." *Blackness in Latin America, Vol. II.* Eds. A. Torres and N. E. Whitten Jr. Bloomington: Indiana University Press.

Townsend, C., 1997. "Story without Words: Women and the Creation of a Mestizo People in Guayaquil 1820–1835." *Latin American Perspectives* 244: 50–68.

Trejo, S. J., 1997. "Why Do Mexican Americans Earn Low Wages?" *Journal of Political Economy* 1056: 1235–68.

U.S. Bureau of the Census, 2000. 2000 Census of the Population: Social and Economic Characteristics, United States Summary. U.S. Bureau of the Census. Washington, D.C.: U.S. Government Printing Office.

U.S. Bureau of the Census, 2003. The Hispanic Population in the United States: March 2002. P20-545.Washington, D.C.: U.S. Government Printing Office.

U.S. Department of Education, National Center for Education Statistics 2000. Early Childhood Longitudal Study—Kindergarten Base Year Data Files and Electronic Codebook. Washington, D.C.: U.S. Department of Education.

U.S. Department of Education, National Center for Education Statistics, 2006. Digest of Education Statistics, 2005. Washington, D.C.: U.S. Department of Education.

United States Department of Education, Office of Civil Rights, 2000. Washington, D.C.: Office of Civil Rights Elementary and Secondary School Survey.

University of California Latino Eligibility Task Force, 1997. "Latino Student Eligibility and Participation in the University of California: Ya Basta! Report #5." Berkeley: University of California Latino Eligibility Task Force.

Valdez, L., and R. Rubalcava, 1972. "Venceremos! Mexican American Statement on Travel to Cuba." In *Aztlán: An Anthology of Mexican American Literature.* Eds. L. Valdez and S. Steiner. New York: Alfred A. Knopf.

Valencia, R., ed., 2002. *Chicano School Failure and Success: Past, Present, and Future.* New York: The Falmer Press.

Valenzuela, A., Jr., 1999a. *Subtractive Schooling: U.S.-Mexican Youth and the Politics of Caring.* Albany: State University of New York Press.

Valenzuela, A., Jr., 1999b. "Day Laborers in Southern California: Preliminary Findings from the Day Labor Survey." Center for the Study of Urban Poverty, Institute for Social Science Research, University of California, Los Angeles.

Valenzuela, A., Jr., 2000. "Controlling Day Labor: Government, Community, and Worker Responses." In *California Policy Options 2001.* Eds. D. J. B. Mitchell and P. Nomura.

Valenzuela, A., Jr., 2001. "Day Laborers as Entrepreneurs." *Journal of Ethnic and Migration Studies* 272: 335–52.

Valenzuela, A., Jr., 2003. "Day-Labor Work." *Annual Review of Sociology* 291: 307–33.

Valenzuela, A., Jr., A. Kawachi, and M. D. Marr, 2002. "Seeking Work Daily: Supply, Demand, and Spatial Dimensions of Day Labor in Two Global Cities." *International Journal of Comparative Sociology* 432: 192–219.

Valenzuela, A., Jr., N. Theodore, E. Melendez, and A. L. Gonzalez, 2006. "On the Corner: Day Labor in the United States." Technical report, UCLA Center for the Study of Urban Poverty.

Valle, V., 1989a. "Ethnic Fight Heats Up at Latino Station." *Los Angeles Times,* May 19, 1, 20, 21.

Valle, V., 1989b. "KVEA Shakeup Fuels Debate at Latino Station." *Los Angeles Times,* June 2, 1, 12.

Valle, V., 1989c. "Shake-Up at Latino Station Sparks Protest." *Los Angeles Times,* June 6, 1, 10.

Valle, V., 1989d. "Community Coalition Threats Compromise KVEA's Future." *Los Angeles Times,* June 30, 19, 20.

Van Deburg, W., 1992. *New Day in Babylon: The Black Power Movement and American Culture, 1965–1975.* Chicago: University of Chicago Press.

Verti, S., 1997. *Para Ti: Canciones Inmortales de Mexico: Homenaje a Juan Gabriel.* Mexico City: Editorial Diana.

Vieth, W., and E. Chen, 2004. "Bush Supports Shift of Jobs Overseas." *Los Angeles Times,* February 10: A14.

Vigil, E. B., 1999. *The Crusade for Justice: Chicano Militancy and the Government War on Dissent.* Madison: University of Wisconsin Press.

Vigil, J. D., 1997. *Personas Mexicanas: Chicano High Schoolers in a Changing Los Angeles.* Fort Worth, Tex.: Harcourt Brace.

Vigil, J. D., 2002. *A Rainbow of Gangs: Street Cultures in the Mega-City.* Austin: University of Texas Press.

Villalpando, R. M., 1989a. "Grupos Mexicoamericanos Acusan al Canal 52 de Desdeñar a Su Auditorio." *La Opinión,* 3.

Villalpando, R. M., 1989b. "Gerente del Canal 34 Achaca a la Prensa Versión de 'Cubanización,' de la T.V." *La Opinión,* 4.

Villarejo, D., D. Lighthall, B. Bade, S. A. McCurdy, R. Mines, S. Samuels, A. Souter, and D. Williams, 2000. "Suffering in Silence: A Report on the Health of California's Agricultural Workers." The California Institute for Rural Studies, Davis, California.

Volpp, L., 2002. "The Citizen and the Terrorist." *UCLA Law Review* 49: 1575–1600.

Waldinger, Roger, and Mehdi Bozorgmehr, eds., 1996. *Ethnic Los Angeles.* New York: Russell Sage Foundation.

Wallace, M., 1991. *Black Macho and the Myth of the Superwoman.* London: Verso.

Walter, N., 2000. "Structural Violence and Work Injury: The Experience of Undocumented Day Laborers in San Francisco." Department of Public Health, University of California, Berkeley. MS: 134.

Walter, N., P. M. S. Bourgois, H. M. Loinaz, and D. Schillinger, 2002. "Social Context of Work Injury among Undocumented Day Laborers in San Francisco." *Journal of General Internal Medicine* 17: 221–29.

Wilds, D., and R. Wilson, 2001. "Minorities in Higher Education 2000–2001, Eighteenth Annual Status Report." Washington, D.C.: American Council on Education.

Will, G. F., 2001. "We Have Been Here Before?" *Newsweek,* June 11.

Williams, C., and J. Windebank, 1998. *Informal Employment in the Advanced Economies: Implications for Work and Welfare.* New York: Routledge.

Williams, C., and J. Windebank, 2000. "Paid Informal Work in Deprived Neighborhoods." *Cities* 174: 285–91.

Williams et al. v. The State of California, 2000. Case No. 312236, Superior Court of the State of California, San Francisco Superior Court.

Williams, L., 1991. "Film Bodies: Gender, Genre and Excess." *Film Quarterly* 444: 3–13.

Wilson, W. J., 1996. *When Work Disappears: The World of the New Urban Poor.* New York: Alfred A. Knopf.

Worby, P. A., 2002. "Pride and Daily Survival: Latino Migrant Day Laborers and Occupational Health." Department of Public Health, University of California, Berkeley. MPH: 92.

Xue, Y., and S. J. Meisels, 2004. "Early Literacy Instruction and Learning in Kindergarten: Evidence from the Early Childhood Longitudinal Study—Kindergarten Class of 1998–1999." *American Educational Research Journal* 41: 191–229.

Yarbro-Bejarano, Y., 1997. "Crossing the Border with Chabela Vargas: A Chicana Femme's Tribute." In *Sex and Sexuality in Latin America.* Eds. D. Balderston and D. J. Guy. New York and London: New York University Press.

Zamora, D., 1996. "Where Are the Latinos in Films, TV?" *Los Angeles Times,* May 20, F3.

Zavella, P., 1997. "The Tables Are Turned: Immigration, Poverty, and Social Conflict in California Communities." In *Immigrants Out! The New Nativism and the Anti-Immigrant Impulse in the United States.* Ed. J. F. Perea. New York and London: New York University Press.

Zavella, P., 2000. "Latinos in the USA: Changing Socio-Economic Patterns." *Social and Cultural Geography* 1(2): 155

Zweigenhaft, R. L., and G. W. Domhoff, 1998. *Diversity in the Power Elite: Have Women and Minorities Reached the Top?* New Haven, Conn.: Yale University Press.

Zúñiga, V., ed., 2005. *New Destinations: Mexican Immigration in the United States.* New York: Russell Sage Foundation.

Contributors

BRENDA D. ARELLANO, a native of New Mexico, graduated from the Gevirtz Graduate School of Education at the University of California, Santa Barbara. Her main areas of research include work on the achievement gap of Latino and language-minority students. Her dissertation focuses on understanding the impact of parental involvement in the achievement of language-minority Latino students in early elementary school. In addition, Arellano Anguiano has worked as a teaching assistant in both the Departments of Chicano and Chicana Studies and Black Studies at the University of California, Santa Barbara. She hopes that one day her work will lead her back home, where she can contribute to the understanding and improvement of Chicano students' academic performance.

LEO R. CHAVEZ is a professor of anthropology at the University of California, Irvine. His research examines various issues related to transnational migration, including immigrant families and households, labor market participation, motivations for migration, the use of medical services, and media constructions of immigrant and nation. He is the author of *Shadowed Lives: Undocumented Immigrants in American Society* (Harcourt Brace Jovanovich, 1992, 1997), which provides an ethnographic account of Mexican and Central American undocumented immigrants in San Diego County, California, and *Covering Immigration: Popular Images and the Politics of the Nation* (University of California Press, 2001), which is the culmination of his interest in the ways immigrants are represented in the media and popular discourse in the United States.

YVETTE G. FLORES is a professor at the University of California, Davis as well as a research psychologist and licensed psychologist. She has done postdoctoral work in health psychology, in particular in substance abuse treatment outcome research and intimate partner violence. Her current research examines intimate partner violence among Mexicans on both sides of the border. She is also part of a NIA-funded study of care giving among spouses and adult children of Anglo and Latino elderly with dementia, and a NIMH-funded study of HIV prevention among sex workers along the U.S.–Mexico border. Her publications reflect her life's work of bridging clinical psychology and Chicano/Latino studies, as she foregrounds gender, ethnicity, and sexualities in her clinical, teaching, and research practices.

RAMÓN A. GUTIÉRREZ is the Preston and Sterling Morton Distinguished Service Professor of History and director of the Center for the Study of Race, Politics, and Culture at the University of Chicago. He is the author of many publications, among them *Contested Eden: California before the Gold Rush* (1998), *Mexican Home Altars* (1997), *When Jesus Came the Corn Mothers Went Away: Marriage, Sexuality and Power in New Mexico, 1500–1846* (1991), and is currently working on a synthetic history of the Chicano movement.

AÍDA HURTADO is professor of psychology at the University of California, Santa Cruz. She received her B.A. in psychology and sociology from the University of Texas, Pan American, and her Ph.D. in social psychology from the University of Michigan. Her main areas of expertise are in the study of social identity (including ethnic identity), Latino educational issues, and feminist theory. Her books include *The Color of Privilege: Three Blasphemies on Race and Feminism* (University of Michigan Press, 1996); *Voicing Feminisms: Young Chicanas Speak Out on Sexuality and Identity* (New York University Press, 2003, honorable mention for the 2003 Myers Outstanding Book Awards given by the Gustavus Myers Center for the Study of Bigotry and Human Rights in North America); *Chicana Feminisms: A Critical Reader* (coedited with Gabriela Arredondo, Norma Klahn, Olga Nájera-Ramírez, and Patricia Zavella, Duke University Press, 2003). Her latest book is *Chicana/o Identity in a Changing U.S. Society. ¿Quién soy? ¿Quiénes somos?* (coauthored with Patricia Gurin, University of Arizona Press, 2004).

OLGA NÁJERA-RAMÍREZ is professor in anthropology at the University of California, Santa Cruz. She received her Ph.D. from the University of Texas, Austin. Author of *La Fiesta de los Tastoanes: Critical Perspectives in a Mexican Festival Performance,* she also produced the award-winning video, "La Charreada: Rodeo a la Mexicana." Her most recent work includes two coedited volumes, *Chicana Traditions: Continuity and Change* (University of

Illinois Press, 2002) and *Chicana Feminisms: A Critical Reader* (Duke University Press, 2003).

CHON A. NORIEGA is professor in the University of California, Los Angeles Department of Film, Television, and Digital Media, and director of the UCLA Chicano Studies Research Center. He is author of *Shot in America: Television, the State, and the Rise of Chicano Cinema* (University of Minnesota Press, 2000) and editor of nine books dealing with Latino media, performance, and visual art. For the past decade, Noriega has been active in media policy and professional development, for which *Hispanic Business* named him as one of the Top 100 Most Influential Hispanics. He is cofounder of the five-hundred–member National Association of Latino Independent Producers (established in 1999) and serves on the board of directors of the Independent Television Service, the largest source of independent project funding within public television.

ARMIDA ORNELAS is an associate professor of Political Science at East Los Angeles College (ELAC). Her research and teaching interests focus on the transfer structure, process, and culture and their impact on Latina/o students. She is currently the director to the *Adelante,* First Year Experience Program.

MANUEL PASTOR JR. is professor of Geography and American Studies & Ethnicity and director of the Program for Environmental and Regional Equity at the University of Southern California. His most recent books include *Searching for the Uncommon Common Ground: New Dimensions on Race in America* (W.W. Norton, 2002), coauthored with Angela Glover Blackwell and Stewart Kwoh, and *Up Against the Sprawl: Public Policy and the Making of Southern California* (University of Minnesota Press, 2004), coedited with Jennifer Wolch and Peter Dreier. He is currently working on issues of environmental justice with support from both the California Endowment and the California Wellness Foundation, and on the relationship between community building and regional strategies with the support of the Hewlett and Ford Foundations.

RUSSELL W. RUMBERGER is professor of education at the University of California, Santa Barbara and director of the University of California Linguistic Minority Research Institute. He has conducted academic and policy research in two areas of education: education and work and the schooling of disadvantaged students. His research in the area of education and work has focused on the economic payoffs to schooling and on the educational requirements of work. His research on at-risk students has focused on several topics: the causes, consequences, and solutions to the problem of school dropouts; the causes and consequences of student mobility; the schooling of English-language learners; and the impact of school segregation on student achievement.

DANIEL G. SOLÓRZANO is professor of social sciences and comparative education in the Department of Education at the University of California, Los Angeles. He also has a joint appointment as professor in the Chicana and Chicano Studies Department at the University of California, Los Angeles. His teaching and research interests include: sociology of education; critical race theory; Latino critical race theory (LatCrit); and race, gender, and class relations, with a special emphasis on the educational access, persistence, and graduation of underrepresented undergraduate and graduate students of color in the United States.

ENRIQUETA VALDEZ CURIEL is associate professor of qualitative health research at University of Guadalajara Medical School, Mexico. She received her M.D. from the University of Guadalajara and her master's degree in community development from University of California, Davis. Her current research includes areas of folk medicine, intimate partner violence, and the use of education-entertainment techniques as educational tools.

ABEL VALENZUELA JR. is a professor in the Department of Chicana/o Studies and Department of Urban Planning, and director of the Center for the Study of Urban Poverty at the Institute for Social Science Research at the University of California, Los Angeles. His disciplinary base is urban sociology and planning. He has published numerous articles on immigrant settlement, labor market outcomes, and inequality, including coediting (with Lawrence Bobo, Melvin Oliver, and Jim Johnson) *Prismatic Metropolis: Inequality in Los Angeles* (Russell Sage Foundation, 2000). He is currently under contract with the Russell Sage Foundation to publish his recent work on the social and labor market processes of day laborers—immigrant men who solicit temporary daily work in open-air markets such as street corners, empty parking lots, and storefronts.

PATRICIA ZAVELLA has a Ph.D. in anthropology from the University of California, Berkeley, and is professor of Latin American and Latino Studies at the University of California, Santa Cruz. She has published extensively in Chicana/o and Latina/o studies and feminist studies on women's work and domestic labor, poverty, family, sexuality and social networks, ethnographic research methods, and transnational migration of Mexicana/o workers. She recently coedited *Women and Migration in the U.S.-Mexico Borderlands: A Reader.* In 2003 the National Association for Chicana and Chicano Studies named her Scholar of the Year.

Index

abuse: alcohol, 207; economic, 185; emotional, 186; employer, 35, 37, 38, 52, 56; physical, 185, 205, 212; policy and, 213; precursors to, 207; psychological, 185, 195, 208, 214; report, 211; sexual, 184, 208; verbal, 200, 207. *See also* violence
achievement gap, 61–74; effects of language and socio-economic status on, 73; in reading and math, 69; Latino as compared to white, 68
Acuña, Rodolfo, 105
Advanced Placement (AP), 78–93; in public high schools, 84. *See also* education
affirmative action: as it transpired, 111; bias of the media on, 156; Federal Communications Commission, 165; Grutter type of, 81; Michigan case, 80; reaffirming, 87; Richard Rodriguez decried, 107; undermined, 166
African American: AP applicants, 90; and dependency theory, 95; experience, 102; and internal colonialism, 110; in Mississippi, 109; and racism and segregation, 95; radicals, 96; student population, 86; white historical advancement at the expense of, 105; women more likely to reflect on social identities, 113
age: of college student identity study respondents, 113; of day laborers, 45; of intimate violence study participants, 191, 192, 212; and political activity of children of immigrants, 4; and poverty rates, 75n4;

and the white population, 1; of women when first migrated, 210
Aguirre, Adalberto, 79
Alexander, Karl L., 63, 64
Almaguer, Tomás, 98, 105, 107
Amin, Samir, 99
Anzaldúa, Gloria, 107, 108, 115, 126
Aparicio, Frances A., 10
APSAI, 83–85, 87
Arellano, Brenda D., 8, 75n10
Armor, David, 63
Ashton, Patricia, 64
Asian American: income, 22; population, 86; student performance, 61
assimilation: attitudes about, 149; California style, 108; cultural and structural, 11, 111; European, 94; fears concerning a lack of, 137; models of, 8; requires that immigrants use English, 10; Richard Rodriguez' opinions on, 107
Atlantic Monthly, 10, 138, 149
Aubry, Erin J., 36
August, Diane, 63
Aztecs, 99, 106, 152, 153
Aztlán, 99, 152

Bada, Xóchitl, 4
Barnes, Wendy S., 64
barrios and *colonias*, 105, 106, 110. *See also* ghettoes
barter (economy), 46, 52, 55
Bauman, Richard, 177

Benner, Chris, 32
Bennet, Kymberley K., 64
Benton, Lauren A., 41
Berry, Barnett, 63
Betts, Julian R, 63, 64, 73
bilingual education, 4, 33; Chicano demands for, 97; and the Latino image, 156
biotechnology, 15; bioengineering, 17
black: consciousness, 97; ghettoes, 102; power, 97. *See also* African American
black nationalists, 9; Black Panther Party, 97, 98; *Black Power,* 102; Black Power Conference of 1967, 99; Black Power movement, 110
Black Nonviolent Coordinating Committee, 96
Blauner, Robert, 102, 105
Bohrnstedt, George W., 73
Bok, Derek, 111
border: Arizona-Mexican, 154; Bush politics on, 4; U.S.-Mexican border, 140; crime on, 140; crossing, 126, 209; disappearing, 147, 148, 150, 151; family on both sides of, 210; guardians of, 141; partner violence on, 12, 184, 195; problems on, 108; *ranchera* audiences on both sides of, 169; sex workers on, 244; site of "feminicide," 116; women's shelters on either side of, 213
Borderlands/La Frontera, 108
Bowen, William G., 111
Brooks-Gunn, Jean, 64
Brown, Bradford B., 62
Brown, Elaine, 110
Brown, Marianne P., 40
Brown Berets, 97–99
Bryk, Anthony S., 66
Buchanan, Patrick, 134, 135
Burchinal, Margaret, 64
Bureau of Labor Statistics (BLS), 41, 42
Bush, George W., 4

Calderon, Jose S., 40
California State Department of Education, 64, 84
California State University, 9, 31
Callahan, Rebecca, 63
Camarillo, Albert, 106
capital: labor market and human, 49; structural and human, 45, 48
capitalism, 100; capitalist class, 105
Carmichael, Stokely, 96, 102, 110
Casanova, Pablo González, 101

Castaneda et al. v. University of California Regents, 90, 91
Castells, Manuel, 39
Castillo, Anna, 115
center-based child care, 74; center-based preschool, 72
Cerritos, 83
Chandler, Jean, 64
Chapa, Jorge, 78, 79
Charleton, Kelley, 74
Chávez, César, 109
Chavez, Leo R., 10
Cherríe, Moraga, 107, 108, 115, 126
Chicago, 37, 57n1, 96, 118; 122
Chicano movement, 9, 94; comparison between movements, 110; debates on, 108; decolonization and, 99; failure of, 107, 108; ideological influences, 98; legacy of, 94; media activism during, 158; respondent's involvement in, 125; separatist perceptions of, 153; theoretical concerns, 9, 108; use of Latin American dependency theory, 95
Chicano/Brown Power Movement, 97, 104
child care: state subsidized, 8, services, 29
Chinese Revolution, 98, 99
citizenship, 95, 111; full, 112
civil rights, 33; movement, 95; tangible results of movement, 110
Clark, Kenneth, 102
Cohen, Jacob, 67, 75n14
Coleman, James S., 70
Coleman Report, 70
colonialism, 95, 98, 99, 105; colonial oppression, 103; colonial subjects, 103. *See also* internal colonialism
college and university admissions, 78, 84, 85; use of race in, 80; *Bakke v. Regents of the University of California,* 80; African American, Latina/o, and Native American students, 81; Grutter type (and Gratz proof), 81; Latina/o students' disadvantage in, 90; minority applicants' equal opportunity to compete for, 90; process, 93; UC/CSU, 87, 88
college preparatory curriculum, 81, 84, 90, 92
Community-Based English Tutoring (CBET), 74
community college, 79, 90
consciousness: about gay issues, 121; and commitment, 125; as a developmental

process, 127; gender, 122; of heritage and language, 104; identification and, 114; informed by lived experience, 124; as leading to social action, 113; about oppression, 121

Conflict Tactic Scale (CTS), 183, 186, 188–91

Congress, 55, 96, 138

Cooper, Harris, 74

Cornelius, Wayne A., 8

corporate/business elite, 5, 164

Cotler, Julio, 101

credentialed teachers, 9, 84, 85, 87–89

Crenshaw, Kimberle W., 82

critical race theory, 78, 82

Cruse, Harold, 101

Cuban Revolution, 98, 99, 102, 103

culture: ethnic Mexican and Mexican American movies stars, singers, and athletes, 5, 10; school culture, 92

cultural: capital, 134; deficiency, 106; expressions, 10; integrity, 133; isolation, 101; memory, 10; nationalist, 106, 110; production, 12; roots, 134; starvation, 101; studies, 12

Current Population Survey (CPS), 18, 20, 42, 43n7, 146

Currie, Janet, 72

Danenberg, Anne, 63

Daniel et al. v. State of California, 90, 91

Darling-Hammond, Linda, 63

Delgado, Richard R., 82

Delgado Bernal, Dolores, 82

democracy: 95, 150

dependency in Latin America, 9, 102

dependency theory, 9, 99, 101

discourse, 10, 83, 133–154

discrimination: and colonization, 103; and poverty, 17, 23; various forms of, 81–83; in voting, 96

Disney, 160

diversity: in California schools, 89; and cultural programming in school, 122; ethnic student, 87; of immigrants, 137; and university admissions; efforts toward, 163

Doctorate Records Project of the National Research Council, 93n2

domestic violence. *See* intimate partner violence; sexual abuse

Domhoff, G. William, 4, 6

Domina, Thurston, 64

Donato, Ruben, 79

Dornbusch, Sanford M., 62, 64

Dwyer, Rachel E., 30

East Los Angeles: Chicanos in, 97; racial perceptions of respondents from, 119; in relation to internal colonialism, 110; serving the community of, 98

economy: boom in the Los Angeles, 37; California's "new," 15, 17, 28, 29; and expansion, 154; experienced downturns, 138; global, 61, 100; greatest number of job openings in, 30; Harlem's, 102; Indians coerced into a monetary, 101; informal, 9, 40, 57n2; Latinos in, 31; secondary sector of, 42; state economy, 34; strength of, 16, 18, 19

economic recession, 15, 17–19, 27, 138

economic upward mobility, 3, 8, 108, 110

economists, 95, 99, 101

education: adult, 32; cultural model of, 64; discrimination in, 96; effect of families, schools, and communities on, 63; effects on upward mobility, 3; field of, 82; and immigrant status, 17; inequalities in, 95; leakages in pipeline, 8; and low earning, 22; outcomes in, 62, 74; parental socioeconomic status and achievement in, 63; parenting styles affects on, 64; policy, 61, 71, 74; predictors of student achievement in, 66; and real wages, 23; and resources, 9; social justice in, 82; structural and cultural aspects of, 82; wage prospects and, 46

educational achievement; educational pipeline and, 129; factors that contribute to gap in, 62–65; gap in, 3, 7, 8; laborers lack of, 95; Mexican American's relatively low, 6

educational pipeline, 9, 78–80, 93, 129

Edwards, Jeffrey R., 39

El Plan de Santa Barbara, 104, 105

El Plan Espiritual de Aztlán, 104, 106

Elmore, Richard F., 61

emotional attachments to group membership, 114

employer abuse, 36. *See also* abuse

employment: access to, 3, 94, 95; business cycles and contingent, 21, 36–54; deregulated, 158; and English proficiency, 210; informal, 8, 15, 39, 44, in film and television, 11, 159; Latino rates of, 16; Latinos' levels of, 6; losses, 20; networking and, 32;

opportunities, 74, 155, 161–63, 166, 167n17; polarized, 34; public service, 128; Silicon Valley's, 18; workers' skills and, 24. *See also* labor; work

empowerment, 6, 9, 97, 103, 123, 124

English: backgrounds, 58, 63, 72; dominant, 73, 74; employers prefer workers who can communicate in, 47; English-speaking Californians, 152; English-speaking Canada, 144; immigrants' lack of, 43, 44, 49; language proficiency, 7, 9, 43–50, 61, 66, 150; language proficiency test, 64; literacy skills of parents, 74; non-English backgrounds, 76n16; as primary language, 3, 4, 63, 150; training for adults, 32

Esbenshade, Jill, 40

ethnic studies, 10, 12, 82

Entwisle, Doris R., 63, 64

exploitation: colonial, 100, 103; external administration and, 95; immigrants came escaping, 102; informal labor and, 55; of laborers, 95; patterns of, 106; of racial and minority groups, 105

Falcón, Luis M., 32

Falcone, Michael, 90, 92

families: attributes of students and their, 62–74; average size of Mexican, 146; displacement of, 172; economic opportunities for, 136; economic struggles of, 119–21; and home ownership, 34; immigrant men reuniting with, 210; mixed heritage, 117; violence in, 184; values of, 191

farmwork and farmworkers, 2, 30, 53, 109, 192

Federal Communications Commission, 158–161, 164, 167n25

Feige, Edgar L., 39

feminist: of color, 117; debates amongst, 107, 115; identification as, 112, 120; movement, 121; who protested the masculinist Chicano movement, 107

Fenstermaker, Sarah, 115

Fernandez-Kelley, Patricia, 40

Finn, Jeremy D., 64, 73

Foucault, Michel, 135

Fowler, Edward, 38

Fox, Jonathan, 4

Fraleigh, Michael J., 64

Fregoso, Rosa Linda, 115

Fuhrman, Susan H., 61

Fuller, Bruce, 74

Gallimore, Ronald, 64

Gándara, Patricia, 63, 64

Garcia, Alma M., 107

Garcia, Anna, 40

Garcia, Eugene E., 78, 79

Garcia, Ignacio M., 109

Ghilchrist, Jim, 135

Giamo, Benedict, 38

Gill, Tom, 38

Goldenberg, Claude, 64

Gonzales, Rodolfo "Corky," 103, 104, 109, 110

Goodman, Irene F., 64

Gorey, Kevin M., 74

government regulation, 52, 54, 57n3

GPA, 84, 85, 91, 92

grass-roots movements, 95, 107, 110

Greenwald, Ron, 64

Griffith, James, 64

Griswold de Castillo, Richard, 106

Guadalajara, 194, 195, 205, 215n4

Guatemala, 47, 57

guest worker program, 2, 154. *See also* immigration

Guevara, Ernesto "Che," 98

Gunder Franklin, André, 99, 100

Guo, Guang, 63, 64

Gurin, Patricia, 114, 116, 119, 121, 125

Gutiérrez, Ramón A., 94

Hamilton, Charles V., 102

Haney-López, Ian, 97

Hanushek, Eric A., 73

Harlem: blacks in, 110; economic structure of, 102; riots in, 96

Harris, Kathie M. 63, 64

Hayes-Bautista, David, 4, 24

Head Start, 69, 72, 76n19,

health: care, 3; insurance, 33–35; services, 3, 146, 185, 212

Hedges, Larry V., 64

Hemphill, Lowry, 64

Henson, Kevin, 41

higher education: Chicanas attending, 118; financial aid and, 128; exposure to knowledge and activism in, 124; middle-class identity, 119; pipeline and, 129; policy, 127; as transformation, 124

high school: California's overall enrolment in, 83, 84; diploma, 6, 45; degrees, 32; dropping out as related to retention (being held back) in, 76n20; dropout, 7; enrollment in Advanced Placement courses, 81, 83–86; ethnic organization membership, 214; graduates, 77, 78; learning taking place in, 63; students denied access to AP courses, 90; urban public 9;

high tech, 17, 18, 29

Hill Collins, Patricia, 115

hiring sites: 52, curbside, 42; open-air, 37, 38

history, 13, 82, 127, 136, 144

Holmes, Deborah L., 64

Hope Franklin, John, 96, 99

Houseman, Susan N., 42

housing: affordability and workers' income, 36, 104; arriving immigrants and search for, 209; California's high price in, 22; day workers and sharing of, 50; development, 96; equality and access, 110; fair, 95; and home ownership, 34; government commitment to, 110; movement's affect on, 94–96

Howes, Carollee, 64

Huntington, Samuel, 133–35

Hurtado, Aída, 10

Ibarra, Maria, 40

identification: class, 113; and consciousness, 114, 117, 126; definition of, 119; respondent's social, 118

identity: American traditional, 133; identity-based syllabi, 110; construction of social, 112; multicultural college-going identity, 92; national, 133, 136; racial, gender/sexual, and class identities, 10; new identities, 10

ideology, 82, 99, 106, 138

immigrants: assimilation of European, 94; growing occupations with greatest financial potential for, 30; households of, 28; and Mexican identity consciousness, 116; occupational concentration of, 29; representations of, 135, 136–54; and status, 17, 28, 32, 54; and women's traditional occupations, 57n2; work ethic of, 136

immigration: challenges and opportunities posed by, 189; CPS collecting date about, 34; discourse on, 133–154; educational attainment by ethnicity and, 24; education as related to, 23, 24; fear of Mexican, 135; household income and recentness of, 16; policy and regulation of, 1, 4, 11, 137, 213, 214; and uncertainty about status, 207

immigration law of 1996, 138

income: African American household

income, 20, 35n9; Asian American household income, 20, 35n9; and college students' conceptions of what constitutes "middle class" status, 19; disparities as difficult to overcome, 74; distribution in California, 18; distribution in Latin America, 100; Filipino versus other Asian Americans household incomes, 22; in Harlem, 110; lack of AP classes in Latino communities with low, 89; Latino, 31; Latino compared to whites, 16, 23; leader in low, 21; Los Angeles districts with low, 86; low-wage worker, 20; mean for day laborers, 53, 55; pooling household, 28; sources of work in low-income areas, 48; supplementary, 42; tax revenues, 18; unstable, 8

Inda, Jonathan Xavier, 139

industrial development, 31, 41, 43, 45, 100

industry: construction, 46, 56; gardening, painting, cleaning and maintenance, 47; Latin American government support of national, 100; textile and garment, 56

informalization 55, 56

internal colonialism, 9, 94, 95, 101–10

intersectionality: and education, 82; emerging theories on, 112, 115–18, 123; and political transformations, 125, 126

intimate partner violence (IPV), 183–85, 188, 189, 207–215; emotional violence, 186

Jencks, Christopher, 70

Jepson, Christopher, 73

jobs: creation patterns, 23; low-pay, 42–44; secondary-sector jobs, 39; skills 45, 47. *See also* labor

Kain, John F., 73

Kalleberg, Arne L., 39, 41

Kerr, Clark, 77, 78, 90, 93

kindergarten, 64, 65; Latino kindergartners, 68, 71, 72; Latinos begin more than two months behind white students, 67; teacher-assessed learning behaviors in black, white, and Latino students in, 64

King, Martin Luther, Jr., 96, 98

knowledge: conceptual and procedural, 64; experiential, 82

Kotkin, Joel, 34n3

labor:

—cheap/low-wage labor, 101; competition for, 46; organized, 109

—contingent, 40–42, 47, 50, 56
—day labor, 7, 14, 36, 39, 43; defining, 57n1; growth in, 56, as a gendered informal economy, 57; non-day labor, 45–47; quality of non-day labor jobs, 49; in Los Angeles, 40, 43–64
—immigrant (Mexican/Latino) labor, 2, 7; labor-market disadvantage, 37, 39; recruitment and repatriation of, 106; in relation to assets, 17
—informal labor, 3, 43
—labor market: generalized market, 16, 31; service sector, 29; urban, 37
—labor standards, 17, 33; and rights, 32; basic, 31
—labor skills: low, 51, 56, 101; hard and soft, 25; trade, 46; maximize their, 47. *See also* jobs
Ladson-Billings, Gloria, 82
Laine, Richard D., 64
language background, 68, 71. *See also* English: language proficiency
Larson, Katherine L., 63
Latin American theories of dependency and underdevelopment, 95, 100
Latino-themed programming, 163–165
law: border fence and, 154; corporate media and, 164; federal civil rights and, 90, 96; immigration, 2, 3, 47, 115, 138, 213; as related to unequal education, 91
Lawrence, Charles R., 82, 111
Lee, Jaekyung, 62, 63
Leete, Laura, 32
legal status, 3, 7, 44, 48–49, 51
Leiderman, P. Herbert, 64
lesbian, 108, 115, 117, 120
Liang, Xiaoyan, 74
Light, Ivan, 36, 42
Lin, Jan, 40
López, Elías, 6
López Tijerina, Reies, 109
Los Angeles, 11, 13, 14, 18, 24–25, 32, 43–45, 56
Los Angeles Day Labor Survey of 481 workers in 1999, 7, 43
Los Angeles Living Wage Ordinances, 53, 57n5
Los Angeles Unified District (LAUSD), 83–87

Machismo Scale, 189, 191
Magnuson, Katherine A., 63

Marcelli, Enrico A., 32, 51
Markman, Jacob M., 73
Markman, Lisa B., 64
Marr, Mathew, 38
Martin, Sally S., 64
Martinez, Ruben O., 79
Marxism, 94, 102
master status, 113, 114
materialist analysis, 107, 108
Matsuda, Mary J., 82, 111
Maxwell-Jolly, Julie, 63
McCarthy, Eugene, 102
McClelland, Megan M., 64
media: media conglomerates (operate in global and state-deregulated space), 11; Mexican American media activists, 11, 158; reforming, 157
Meisels, Samuel J., 64
melodrama, 11, 168, 171–73, 179
mentoring program, 112, 128
mestizo (mixed race), 101, 104; Cherríe Moraga's, 108; heritage families, 117; knowledge that Latina/os are, 119; respondents are, 123
middle class, 16, 25, 33; Chicanas that see themselves as, 112, 119; homes, 110; income levels of the median household, 18, Latinos, 72; Mexican American, 107
migration: benefits of, 190; and cultural expression, 10; rural to urban migration, 11; stressors of, 209; transnational, 12. *See also* immigration
militant action, 97, 106
Milkman, Ruth, 30
Min, Pyong G., 42
minimum wage: determining, 52, 53; economic growth and, 20; and the federal rate, 55; increases in, 25, 32; laborers setting of, 52, 53; pay falling below, 40; and state as compared to federal, 33; workers paid slightly above, 48; yearly income for earners of, 55
Monfort, Franklin, 79
Montez, Carlos, 97
Moreno, Jose F., 78
Morrison, Megan M., 64
Moss, Alfred A., Jr., 96, 99
Mozingo, Joe, 36
Muhlenbruck, Laura, 74
multiculturalism, 122, 135; ethnic diversity, 89; multicultural subject, 126. *See also* diversity

multiple oppressions, 123. *See also* intersectionality
Murphy, Patrick J., 32

Nájera-Ramírez, Olga, 11
Nardone, Thomas, 41
narratives: Cherríe Mendoza's lyrics and, 171; Lydia Moraga's, 108; migration, 211; of a nation of immigrants, 136; Quebec, 145, 149, 151, 152
nation, threat to, 134, 137
national identity, 11, 135
nationalism: appeal of, 96; brown power as the first, 97; calls to, 107; Chicano, 108, 150; economic, 100
National Center for Educational Statistics (2006), 61, 64, 75n4
nativists, 3, 4, 11, 157, 158
Navarro, Armando, 109
networks: establishing, 56; lack of, 49; role of, 17, 23, 31, 38–39, 50
New Mexican Alianza Federal de Mercedes, 104, 109
New Republic, 10, 138, 147
Newsweek, 10, 145, 146, 154
non-working poor, 28, 31, 34. *See also* employment; labor; poverty; work
Noriega, Chon A., 11

Oakes, Jeannie, 79, 86
Ogbu, John U., 62
Olson, Linda Steffei, 63
Orfield, Gary, 79
Ornelas, Armida, 9, 81, 82, 90
Ozuna, Erika, 34n3

Palardy, Gregory J., 62, 63
Pannozzo, Gina M., 64
Paredes, Américo, 170
Parker, Robert E., 36
Passel, Jeffrey, 152
Pastor, Manuel, Jr., 6, 7, 26, 32, 43n8, 51
pay: cheap/low wage, 2, 28, 54; irregular, 46; low rate, 49, 54, scale for day labor work, 52
Peck, Jamie, 36, 48. 54, 57n1
Peisner-Feinberg, Ellen, 64
Peña, Manuel, 169
performance, 168–80
Peru, 45, 101
Phillips, Meredith, 70
Pianta, Robert, 64

police: brutalization by, 95, 96; surveillance, 104, 109
political: activism, 111, 112; engagement, 103, 127; mobilization, 122, 123
Polivka, Anne E., 41
population: data, 20, 22, 26, 41, 42, 86; Latino population in Los Angeles County, 18, 142; Latino urban, 2–10, 30, 161; Mexico's, 142
Portes, Alejandro, 39–41
post-secondary education, 79, 90. *See also* education
post–World War II period, 41, 99
poverty: Current Population Survey (CPS), 18, 20, 42; federal poverty line, 21; Latinos overrepresented, 26; Latinos represent over half of the working poor, 27; non-working poverty, 24, 25; rate for Latinos, 7, 16, 21, 22; status, 61; systemic effects of, 95
Prebisch, Raúl, 100
Proposition 187, 3, 4, 152
Proposition 227, 4, 74
public sphere, 156, 157

Quesada, James, 40

race: and inequality, 82; relations: 95, 101. *See also* racism
racial: background, as related to student learning, 64; background and class, oppression, 107, 108; division, 105; domination, 108; make-up, 83; status, 108
racialization, by families, 119
racism: and access to AP classes, 82; affirmative action and, 93; cheap labor as related to, 101; daily effects of, 99; internal colonialism and, 9, 95; intersectionality and, 117; masculine resistance to, 109, 110; structural versus individual forms of, 102, 105
Ramirez, Ralph, 97
Raudenbush, Stephen W., 66
Reardon, Sean F., 62
reconquest/*reconquista*: aftermath of the U.S.–Mexican war and, 139; metaphors of (Quebec), 135, 142, 147; in public discourse, 10; rhetoric of, 155; vanishing borders and anxieties about, 151
Reese, Ronald, 64
representation, 10, 110, 135
Reyes, Belinda I., 74

Reyes, David, 36
Riegos, Cristina, 40
Ritter, Philip L., 64
Rivkin, Steven G., 73
Roach, Elizabeth, 36
Roberts, Donald F., 64
Rodney, Walter, 99
Rodriguez, Gregory, 35n11
Rodriguez, Richard, 107
Rosenblatt, Robert A., 36
Rothstein, Richard, 62, 63
Rove, Karl, 4
Rubalcava, Roberto, 103
Rueben, Kim S., 63
Rumberger, Russel W., 8, 62–64, 67, 75n10, 76n19, 78
Ryan, Allison m. 73

Sanchez, David, 97, 99
Sandoval, Chela, 115
Sassen, Saskia, 40, 41
Schacter, John, 64
schools: high-concentration Latino, 74; private as compared to public in achieve-ment, 71; socioeconomic composition of, 72; professional school, 79. *See also* achievement gap
Scoggins, Justin, 26
segregation, in California, 73, 95
Segura, Denise, 115
Selee, Andrew, 4
sexual abuse: comparison between North-ern California and Tenamaxtlán in, 212; factor analysis that includes, 194, 200; forms of violence suffered including, 184–87, 188; lower rates on both sides of the border, 212; *machista* views and, 202; psychological and verbal abuse, 12; "vent-ing" and, 208
Shanahan, Timothy, 63
Singer, Judith D., 74
skin color, 113. *See also* white: skin privilege
Smith, Vickie, 41
Snow, Catherine E., 64
social movement, 113. *See also* black, power; civil rights; Chicano movement; feminist
socio-economic status (SES): affects on achievement gap, 69, 72; lower for Lati-nos than white students, 68; as related to student learning, 64
Solórzano, Daniel G., 9, 78, 79, 81, 82, 86, 90
Southwest, 103, 106, 109

Spanish: language loyalty, 11; speaking households and economic disadvantage, 73
standardized tests (SAT and ACT), 84, 133
Stavenhagen, Rodolofo, 101
Stecher, Brian M., 73
Steinberg, Larry, 62
Stepick, Alex, 40
stereotypes: of culture of poverty, 170; gen-der; 12, 168; of immigrant men, 146; of Mexican masculinity, 169, 178, 179n3; of migrating Mexicans, 148
stigmatization, 117, 126
Stipek, David, 64
students, 70, 86. *See also* education
summer programs, 74, 76n22

Tajfel, Henry, 112, 114, 116
Tate, William F., 82
tax: employment and, 42; of payroll, 40, 47, 55; poll, 95; revenue, 31
telecommunications, 5, 155, 158
Telecommunications Act of 1996, 158, 164
Tenamaztlán, Jalisco, 12, 183, 189–91, 205, 212
Texas, 96, 103
Theodore, Nik, 36, 47, 54, 57n1
Thernstrom, Abigail, 62
Thernstrom, Stephan, 62
third world, 102, 105
Thomas, Duncan, 72
Thomas, Jim J., 39
Thoreson, Amy, 63
Thum, Yeo Meng, 64
Tierney, William G., 82
Tilly, Chris, 41
Townsend, Camilla, 38

UCLA Daily Bruin, 79, 90
unemployment: Anglo and African Ameri-can rates, 35n14; bouts of, 51; in Califor-nia, 13, 15–18; day worker reciprocity dur-ing periods of, 49; Latino 43; Mexicans in the United States as related to, 103; Mexico's high levels of, 141; patterns by race, 27, 28. *See also* employment; labor; work
unions: 24, 33; Chávez's organizing strate-gies, 109; prevent workers' attempts to unionize, 42
University of California systems, 9, 31, 78
urban: ghettoes, 9, 99, 101, 103, 105; labor market, 37; Latino population, 89, 161, 191;

migration, 11, 169; public schools, 9, 86, 93; settings, 89, 98, 189; urbanization, 141

U.S. Bureau of the Census, 79, 84

U.S. Department of Education, 61, 64, 75n4, 84, 91

Valdez, Luis, 103

Valencia, Richard R., 78, 79

Valentine, Jeff C., 74

Valenzuela, Abel, Jr., 7

Valenzuela, Arlene, 36, 38, 40

Vanackere, Martine, 38

Van Deburg, William L., 99

Vigil, James Diego, 79, 109

Voelkl, Kristine E., 64

voting in U.S. elections: and blacks in the South, 95; ethnic Mexicans and, 2, 5; fear of Mexican immigration and, 152; generational change and, 12; patterns of, 110; proof of citizenship and, 4; proposition 227 and, 156; registration drives and, 95; Republican party and, 5; rights, 96; safeguarding women's rights, 121; workers and, 33

wages: casual versus formal, 55; contracts, 109; differential between two countries, 142; equal, 122; and their fluctuation, 20; Latinos lowest in, 16; Mexican immigrant, 6–8; negation, 50; paid in cash, 56; poverty and, 24–25; prospects, 46; real, 23; reservation, 53; starvation, 103; training and, 32–43; willing to work any job for a, 51. *See also* minimum wage

Waldfogel, Jane, 63

Waldinger, Roger, 51

Wallace, Michelle, 110

Walter, Nicholas, 40

Weigel, Daniel J., 64

welfare, 25, 74, 139, 143

West, Candace, 116

white: power, 102; skin privilege, 95, 103, 105

Williams, Colin C., 39, 40

Wilson, William Julius, 24

Windebank, Janice, 39, 40

women's studies, 82, 124

Worby, Paul A., 40

work: experience 45; home-based, 41; involuntary part-time work, 43; motivation to, 43; opportunities for, 47; safety standards in, 40; temporary agencies and, 42. *See also* employment; labor

Yosso, Tara J., 78, 79, 82

Zabin, Carol, 35n8

Zweigenhaft, Richard L., 4, 6

The University of Illinois Press
is a founding member of the
Association of American University Presses.

Composed in 10.5/13 Adobe Minion Pro
by Jim Proefrock
at the University of Illinois Press
Manufactured by Cushing-Malloy, Inc.

University of Illinois Press
1325 South Oak Street
Champaign, IL 61820-6903
www.press.uillinois.edu